Women's Poetry of Late Imperial China

Women's Poetry
of Late Imperial China

TRANSFORMING THE INNER CHAMBERS

Xiaorong Li

A China Program Book
UNIVERSITY OF WASHINGTON PRESS   *Seattle and London*

THIS BOOK IS MADE POSSIBLE BY A COLLABORATIVE GRANT FROM THE ANDREW W. MELLON FOUNDATION.

This book was supported in part by the China Studies Program, a division of the Henry M. Jackson School of International Studies at the University of Washington.

This book was also supported by the Association for Asian Studies First Book Subvention Program.

© 2012 by the University of Washington Press
17 16 15 14 13 12   5 4 3 2 1

All rights reserved. No part of this publication may be reproduced or transmitted in any form or by any means, electronic or mechanical, including photocopy, recording, or any information storage or retrieval system, without permission in writing from the publisher.

University of Washington Press
PO Box 50096, Seattle, WA 98145, USA
www.washington.edu/uwpress

Library of Congress Cataloging-in-Publication Data
Li, Xiaorong, 1969 May 25–
Women's poetry of late imperial China : transforming the inner chambers / Xiaorong Li.
p. cm. — (A China program book)
Includes bibliographical references and index.
ISBN 978-0-295-99205-1 (hardcover : acid-free paper)
ISBN 978-0-295-99229-7 (pbk. : acid-free paper)
1. Chinese literature—Women authors—History and criticism. 2. Chinese literature—Ming dynasty, 1368–1644—History and criticism. 3. Chinese literature—Qing dynasty, 1644–1912—History and criticism. I. Title.
PL2278.L49 2012
895.1'099287—dc23   2012011200

The paper used in this publication is acid-free and meets the minimum requirements of American National Standard for Information Sciences—Permanence of Paper for Printed Library Materials, ANSI Z39.48 1984.∞

*This book is dedicated to my grandmother
Wang Dongmei (1911–2010), who raised me. She
did not have the opportunity to receive a formal
education and remained illiterate throughout her life,
but she was profoundly cultured and had a big heart.*

*It is also dedicated to my teacher Professor
Grace S. Fong, who led me to the field of women's
literary culture in late imperial China.*

CONTENTS

Acknowledgments — ix

Introduction — 3
1. The Green Window: The Boudoir in Poetic Convention — 20
2. A New Feminine Ideal: The Case of *The Anthology of Correct Beginnings* — 52
3. Convention and Intervention: The Lyrical World of Gu Zhenli — 86
4. Inside Out: The Gui in Times of Chaos — 115
5. The Old Boudoir and the "New Woman": The Late Qing and Early Republican Era — 145
Conclusion — 179

Notes — 187
Glossary of Chinese Characters — 211
Bibliography — 215
Index — 231

ACKNOWLEDGMENTS

The journey of the making of this book started at McGill University, where I met Professor Grace S. Fong and took her course "Ming-Qing Women's Writings" in 1999. When she recommended this course to me, I can still remember blurting out, "Were there women writers in the Ming-Qing period?!" Before going to McGill, I graduated from the Department of Chinese Language and Literature at Peking University, one of the best universities in China, but I had learned about only a handful of women writers from earlier periods. Women writers of the Ming-Qing period? Unheard of. With an understanding smile, Professor Fong replied, "Well, you should come to my class then." I did and have ever since been exploring this forgotten part of China's literary past.

The years of training I received at McGill were crucial to the making of this book. From basic research knowledge and skills to how to become a serious scholar, Professor Fong has been an unflagging guide. I am deeply grateful, not only for her scholarly inspiration, but also for her sustained support of my career. She opened up a brand-new world to me and played a fundamental role in helping me reestablish my career after I immigrated to Canada in 1998. I can never thank her enough. Adding to this good fortune, I am also blessed to have had Professor Robin S. Yates's advice on the field of Ming-Qing history. His insights as a historian have led me to always pursue further the historical and critical issues relevant to my study. My heartfelt thanks also go to Professor Thomas Lamarre, for comments on my thesis proposal that have remained helpful in refining the approach adopted in this study, and to Professors Kenneth Dean, Hajimei Nakatani, and K. M. Sibbald, for serving on my dissertation examination committee and making suggestions for revisions that have been incorporated into this book. I want to thank Professor Dean, in particular, for his assistance on many other academic occasions. It would have been impossible for me to come this far if not for their support. I wish also to acknowledge my fellow students and friends at McGill, James Bonk, Paola Carrozza, Alvin Chung, Jie Ding, Ping Fu, Qiaole Huang, Young Kwon, Fan Lin, Yonghua Liu, Diane Lemire, Sara Neswald, Margaret Ng, Sufeng Xu, and Yimin Zhang, who made my years of graduate study pleasant and unforgettable. All have been a precious source of inspiration and peer support.

This scholarly undertaking is also indebted to a number of other institutions and individuals. First, I would like to acknowledge the Social Science and Humanities Research Council of Canada's Four-Year Doctoral Fellowship, 2000–2004, and the Chiang Ching-Kuo Doctoral Fellowship, 2005. During my doctoral studies, I also benefited from the 2004 Mellon Dissertation Workshop at Washington University in St. Louis hosted by Professor Robert Hegel. In 2005, I landed my first job at Swarthmore College, where I was able to move on to the next stage of my career. I want to thank Alan Berkowitz, Haili Kong, Carole Netter, and Kirsten Speidel for their friendship. In 2008, the University of California, Santa Barbara, offered me my current job, which I hope will be my last. I am deeply grateful for the generous support of the department and the university in the forms of course release and research funds, including the Career Development Fund, Individual Research Fund, and Hellman Fellowship. I have been especially blessed to have Professor Ron Egan, a real gentleman and scholar, as my mentor and friend. He has graciously read my work and offered valuable suggestions. Professors John Nathan, Yunte Huang, and Anthony Barbieri-Low have also helped in various ways. During the writing of this book, I belonged to a book-writing group with ann-elise lewallen, Christina McMahon, Mhoze Chikowero, and Teresa Shewry. I benefited a great deal from their criticism and suggestions.

Beyond the campuses with which I have been affiliated, I would like to thank Professor Wilt Idema, the external examiner of my Ph.D. dissertation, and Professor Ellen Widmer who read the dissertation and the introductory chapter of my book manuscript. Both gave me specific advice on how to expand on my subject. Liang Ying, the librarian at Shanghai Library, kindly assisted me many times in finding the materials I needed. I also want to acknowledge pioneering scholars in the field of late imperial Chinese women's culture and history, such as Kang-i Sun Chang, Beata Grant, Wilt Idema, Grace S. Fong, Dorothy Ko, Susan Mann, Maureen Robertson, and Ellen Widmer, whose works were particularly inspirational. Without their studies, there would have been no way to chart the territory of this book.

For the publication of this book, my special thanks go to my editor, Lorri Hagman, who was extremely enthusiastic and efficient in responding to my initial proposal, arranging the review of my manuscript, and managing all other matters. The two anonymous readers of my manuscript were also incredibly expeditious and provided incisive comments and suggestions that have helped me improve the final version. Tim Roberts was the managing editor, and Laura Iwasaki did a wonderful job of copyediting. I also wish to especially thank Jim Bonk, my former fellow student and friend, who was always available to meticulously check the errors and awkwardness of my English and to make sure my points were more clearly expressed. I also remember Kim Trainer, who helped edit two chapters of my dissertation. For the illustrations, I want to thank Hui-shu Lee for her help.

The intervening years between the dissertation and the publication of this book were the most difficult of my life. In addition to other family crises, both my parents were seriously ill; however, they gave me their unfailing support even though their health was failing. They often said that good news coming from me always cheered them up. I am terribly regretful that they did not live to see the publication of this book. In spite of sorrow over our not-till-the-end journey, I am grateful for Lanqing Han's love and support when I was a graduate student. Finally, I wish to thank my bosom friends Gao Hongmei, Liu Xiudong, Wang Jing, Zhang Huihong, and Zhang Xiuli, who comforted and encouraged me from time to time when I was facing difficult moments.

Last but not least, I want to send two words to cheer myself up: onward and upward!

Women's Poetry of Late Imperial China

Introduction

On a spring day in 1929, Hu Shi (1891–1962), one of the most prominent writers and scholars of twentieth-century China, was at home examining a comprehensive catalog of Qing women's writings edited by Shan Shili (1863–1945). Despite his amazement at the sheer number of women poets recorded in the catalog, Hu Shi wrote a preface in which he came to this stunning conclusion: "In my opinion, the literary achievement of women in the past three hundred years is indeed poor, and most of their writings are worthless." The reason, he suggested, is that most of the texts in Shan Shili's catalog are poetry on the theme of women's activities in the inner chambers.[1] As a cultural giant of the May Fourth Movement, Hu Shi was intolerant of old literature that did not accord with his new cultural agendas. His sweeping critique of women's poetry of the recent past may have been partially responsible for its marginalization in the modern compilation of Chinese literary history.[2] It was not until the past two decades, more than half a century after Hu's comments, that exciting scholarship on women's literary practice in late imperial China (ca. 1600–1900) began to emerge. Informed by feminist and other critical agendas, social and literary historians have striven to rediscover women's texts and to show their significance in providing new perspectives on the lives of women authors and the recent Chinese literary past. It turns out that the previously invisible and silenced female half of society was actually an active cultural community whose achievement is far from "poor."[3]

In reevaluating the texts, however, we cannot simply dismiss Hu Shi's low opinion; instead, we should inquire into the reasons for his opinion and take them into account when developing critical models. Hu Shi's glimpse into Qing women's writings, though impressionistic and oversimplified, does have a certain degree of evidential support. First of all, the poetic genre is by default the one in which women were most active. Furthermore, the shared features of their poetry are indeed striking: from similar thematic choices and styles, to recurrent images, to the fact that many of these poems are related to women's lives in the inner chambers. The recurrence of certain themes and patterns is not unique to women's texts but has been often discussed in literary criticism dealing with originality and imitation or intertextuality.[4] However, in developing critical models for women's writings, one should ask: What are the important ways in which women participate in literary practice as a socially and culturally determined group? How should we interpret distinct features pertaining to women's texts? To what extent should we recognize gender difference in literature by women?

This book addresses these critical issues by tracing the development of the *gui*, meaning the boudoir or the inner chambers, topos over the three hundred years identified by Hu Shi—a period that witnessed the most significant developments in late imperial Chinese women's writings. The period covers the last decades of the Ming dynasty (1368–1644), the entire Qing (1644–1911), and the early years of the Republic (1911–49). Whereas Hu Shi overlooked the subtle and new meanings that women authors attached to the *gui* and ultimately dismissed their poetry on the *gui* as "worthless," the *gui* elucidates and was fundamental to a dynamic poetics that brings into relief recurrent themes, motifs, and imagery pertaining to women's texts, sheds light on the levels of mediation of women's textual production by the literary tradition as well as ideological and sociohistorical conditions, and serves as a measure of their creativity in expanding conventional poetic space.

During the late imperial period, women continued to be consigned to the *gui* by Confucian social and gender norms. Most of the women writers in this time were from elite families who were observant of the principle of sex segregation and able to afford the expense of accommodating female family members in the inner chambers. Consignment to the *gui* influenced women as both social and writing subjects. The *gui* not only was a physically and socially bounded location within which women were supposed to live but also constituted a discursive space in which both men and women articulated their ideas about gender, sexuality, femininity, and women's subjectivities. It became a significant determinant in women's approaches to representing their gendered positions and experiences in the late imperial period and beyond.

Social historians such as Dorothy Ko and Susan Mann have shown the complex ways in which women both depended on and negotiated their gender boundaries in cultivating a distinctive women's culture.[5] Women's interaction with the multileveled conception of the *gui*, however, has not yet been closely examined from the standpoint of women's literary production. In their pioneering studies, literary historians such as Maureen Robertson and Grace S. Fong have offered important theoretical insights into women writers' negotiation with conventional poetics in the *shi* and *ci* genres.[6] The boudoir as a conventional setting in feminine poetics underlies their analysis, and both authors offer many insights on which this study can draw, but neither focuses on the conception of the *gui* itself.[7]

Although the parameters of women's poetry are not signified only by the *gui*, by making it a focus and framing device, this study identifies a core area in which to examine women's connections to and the innovations they introduced to preexisting feminine poetic tradition. Women poets in late imperial China constructed a poetics that simultaneously was within the tradition and derived from their subjective positions and perspectives. Although the framework of the *gui* does not supersede other "particularized gendered subformations," with its multiple significations associated with female gender, it is crucial for our understanding of the distinctive poetics of women who were active writers during this period.[8]

THE *GUI*: THE NORMATIVE GENDER LOCATION

The Chinese character *gui* etymologically means "the small gate of the inner courtyard, palace, or city."[9] It is most often used in combination with other elements to form a range of words associated with the inner apartments, space, or sphere, such as *guige* (inner chambers), *guikun* (inner quarters), and *guifang* (bedrooms).[10] Moreover, due to its association with inwardness, it has long been associated with the female gender. By the late imperial period, the term *gui* had come to embrace a nexus of meanings: the physical space of the women's chambers, a defining social boundary for the roles and place of women, and a spatial topos evoking feminine beauty and pathos in the literary imagination. All of these meanings are crucial to the concerns of this study. While the Chinese term *gui* may be used in an inclusive and general sense, depending on the context, "the inner chambers" is a more abstract and broader concept that refers generally to the space of the inner or domestic sphere to which women were supposed to belong and "the boudoir" represents an even more private and narrower space composed of women's apartments in the inner chambers, that is, the bedrooms and dressing rooms.

The consignment of women to the inner chambers originated from the ideal of physically and socially separating the sexes. The recognized, earliest source of this idea is the Confucian ritual and ethical classic the *Book of Rites* (Li ji), dating to the Han dynasty (202 BCE–220 CE), which notes: "While men live in the outer, women live in the inner sphere." It goes on to say, "From the age of seven, a boy and a girl would not sit together or share a meal." A boy "from the age of ten would seek instructions from an outside teacher," but "a girl from the age of ten should not go outside."[11] The section "Regulations for the Inner Sphere" (Nei ze) in the *Book of Rites* goes further, elaborating on the behavior codes of sex segregation. These principles were repeatedly quoted verbatim or rephrased in the moral instructions of later ages. The *Analects for Women* (Nü lunyu) by the palace woman Song Ruozhao of the Tang (618–907), for example, rephrases the idea stated in "Regulations for the Inner Sphere": "Inner and outer, each has its place. Males and females gather separately. Women do not peek outside the walls nor step into the outer courtyard. If they go out, they must cover their faces. If they do peek, they conceal their forms."[12] Another influential source reiterating the separation of spheres is "Miscellaneous Proprieties for Managing the Family" (Zhi jia), by Sima Guang (1019–1086). This work is considered a signpost of the Song dynasty's (960–1279) increasing attention to gender distinction associated with spatial terms.[13]

The idea of gender separation was supposed to be not only embodied with physical boundaries but also extended to the division of labor. Men were supposed to be in charge of social and public affairs, whereas women were called to mind domestic matters. As the *Book of Rites* emphasizes, "Men should not discuss affairs of the inner sphere; women should not discuss affairs of the outer sphere."[14] Presuming the separate spheres between males and females, the Han classic *Precepts for Women* (Nü jie), by Ban Zhao, provides specific codes by which women were to conduct themselves in the domestic sphere.[15]

The above-mentioned moral instructions, among others, were recognized as orthodox sources on gender division in late imperial society. Elite men and women drew on these sources to construct the cultural ideal of the segregated women's quarters and female propriety. Together, *Precepts for Women*, *Instructions for the Inner Quarters* (Neixun), by the Ming Empress Xu, *Analects for Women*, and the *Record of Female Exemplars* (Nüfan jielu), by Wang Jiefu (Chaste Woman Wang) of the Ming, constituted the so-called Four Books for Women (Nü sishu), a standard curriculum of didactic texts for women established by the late Ming.[16] These books were recognized as the quintessential works on normative womanhood and were "required reading for the daughters of all upper-class families."[17] Despite different emphases and temporal origins, these moral classics clearly set forth the separate spheres—male: outside, female: inside.

The ideal material expression of these ethical principles was a Chinese house built to provide "the physical frame of women's lives and [give] concrete form to the separation of men's and women's domains."[18] The women's sphere was located within the inner quarters. Enclosed by high walls, the house ensured that women were kept out of public view. As a girl grew up in such a house, she learned about her proper place and roles within society. The Chinese house was not merely a shelter made of materials but also "a cultural template": it was a learning device, a space imprinted with ritual as well as political and social messages.[19]

There is little evidence that these ideological principles were put into practice, but there is evidence of the elite's insistence on gender distinction in everyday life. A father of five daughters and a believer in the ethical values espoused by the Cheng-Zhu school of Neo-Confucianism, Chen Hongmou (1696–1771), compiled *Inherited Guide for My Daughters* (Jiaonü yigui) in 1742 in order to instruct the women in his family on their proper roles and daily conduct.[20] In his guide, he sees women's major role as managing the household in order to ensure the prosperity and propriety of the patrilineal family. In addition to the old doctrines of sexual segregation, he gives the women of the house specific pieces of advice such as: "If women do not know how to cook and do not enter the kitchen, they cannot effectively manage the household; if women are enabled to make companions and form clubs, showing their bodies and faces in public, they cannot order the household."[21] Chen's book was widely recognized and reprinted repeatedly during the Qing and Republican periods.[22] But his was only one among many expressing similar views. Female seclusion was always the first and foremost concern of "household instructions" (*jia xun*), a practical genre established in the mid-Ming.[23] Gender distinction had become a core belief by the mid-Qing.[24]

However, drawing on different sources, new trends in historical studies have uncovered shifts of consciousness and discrepancies between reality and ideal principles, especially in the late Ming. Through an examination of the sixteenth-century manual *Regulations for the Inner Chambers* (Gui fan), by the late Ming scholar-official Lü Kun (1536–1618), Joanna F. Handlin illustrates a more sympathetic and pragmatic approach to women's moral issues in a changing society.[25] Dorothy Ko's article on women of the Clear Brook Poetry Club indicates that women from the gentry class also crossed gender boundaries in their literary interaction with a male teacher and leader.[26] In her book *Teachers of the Inner Chambers*, Ko further theorizes a female literary culture based on an expanding women's sphere in the fluid society of seventeenth-century Jiangnan.

From various perspectives, scholars have painted two different pictures of women's relations to the gendered domain of the *gui*, both of which are supported by strong evidence and arguments. Their divergent points of view reveal the complexity of the issue. A better position from which to discuss it may be found by taking into account both visions of gender boundaries associated with the *gui* and revisiting Lü Kun's thoughts about women in his *Regulations for the Inner Chambers*, a didactic work designed specifically to be read by women. The fact that Lü Kun uses the *gui* as a framework for expounding the major principles asserted in earlier classics, makes his manual an essential work for examining how the ideological concept of the *gui* was established and its implications for women's place in society in the late imperial period.

Lü Kun explains in his preface that he compiled *Regulations for the Inner Chambers* as a reaction to what he perceived as the degenerate behavior of women, whether the vulgar speech of village women, the extravagant lifestyle of wealthy women, or women's difficult relationships with other family members. In his preface, he also frowns upon women's participation in literary activities.[27] Lü Kun's criticism of the disappointing behavior of women reveals the gap between orthodox principle and social reality. She Yongning, who contributed a preface for the manual, points out, "There are so many transgressions of the principles for the inner sphere; the way of the world is

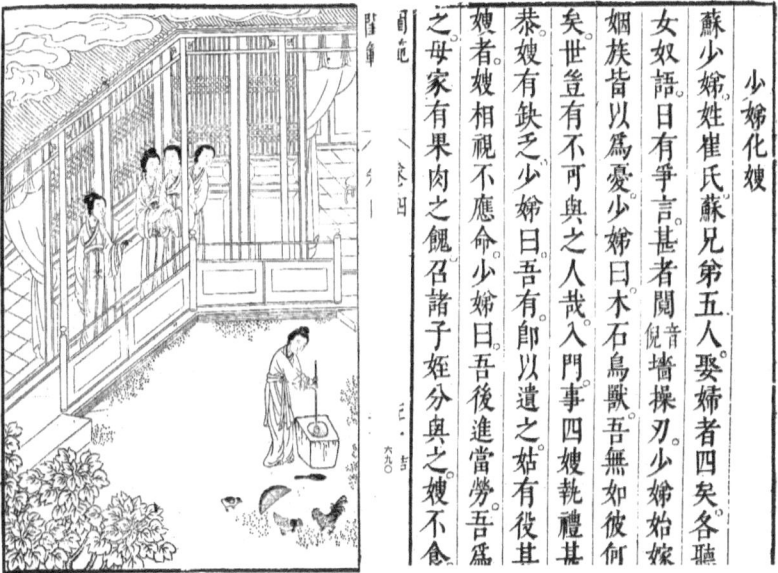

Figure 1.1a-b "The Younger Sister-in-Law Serving as a Role Model for the Older Ones" (Shaodi hua sao), reprinted from Lü Kun, *Guifan*, 4.690-91.

daily getting worse."[28] Troubled by the fact that "the person dwelling within the inner quarters" (*guimen zhong ren*) discarded rituals and behavior codes, Lü Kun hopes his manual can provide moral guidelines that she can uphold, recite, and learn.[29]

Although Lü Kun's didactic text may not fully represent social reality, his moral instructions framed by the notion of the *gui* indicates that the *gui* had become a recognized discursive field in dominant ideological discourse for reiterating gender boundaries and constructing the female subjectivity. The preface writers for the different editions of *Regulations for the Inner Chambers* insisted on the *gui* being inscribed with moral codes, turning it into a locus for defining women's proper roles in society. As She Yongning claims, "There must be regulations in the women's chambers."[30] They compiled and reprinted Lü Kun's manual in order to continuously spread "old values." The first *juan* of the manual is a large collection of quotations from Confucian classics such as the *Book of Rites*, with Lü's annotations and interpretations. Lü's written commentary, however, reiterates gender division without offering any suggestions for bringing about change. Despite the subtle changes in Lü's approach to women's issues, the basic values he reasserts are unchanged. Lü Kun's strategy in promoting these ideas is adaptive; he made *Regulations for the Inner Chambers* more user-friendly with illustrations and annotations. But these approaches can be viewed as efforts to make his didacticism more effective and more widely received. In encouraging women to be "expedient" in case of emergency, he is calling for a restricted moral autonomy that remains within the boundaries of orthodox values.

The subject targeted by *Regulations for the Inner Chambers* is explicitly termed the *guiren* (the person dwelling within the inner quarters)."[31] The *gui* is the defining element in both of these terms. Because the *gui*, as a physical space, was possible only in the ideal Chinese house, the terms suggest a class prerogative. It is clear that the majority of women in the late imperial period would not have had the means to live in the ideal house capable of accommodating a *gui*. Elsewhere, in his *Records on Practical Government* (Shizheng lu), as quoted by Handlin, Lü Kun does seem to recognize class as a mitigating factor. Unlike his contemporary Hai Rui (1514–1587), who insists that all women should remain inside the home, Lü Kun maintains a tolerant attitude toward lower-class women working outside their homes as wine vendors and weavers. He even suggests that they contribute to the local economy.[32] However, he does not address the classist issue in his manual. Nor do other assertive preface writers specifically define the *guiren* in terms of social class. The ambiguity of class in constructing the regulations for the women's chambers makes it appear that Lü Kun intended these regulations to be socially inclusive. In making his manual easier to understand, he also aimed at a more general female audience. Indeed, the *guiren* subject appears to be synonymous with the generic notion of women vis-à-vis men. This is not surprising, given that the *gui* was discursively constructed rather than reflective of the actual situations in which women found themselves.

In addition to the ideological-didactic construction of the *gui* as women's proper social place, the image of women and the space of the women's chambers had long been part of Chinese literary imagination. Among all the major literary genres, boudoir poetry had assumed the longest-lived and most important place in Chinese literary history, with the earliest examples dating to the Han period. Most commonly, male literati used the image to exercise their imaginations about female sexuality and emotion. The setting of the inner chambers was aestheticized and the image of women objectified in poetic forms mainly to serve their desires and interests.[33] The literary construction of women's boudoir life was remarkably different from that in Confucian gender ideology, but it likewise strengthened the association between women and the inner sphere. The sensual depiction of the feminine setting, which is typical of the literati poetic imaginary, emphasizes "a closed and enclosed environment, in which the female dweller is typically portrayed as static and passive." The representability of domesticity with stock images makes the concept of "the inner" (*nei*) more than an ethical concept.[34]

Despite degrees of complexity in actual situations, the *gui* had become both a real and an imaginary place for women.[35] Moral instructions for women as well as other discourses centered on the *gui* provide clues for constructing female subjects in both social formation and discourse. They generated conceptualized gendered positions into which women could be interpolated. In other words, the *gui* was molded into a symbol of women's sexual status and gender position and became a recognizable signifier in late imperial Chinese social and cultural practices. Women inevitably brought these meanings into their poetry even as their strategic uses of these meanings differed.

THEORIZING A POETICS OF THE *GUI*

Consignment to the *gui* determined, shaped, and constrained not only women's lifestyles but also their relationship to literary power and discourse. It has been a commonplace that in premodern China women in general were ideologically and institutionally excluded from the public sphere of intellectual and literary activities. However, it was the belief in and practice of the gendered distinction between the inner and outer spheres that left women without a legitimate place in literary practice. The visibility of writing women in the late imperial era therefore generated heated debates on the issues of women's talent and virtue, exemplified in the famous debate between Zhang Xuecheng (1738–1801), who opposed women writers, and Yuan Mei (1716–1797), who supported them.[36] Many writing women were actually struggling (or claimed to be doing so) with the question of whether or not to write. Like Western women writers such as Emily Dickinson (1830–1886), writing women in late imperial China suffered from "the anxiety of authorship." As Sandra M. Gilbert and Susan Gubar observe in *The Madwoman in the Attic*, this anxiety was unique to female authors because they lived in "a culture whose fundamental definitions of literary authority are overtly and covertly patriarchal."[37] Although Gilbert and Gubar's study is about Western women writers, their observation can be applied to the situation of late imperial Chinese women poets. The *gui* in the context of Chinese culture institutionally defined a patriarchal condition that excluded women from the public sphere of writing.

Even though many women crossed the boundaries and engaged in writing, they entered into literary practice on a different footing than men. The *shi* and *ci* genres had been constructed within male social, political, and cultural practices long before women entered the field in significant numbers. The poetic treatment of the images of women and the boudoir, whether for aesthetic appreciation or political-erotic allegory, had been an influential and far-reaching literati tradition, from early times up until the Qing period. It left behind a vast repertory of vocabulary, imagery, themes, and motifs centered on the images of women as well as their emotional world and life settings. Women poets to a large extent relied on the repertory of available representations in writing about themselves. The most easily identifiable textual feature is their heavy reliance on conventional codes and formulaic descriptions developed in the literati boudoir literature, such as terms describing women's garments, ornaments, and the boudoir setting. Women also derived textual positions and voice from the literati inscription of femininity. This feature in women's poetry is particularly evident in their employment of the literati topoi of boudoir lament. Speaking through recognized poetic conventions, some texts by women are barely distinguishable from those of their male predecessors. This similarity suggests that women writers found an important channel that connected them to the literary past.

Although women's literary imaginations could go as far as those of their male counterparts, the inner chambers often circumscribed the field in which they could develop a distinctive literary culture. Familial and female homosocial life was an important channel of poetic production. Daily activities in the inner chambers provided a primary source apart from books and hearsay from which to draw inspiration for poetic themes and motifs. The fact that they spent most of their time in the inner chambers while male family members left home for education and career explains why women often echo the traditional boudoir lament in their poetry. This also explains why domestic activities such as weaving, cooking, and sewing disproportionally outnumber other subject matter in the thematics of women's poetry, as Hu Shi observed.

Writing women nonetheless demonstrated their literary agency and creativity—when assuming the place of writing subjects, they did not merely perpetuate the literary tradition but rewrote it from their subjective positions and according to their social and cultural experiences. When she had the opportunity to wield the brush, a woman, consciously or unconsciously, had to make a difficult yet compelling choice: how to present herself to the intended or possible reader (even if she was writing to herself). Due to the belief that "poetry expresses one's intent" (*shi yan zhi*), a prevalent cultural assumption about the poetic genre in Chinese literary history, a poem was presumed to be a record of historical experiences and an expression of the author's intent. It was supposed to be read in relation to the poet.[38] In other words, a woman's poetry was perceived as a self-representation within her historical context; she was responsible for the meaning of the text that bore her name. To represent herself properly and "truthfully," she had to make choices—what to write, what not to write, and how to write.

Numerous female subjects and multiple ideologies and discourses were involved in constructing the feminine space of the *gui*. Along with the *guiren* subject, other discourses centered on women in late imperial China's social and cultural life also produced an array of female subjects associated with the *gui*, such as, to name a few, *guixiu* (the talented of the inner chambers), *guiyan* (the beauty of the inner chambers), *guiwa* (the girl of the inner chambers), and *guiying* (the eminent of the inner chambers). While the common morpheme *gui* always functions to indicate that the subject is female, the second morpheme in each term suggests some other quality. In particular, moral teachings on female gender boundaries and literati imaginations of the boudoir provided different and even contradictory messages. For example, the unconventional writer Li Yu (1610–1680) deliberately subverts the presumption that female seclusion can facilitate true virtue.[39] His erotic novel *The Carnal Prayer Mat* (Rou putuan) sharply satirizes the strict Confucian scholar Master Iron Gate (Tiefei Daoren), who has compelled his daughter to live in seclusion, only to have her eventually elope with a male seducer. Compared with didactic books and their moralizing, literary discourse is both more diverse and more complicated.

Both a "subjected being" and a "free agent," the writing woman might have found herself caught between different subject positions,[40] but she had a certain degree of autonomy in choosing those positions that she found most compelling and rejecting those that she found irrelevant or distasteful.[41] The writing woman's ability to make alterations and changes through literary means, however conditioned and constrained, underscores her creativity. Construction of new feminine subjectivities, such as the emergence of the *guixiu* identity redefined according to its contemporary cultural ideal, is one of the major forces underlying women's transformative poetics of the *gui*. A woman's modifications of literary conventions testify to her agency and creativity in engaging with power structures that dictated language and symbol-making practice. Writing, even in the restrictive poetic genre, provided women with new possibilities for self-understanding and projection. Women, based on their subjective experiences and positions, interact with the *gui* as a feminine and erotic space in the preexisting poetic tradition and as a proper social place for women.

Reiteration of the textual positions and artistic effects in the preexisting boudoir poetics is a prevalent mode of articulation by women poets. This type of writing is centered mostly on conventional themes such as the boudoir lament and the seasonal scenery of the boudoir. The poems may not refer to the poet's actual life experience but read like exercises in conventions of the genre. Women's poetry of this kind is informed largely by women's textual experience of the boudoir as learned from the literary past. However, we should not treat it simply as an imitative exercise of the literati; it may reveal aspects of the culturally constructed nature of women's gender consciousness and may still express their interests and desires.

Informed by their subjective experiences and the unprecedented development of women's literary culture in the late imperial era, women poets also created new modes of representing their lives related to the *gui*, modes that did not exist in male-authored representations or women's writings of earlier times. A critical mass of writing women in late imperial China, especially in the Qing, re-created some distinct, "female" textual territories by projecting their subjective experiences and perspectives.

Late imperial Chinese women reconstructed the *gui* as an ideal place for women within existing social orders. In other words, Ming-Qing women writers "reclaim the boudoir as their own domestic space" by turning the lonely corner of the boudoir into "a de-eroticized place of work, leisure, and companionship with other women."[42] The abandoned-woman persona is replaced by a content, active, and cultured *guixiu*, a newly minted feminine identity. The parameters of the *gui* are significantly broadened, from the narrow boudoir to the more spatial and lively inner chambers.

In expressing their feelings about women's proper place, some female poets were not afraid to go against the tide. For these women, life in the boudoir was a living nightmare, and their poetry articulated their resentment and bitterness about their plight as women cloistered in the *gui*. This mode of writing demonstrates a subversive tendency toward deconstructing the inner chambers as the cultural ideal.

Another mode of women's poetic articulation regards the *gui* in collision with the outside world. While most *guixiu* lived in the inner chambers most of the time, women sometimes did venture out for travel, pleasure, work, or flight from a war-torn region. In times of tragic or dramatic social changes such as the Ming-Qing transition (in the mid-seventeenth century) and the Taiping Rebellion (1850–64), the *gui* could collapse into a world of chaos, forcing women to confront historical transitions and political disasters. Women living through social upheavals were deeply affected, and they brought their broader social and political experiences into the poetic space of the *gui*. The *gui* appears in their writing as inconsequential, a "small window" that frames their perspective on broader historical changes, a shrunken space that they examine from a great distance. Some even decided to break free from the *gui* in order to devote their lives to national or political movements.

Variables in women's depictions of their *gui* reflect the female subject's positioning in relation to the normative gender location. These poetic modes result from a combination of continuity (the *gui* as a social norm and literary convention), on the one hand, and contingency (women's changing subject positions and sociohistorical experiences), on the other. Although these modes by no means exhaust the complexity of women's depictions of their lived experiences in the *gui*, it is still productive to identify them and analyze their origins, modalities, and significance in relation to literary traditions and gender norms in social, historical, and personal contexts. Underlying these major modes of articulation are complicated relationships between the writing subject and the age-old poetic tradition, relationships affected by different social and historical factors as well as personal backgrounds and experiences. Analysis of each mode's intersections with literary traditions and varying historical contexts reveals much about the processes of women's poetic production, or the unique ways in which women participated in the production of meaning from their gendered perspectives.

A FEMALE LITERARY TRADITION?: A DIALOGUE WITH WESTERN FEMINISM

These major modes of women's articulation about the *gui* point to a striking coherence of women's texts produced in the late imperial era. Importantly, the coherence of women's texts is not unique to late imperial China. Western feminist scholars have also encountered "an imaginative continuum, the recurrence of certain patterns, themes, problems, and images from generation to generation" and "the coherence of theme and imagery" in nineteenth-century works by women in the West. They have therefore argued for a "distinctively female literary tradition."[43] However, this approach has also been criticized by postmodernist female thinkers as a tendency to seek an essential female identity and style.[44] After being vigorously attacked by postmodernist critics, the agenda of establishing a female literary tradition seems to have lost its inspirational power.

Directly related to the notion of "a distinctively female literary tradition," another controversial notion in Western feminist criticism, "women's experience," has been criticized as "a biologically based essentialism" and "an inadequate biographically based approach." Critics argue that the term "gynocritics" implies a traditional humanist position, assuming the text to be a "transparent medium" through which human experience can be seized. It bears the weakness of all experientially based positions: inadequate attention to the literariness of women's works, inability to appreciate modernist and avant-garde texts, and neglect of the mediated nature of women's self-expression.[45] All these criticisms rightly point to the limitations of a reflectionist model.

Revisiting these issues decades later, however, it is still important to consider how to interpret or understand "the coherence of theme and imagery that we encountered in the works of writers who were often geographically, historically, and psychologically distant from each other."[46] The notion of women's experience is a valid basis for feminist literary analysis to the extent that it is taken as a sociocultural category evolving with its historically specific context and as a ground for the formation of female subjection and subjectivity. As an institution of gender, the *gui* determined the ways in which women participated in literary production, and to identify the common experiences of a certain group of women that help constitute meanings attached to the female gender is not to pointlessly pursue "an ideal of quintessential female experience."[47] Women in a historically specific context indeed share some common political, social, and cultural experiences. Taking women as a critical category, our first task must be "to plot the precise cultural locus of female literary identity and to describe the forces that intersect an individual woman writer's cultural field."[48] More than a cultural locus of female literary identity, but definitely a cultural field that encompassed all the major forces that influenced the lives and works of women writers in late imperial China, the *gui* provides such a locus for studying the ways in which women of this particular era participated in poetic production.

SOURCES AND STRUCTURE

The five chapters of this book introduce the major modes of articulation in poetry while acknowledging the internal patterns by which these different poetic modes relate to one another and the particular historical and personal circumstances under which they were generated. Although this study is confined to the analysis of women's textual strategies on a literary level, its major framework and organization of references are informed by an investigation of the historical conditions and circumstances under which the texts were produced. It is assumed that nuances in women's historical, cultural, and individual experiences played an instrumental role in shaping women's changing perceptions of their *gui* and the meanings of their texts. Texts do not necessarily mirror their authors' life experiences, but our reading of these texts can be illuminated by considering the historical conjunctures in which they were produced. Women's writing is a product of their broader social and cultural contexts as well as a reflection of their individual experiences and perspectives.

The term "Ming-Qing" in phrases such as "Ming-Qing women's poetry" or "Ming-Qing writing women" is used here in a loose sense, referring to the late imperial period from about 1600 to 1900, when women's literary culture developed. The organization of the chapters reflects the internal relationship between the different modes of articulation adopted by women poets and the positions they take toward the *gui*. This pattern does not necessarily occur linearly in time. While some modes appear to be unique to certain historical moments or individual cases, others are common across time and in multiple cases. For example, the traditional literati mode of boudoir poetry can be found throughout imperial history and even into the Republican era. Furthermore, one of the major sources for this study, *The*

Anthology of Correct Beginnings by Inner-Chamber Talents of the Present Dynasty (Guochao guixiu zhengshi ji), is neither chronological nor reflective of only works of its own time. Even though it was compiled in the 1830s, it includes poems produced in the late Ming and early Qing and may represent even earlier tendencies. For example, the incorporation of female virtues prescribed by Confucian gender ideology into the genre of the boudoir plaint is evident as early as the popular songs preserved in the Dunhuang caves. *The Anthology of Correct Beginnings* is discussed immediately after an examination of the preexisting boudoir tradition, not only because it marks the culmination of a major revision of the older convention, but also because it represents a norm of women's poetics that can be read in contrast to other modes of articulation, whether taking place before or after. In contrast to the feminine ideal represented in *The Anthology of Correct Beginnings*, women's articulations on their displacement from the *gui* and resentment of gender inequality during times of disorder were voiced in a similar mode, whether during the Ming-Qing transition or the Taiping Rebellion. As literary expression, each of the modes has its own complex relationship with time.

Most of the women writers studied here were active in the Qing. This reflects the natural outgrowth of women's literary culture in late imperial China, a development that had reached its peak by the mid-Qing. Testifying to the primacy of the Qing, 4,000 among the total of about 4,300 women authors registered in Hu Wenkai's comprehensive catalog of women's writing in premodern China lived during the Qing and the rest during the Ming.[49] Members of the new literary collective were largely gentry daughters, wives, and mothers, not only because they constituted the majority of writing women but also because they were most directly subject to the gender roles defined by the boundaries of the *gui*. To a much greater extent than the courtesans and nuns who lived outside the family system, they were keen to modify stereotypical images of women that did not reflect their subjective experiences with the *gui*. Thus, this book focuses on this major force behind the transformation of the preexisting boudoir tradition, writing women based in gentry or elite families.[50]

This is not to say, however, that the writings of courtesans and nuns are totally irrelevant to the critical concerns of this study. Whether as a source of inspiration or in the role of author, the courtesan had long been and continued to be active in the writing of boudoir poetry until the decline of courtesan culture in the early Qing. Not surprisingly, most boudoir poems by courtesans were affinitive to the literati tradition. Even the poetry of Liu Shi (1618–1664), who is famous for her individual, intense poetic voice, does not express a strong interest in altering the conventional meaning of the boudoir. Women often became nuns in their later years, so nuns also touched on motifs related to the *gui* when reflecting on their departure from domestic life and entry into religious pursuits.[51]

Sources fall into two main categories: male-authored and female-authored writings on the *gui*. Theoretical considerations have guided the selection of several groups of poetic writings produced in different historical moments and personal contexts. Works from both the *shi* and *ci* genres are included, with attention to particular conventions and cultural implications pertaining to each genre.

Both anthologies and individual collections constitute essential information on the common features of and individual differences in women's writing. Anthologies are by nature selective, for they are put together according to the compiler's implicit or explicit criteria. If the criteria are implemented consistently, anthologies can reveal particular recurring features of women's writing. For example, the poems selected for *The Anthology of Correct Beginnings* strike a reader as very similar in themes, styles, and language. This is important for identifying some common processes of meaning production in women's literary practice. Individual collections provide a sense of completeness and indicate the depth of a poet's writing. They can tell us much about what anthologies have left out: the range of an author's writings, her personal preferences in themes and styles, and, in some cases, information on her life experiences. These two kinds of sources constitute the basis for obtaining close and extensive knowledge about Ming-Qing women's rewriting of the *gui*.

A discursive space intimately connected to both the Chinese poetic tradition and the social prescription of women's place, the *gui* is an important point of departure for studying Ming-Qing women's distinct approach to the writing of poetry. It provides a productive framework for systematically examining interactions between gendered poetics and women's gendered consciousnesses in late imperial China and beyond.

CHAPTER 1

The Green Window

The Boudoir in Poetic Convention

On patterned silk, golden kingfishers;
Fragrant candles melt into tears.
Flowers fall; the cuckoo cries;
At the green window, the remnant of a dream dims.

畫羅金翡翠，香燭銷成淚。花落子規啼，綠窗殘夢迷。

—WEN TINGYUN 溫庭筠

The boudoir as a poetic convention had long been established in both the *shi* and *ci* genres by the late imperial era. These two forms have different generic conventions, but they share some common ground in representing boudoir themes. The concept of topos is useful for studying the status of the boudoir in Chinese poetic tradition. The term "topos," short for the Greek *koinos topos* (literally "common place"), is generally understood as an ordinary or conventional theme or motif in literary studies. Viewing topos as "a form-element in literature that presents a certain setting, with the range of associations that have adhered to it through time and use" is particularly germane in working through the formation of the boudoir topos.[1] The boudoir is just such a poetic element encompassing a constellation of recognized themes, motifs, and images. An examination of the boudoir topos will aid in identifying some of the essential features and constituent elements of the normative poetics and aesthetics of the women's boudoir, a frame of reference that will clarify how late imperial Chinese women as newly emergent writing subjects interacted with the literary convention. A topos is not unchangeable but historically constructed and received. It can be enlarged to include new conventions recognized by writers of later generations.

NEW SONGS FROM A JADE TERRACE: THE ESTABLISHMENT OF THE BOUDOIR TOPOS

Widely recognized anthologies played an instrumental role in genre formation and allow for the identification of generic conventions. The two earliest poetic classics, *Book of Songs* (Shijing) and *Songs of the South* (Chuci), were followed in the Southern Dynasties (420–589) by a third influential anthology, *New Songs from a Jade Terrace* (Yutai xinyong).[2] This work was compiled by the Liang court poet Xu Ling (507–583) under the patronage of the Liang crown prince, later known as Emperor Jianwen, Xiao Gang (503–551).[3] The anthology consists of ten *juan* containing more than eight hundred poems arranged in chronological order.[4] Although the title proclaims it as "new," the collection actually covers a time span from the second century BCE through the early sixth century CE. The "new" in the title suggests, instead, that the anthology was intended to embody a new poetic vogue, the so-called Palace-Style poetry (*Gongti shi*).[5] Whether a conscious reaction to the orthodox view of poetry as expression of one's moral intent or a "new poetics of seeing" enlightened by Buddhist teachings, the emergence of the Palace Style was absolutely a "novel transformation" of Chinese poetry.[6] In any case, the court poets demonstrated a sustained interest in meticulously depicting feminine beauty, psychology, and settings. Although this sixth-century anthology could arguably be understood as "poetry of images" in a more fluid sense, drawing as it does on earlier traditions, it is still safe to say that it was instrumental in establishing the poetics and aesthetics of the boudoir in Chinese literary history.[7]

Women and the boudoir, among all other aspects of elite life during the Liang (502–57), assume a central, if not the only, site of attention in Palace-Style poetry. Even though the early chapters of the anthology include some works in which the speaking voice or persona is of ambiguous gender, there is an increasingly conspicuous tendency in the rest of the anthology to depict feminine beauty and settings. This tendency is likely to have affected the reception of these works. It is not surprising that later critics, such as Wei Zheng (580–643), summed up the poetic style of Emperor Jianwen, the representative of Palace-Style poetry in the following words: "The range of his lucid pieces and artful compositions was confined to pillows and mats; in his elaborate carvings and ornate words, his thoughts were limited to the boudoir."[8] Echoing Wei Zheng, the Ming scholar Hu Yinglin

(1551–1618) also jumped to the following conclusion: "*New Songs from a Jade Terrace* collects only a single body of boudoir poetry."[9] Hu's observation may be an oversimplification of the anthology, which is quite rich in its complexity, but the element of the boudoir is indeed outstanding. He was inspired to mint a new poetic term: a *ti* (style) of the boudoir.[10] For a reader like Hu, boudoir poetry was an established subgenre, in terms of both theme and style.

In his preface, the anthology's compiler, Xu Ling, imagines the goddess-like figure of a palace lady as his reader: extremely beautiful and talented, she can write and devotes all her idle hours to reading "the latest verses," which will soon include those found in Xu Ling's volume.[11] The figuration of a female audience here may be merely a rhetorical prop.[12] Although there are records of writing and reading women active during the period, the argument that the anthology, a crystallization of a palace culture dominated by male poets and audiences, was compiled merely for palace ladies requires further evidence. However, based on *New Songs from a Jade Terrace*, one can say that women were an essential part of this emergent poetics of the Palace Style, whether as a source of inspiration or as active participants. The elaborate description of the beautiful appearance and environment of the woman reader is consistent with the approach court poets took to images of women and the boudoir in their poetry.

Only about ten of the authors of Xu Ling's anthology are identified as women. While some are given only vague identities, such as a certain man's wife, some have historically credible names, such as Bao Linghui (fl. ca. 464), the sister of the famous poet Bao Zhao (ca. 414–466). Whether or not these women actually authored the texts attributed to them, their gender identity complicates the reading of the female voice projected in their poems.[13] However, the nuances in different authors' approaches are not significant enough to affect what we can discern about the formation of the boudoir setting as a topos in the anthology. As part of a selective collection with a specific agenda, the poems in *New Songs from a Jade Terrace* share a high degree of textual conformity in terms of themes and representational codes.

Despite the inclusion of a few female authors in the anthology, the practice of Palace-Style poetry by Xiao Gang's literary coterie reveals a dynamic dimension of the court poets' homosocial competition for describing the female realm and the control of desire and language.[14] However, this does not mean that the whole collection is a self-serving construction by male literati. Their construction of feminine voice and consciousness draws on a common set of resources shared by both genders. For instance, they drew inspiration from folk songs created by active communication between men and women. It would be unfair to claim that literati textual productions absolutely reflect merely male interests.

The poems anthologized in *New Songs from a Jade Terrace* are not all Palace-Style poetry in the narrow sense established by Xiao Gang and his courtiers. In fact, as a project attempting to embrace a new poetic taste, the corpus of the anthology reveals a process of genre formation. The collection can be divided roughly into two groups: the first group of 150 poems, written from the second century BCE to the late third century CE, is "more loosely structured," while the remainder of the poems, written from the fourth to the early sixth century, follows "a stricter conventional pattern."[15] By including poems of similar themes and styles from the Han to the Liang, Xu Ling intended to establish "a genealogy of the Palace Style."[16] As the Qing scholar Wu Zhaoyi notes on *juan* 8 of the anthology:

> In the third and fourth *juan*, the Palace Style begins to appear sporadically; in the fifth and sixth *juan*, it has gradually taken shape; the seventh *juan* is where the emperor from his highness elevates the Palace Style to a privileged place, and all scions sing alike; this *juan* (*juan* 8) are poems in which ministers imitate the style from their lower position, and women follow them in the same style.[17]

Palace-Style poetry represents a synthetic development of broader poetic practices. Many scholars note that Palace-Style poetry is very much "an aristocratic refinement" of early amorous songs such as "Songs of Wu" (Wusheng) and "Western Melodies" (Xiqu).[18] In fact, the emperor and his entourage drew frequently from literati traditions, including earlier literati *yuefu* (Music Bureau songs) and Han ancient-style poems, in creating a distinctive subgenre representing their aesthetic and artistic tastes. *New Songs from a Jade Terrace* includes both the court poets' conscious textual production and the earlier works that inspired them. Thus, the anthology provides a rich source for examining the dynamic process in which the poetics and aesthetics of the boudoir are established through a synthesis of earlier traditions.

The poems of female lamentation produced in the Han and Wei (220–65) periods were a major influence on the formation of Palace-Style poetry. Although the image and voice of the deserted woman can be traced back to the *Book of Songs*, they began to be visibly associated with the boudoir setting, or more precisely the bedchamber (*fang, guifang*), from the Han. The bedchamber seems to have been naturalized as a locus for depicting the situation of the one being left behind, a setting that becomes both a physical and an emotional trap. The earliest extant examples are from "Nineteen Old Poems" (Gushi shijiu shou), several of which are included in the beginning chapters of *New Songs from a Jade Terrace*.[19] The following two are most notably centered on the bedchamber setting and are frequently imitated by poets of later ages.

POEM NO. 2

青青河畔草,	Green, green riverside grass,
鬱鬱園中柳。	Lush, lush willow in the garden,
盈盈樓上女,	Sleek, sleek a girl upstairs,
皎皎當窗牖。	White, white faces her window.
娥娥紅粉妝,	Fair, fair her rouge and powder face,
纖纖出素手。	Slim, slim she shows her white hand.
昔為倡家女,	Once I was a singing-house girl,
今為蕩子婦。	Now I am a playboy's wife.
蕩子行不歸,	A playboy roves, never comes home,
空床難獨守。	My empty bed is hard to keep alone.[20]

POEM NO. 19

明月何皎皎,	Bright moon white, so white
照我羅床帷。	Shines on my silk bedcurtains.
憂愁不能寐,	In sad despair I cannot sleep,
攬衣起徘徊。	I take my robe, get up, and pace.
行客雖云樂,	To travel, they say, is pleasant,
不如早旋歸。	But not as good as coming back home.
出戶獨彷徨,	I go outside, stroll in solitude.
愁思當告誰。	My sad longing to whom can I tell?
引領還入房,	I lean forward, go back to my room,
淚下霑裳衣。	Tears fall soaking my robe.[21]

Although these two poems are both framed by the bedchamber setting, they represent two different approaches. The first one pays much attention to an objective description of the female persona's appearance, whereas the second constructs a subjective voice articulating a troubled inner world. Both address the lonely situation of the persona by mentioning the "empty bed" or restlessness at night, but the effects of their expressions are different. While the speaking voice at the end of the first poem reads more like a tantalizing gesture inviting a companion, the second poem expresses inescapable physical confinement and emotional trouble. In sum, the first poem plays with "the erotic potential of the lonely wife," while the second voices sorrow and grief.[22] These two poems set up two different models that would be emulated by poets of later ages.

However, a crucial issue that must be addressed is the second poem's ambiguity with regard to gender. The poem has typically been interpreted as an expression of the deserted woman's sorrow, but it can also be read as a more generalized grief that is specific neither to the female gender nor to the theme of separation. Nowhere in the poem is this information specified. Even on the rhetorical level, Han and Wei poems centered on the bedchamber setting are not unambiguously limited to the theme of female lamentation. In expressing their troubled emotions, male poets adopted modes of expression similar to those used by the deserted female persona without invoking the figure in their poems. For example, in "Bereavement," a poem mourning his wife's passing, Pan Yue (247–300 BCE) writes:

皎皎窗中月，	White, white moon through a window
照我室南端。	Shines on my room's south end.
清商應秋至，	Clear-tone winds usher autumn in;
溽暑隨節闌。	Sultry heat ebbs with the season.
凜凜涼風升，	Bleak, bleak cold winds rise;
始覺夏衾單。	I begin to feel my summer quilt too flimsy.
豈曰無重紈，	I wouldn't say I have no thick clothes,
誰與同歲寒。	But with whom will I share year's-end cold?
歲寒無與同，	The year's-end cold no one to share with.
朗月何朧朧。	Lustrous moon so glistening!
展轉眄枕席，	I toss and turn, stare at pillow and mat.
長簟竟床空。	The long mattress lies empty on the bed;
床空委清塵，	The bed lies empty, lost to clear dust.
室虛來悲風。	To my vacant room mournful comes the wind.
獨無李氏靈，	I'm alone, have no vision of Lady Li.[23]
仿佛覩爾容。	Vague, faint, I glimpse your face.
撫衿長嘆息，	I stroke my collar, sigh long sighs;
不覺涕霑胸。	Tears unaware soak my breast,
霑胸安能已，	Soak my breast, how can I stop them?
悲懷從中起。	Sad longing wells deep inside me. . . .[24]

In mourning his wife, the major textual strategy the poet adopts is the elaborate description of the lonely bedchamber as a means of reflecting his traumatized inner world. One could read this poem as sorrow expressed by the deserted woman if not for the indication of the speaker's gender identity in the line "I'm alone, have no vision of Lady Li."

New Songs from a Jade Terrace anthologizes many earlier works on themes associated with the bedchamber or domestic settings. But as the court poets developed a new interest in representing women's beauty and psychology for the purpose of artistic and erotic appreciation alongside the old tradition of female lament, they placed images of women and their boudoirs at the front of the poetic agenda, consequently establishing the women's chambers as an aesthetic site in Chinese poetry. The old bedchamber topos comes to be more explicitly associated with the female persona; meanwhile, the specifically gendered term "boudoir plaint" (*guiyuan*) appears for the first time as a poetic title in the anthology.

The court poets' meticulous attention to the portrayal of a beautiful woman and her boudoir is intimately connected with the "celebrating objects" (*yongwu*) mode cultivated in the Chinese literary tradition. Palace-Style poetry is in general "a form of objective description."[25] Although the feelings of the persona are sometimes expressed, they are not individualized. They are still in a descriptive rather than an expressive mode.[26] "Woman" is inscribed as a beautiful object. Her loveliness is portrayed through detailed descriptions of her body parts, such as her eyebrows, fingers, and waist, and, perhaps more important, of her attire and ornaments, such as her silk dress, hairstyle, and hairpins. Titles such as "Embroidery on Her Collar" and "Slippers on Her Feet" speak to the court poets' obsessive fondness for what is perceived as feminine beauty.[27] For poets, "woman is adored when adorned."[28] Xiao Gang's "A Lovely Woman's Morning Makeup" well illustrates this point:

北窗向朝鏡，	At the north window she faces her dawn mirror.
錦帳復斜縈。	Brocade curtains she drapes in a slanting twist.
嬌羞不肯出，	Sweet, shy, unwilling to come out,
猶言妝未成。	She still claims her makeup isn't done.
散黛隨眉廣，	She spreads kohl wide along her eyebrows;
燕脂逐臉生。	Yen rouge appears across her cheeks.
試將持出眾，	No doubt with all this she's sensational;
定得可憐名。	She deserves to be called "Adorable"![29]

By the same token, the boudoir, the women's chamber, is treated with equal attention in palace verses. A woman's bedroom is the most typical site for the poet's imagining of feminine activity and includes by extension her house and backyard. Compared with early love poems, "love moves indoors" to the boudoir as the court poets confine their interest to tamed nature and artificial luxury brought about by the palace lifestyle.[30] No matter whether it is a palace harem, a courtesan's bedchamber, or a forsaken wife's house, women's dwellings generally are referred to as *gui*. Many poems include the term *gui*, in various guises, in their titles, such as "Spring Boudoir," "Cold Boudoir," and "The Moonlit Night in the Boudoir."[31] The boudoir, more often than not, is lavishly decorated with luxurious furniture and utensils. Poems about objects are one major subcategory of palace verses, and boudoir accoutrements such as mirrors, screens, and candles are popular objects with which poets celebrated and evoked the aesthetic and erotic imagination of the women's chambers.

Although Palace-Style poetry is narrowly defined as poetry treating feminine beauty and settings for the purpose of evoking "amorous and sensual feelings" (*yanqing*), most of the poems collected in *New Songs from a Jade Terrace*, including the poems by court poets, are still dominated by the ancient theme of the abandoned woman. Palace-Style poetry carries on the old theme of the female lament but is more concerned with the "playful" representation of female images and boudoir life than with forcefully expressing lamentation.[32] The poets' new poetic taste and descriptive skills led to a renewal of the old story of the deserted woman. In many cases, the old theme is subsumed by a meticulous description of feminine beauty and settings. The poem about the singing-house girl in "Poem No. 2," from "Nineteen Old Poems," becomes the precursor of Palace-Style poetry. This poem sets up the classical formula of the Palace-Style boudoir plaint: a rhetorical complaint about the "empty" room or bed expressed by an elaborately beautiful persona.

The "empty room" (*kong fang*), more often the "empty boudoir" (*kong gui*) in palace verses, and the "empty bed" (*kong chuang*), elements derived from earlier poems of female lament, explicitly or implicitly constitute the most typical scenario in palace poetry tales. The boudoir where the lover is absent yet desired provides the court poet a perfect place in which to exercise his imagination and artistic skills. The boudoir not only functions as the central stage on which to expose the female persona's beauty and mind but also constitutes the very site of aesthetic appreciation, as in Xiao Gang's "Her Hidden Room."[33]

密房寒日晚，	Her hidden room in cold sun grows late,
落照度窗邊。	Declining rays cross the window sill.

紅簾遙不隔，	Red blinds far do not prevent my view,
輕帷半捲懸。	Light drapes hang half rolled up.
方知纖手製，	I know slim hands are tailoring,
詎滅縫裳妍。	Such perfection her finely sewn cloak.
龍刀橫膝上，	Dragon shears lie across her knees,
畫尺墮衣前。	Painted ruler slips down her skirt front.
熨斗金涂色，	Pressing iron, sheen of gilt varnish,
簪管白牙纏。	Needle spool cased in ivory.
衣裁合歡褶，	Cloth cut into joint-love pleats,
文作鴛鴦連。	Designed as nestling mandarin ducks.
縫用雙針縷，	In sewing she uses double needle thread,
絮是八蠶緜。	For padding a silkworm's eightfold thread.
香和麗秋蜜，	Perfume laced with Liqiu nectar
麝吐中臺煙。	And musk exhaling Zhongtai smoke
已入琉璃帳，	Now enter lapis lazuli bedcurtains,
兼雜太華氈。	Suffuse Mount Tai rugs.
具共雕鑪煖，	Besides she has a carved stove warm,
非同團扇捐。	Unlike the round fan rejected.
更恐從軍別，	She fears more keenly wartime separation:
空床徒自憐。	An empty bed and futile self-pity.[34]

Although her room is located in a secluded area and sheltered with blinds and curtains, the poet still tries to slip through with his gaze. He discovers that she is sewing, an ordinary female activity, yet he will find something interesting as he watches. Each detail of the woman's activities and surroundings is being examined: her slim hands, her fine materials and decorated tailoring tools, and the clothes she is making. The images of "joint-love pleats" and "nestling mandarin ducks" reveal the theme of the poem: she is waiting and preparing for a reunion and passionate consummation. Once the theme is revealed, the poet continues to depict the woman's careful tailoring and the luxurious decorations in her room in order to convey the perfect environment for the release of passion and her anticipation of the love union. However, the concluding lines take an abrupt, subversive turn. The poet seems to put the female persona at ease by subverting the allusion to "the round fan"—a symbol of the abandoned woman derived from the story of Ban Jieyu[35]—but he does not foreclose the possibility that she might still end up with an empty bed if her lover is recruited into the army. The delayed unfolding of this sad ending only serves to make a stronger anticlimax. This clever touch helps make this a masterpiece of Palace-Style tale.

Sometimes, the feeling of neglect is depicted through the persona's subjective perception of the coldness of the boudoir. The cold boudoir or the cold night in the boudoir is a common theme in the anthology. Several poems are straightforwardly titled "The Cold Boudoir." It is not necessarily a cold season, but the absence of "him" that makes the solitary woman feel chilled:

行人消息斷，	There is no news from the wanderer,
空閨靜復寒。	The empty boudoir is quiet and cold.
風急朝機燥，	Wind harsh—the morning loom is dry,
鏡闇晚妝難。	Mirror dim—it is hard to apply makeup by night.
從來腰自小，	Her waist was originally slender,
衣帶就中寬。	But the sash now is even looser.[36]

Another poem informs the reader how the coldness of the season becomes unbearable for a woman after her lover is gone:

別後春池異，	After we parted the spring pool looked different,
荷盡欲生冰。	Lotus died, ice seemed to form.
箱中剪刀冷，	In my sewing-box the shears felt cold,
臺上面脂凝。	On the mirrorstand my face-cream froze.
纖腰轉無力，	My slender waist become so frail
寒衣恐不勝。	Can hardly bear the coldness of the clothes.[37]

Everything she sees and touches is cold and frozen. Certainly it is not merely because of the winter, but more the result of her loneliness. The cold boudoir without a male companion becomes for the woman an alien space. Neither of the above poems directly addresses the female persona's emotion; each describes only her appearance and the surrounding environment. Every detail, however, serves to express the grief of separation.

The boudoir is also differentiated according to the seasons. The perceived parallel between the cycle of nature and the span of human life had long been held in Chinese philosophical and literary traditions: human life is as transient as the seasons.[38] The depiction of seasonal boudoirs in palace verses reflects this common perception. Spring and autumn scenes are the two most common motifs because in these two seasons nature undergoes fundamental and visible changes that strike melancholy chords in the abandoned woman.[39] Spring, the season during which everything is flourishing, is an amorous season. Flowers, metaphor of feminine beauty, are brought to bloom by the east wind, sun, and rain, symbols of male love. In Palace-Style poems, however, human love does not smoothly mirror the patterns of nature. Court poets often twist these cultural assumptions in order to express the emotions of yearning or loss. Against the flourishing background of springtime, the boudoir is a place denied access to love; passion is in no way fulfilled:

春宵猶自長，	The spring night is still long,
春心非一傷。	My amorous heart is not broken just once.
月帶園樓影，	The moonlight shapes the shadow of the garden and tower,
風飄花樹香。	The wind brings to me the aroma of flowers and trees.
誰能對雙燕，	Who can face the paired swallows
瞑瞑守空床。	And stay in the empty bed feeling indifference?[40]

The spring night would be short if spent in an enjoyable way. However, the woman in this poem feels that it is painfully long. Her time is wasted under the bright moon and in front of fragrant flowers. A pair of swallows, both a sign of spring and a symbol of love, offers a further heartbreaking contrast to her loneliness. Thus, the rhetorical question raised in the final two lines about the difficulty of going to the empty bed serves as both an assertion of the abandonment plaint and a tantalizing gesture to the male reader.

Autumn is a season of withering: leaves fall, and flowers fade. Nature is finishing one cycle, but passion has not been fulfilled in the boudoir, and the unfulfilled passion grows into a deeper sorrow:

曉河沒高棟，	Dawn River dies on a tall ridge-pole.
斜月半空庭。	The slanting moon halfway over an empty garden.
窗中度落葉，	Fallen leaves cross the window sill,
簾外隔飛螢。	Beyond the blind flitting fireflies are trapped.
含情下翠帳，	Full of love she lowers kingfisher drapes,
掩涕閉金屏。	Tearful shuts the gold screen.
昔期今未反，	My long promised love has not come back,
春草寒復青。	Spring grass though chill is green once more.
思君無轉易，	My love for you is unswerving
何異北辰星。	When will the North Star veer?[41]

This poem is titled "Boudoir Plaint," explicitly indicating its theme. The plaint arises because the woman's lover has broken his promise to return. The mention of the new growth of "spring grass" suggests that spring is imminent and that she has been waiting a long time for their reunion. Time passes meaninglessly in the lonely boudoir. The seasonal changes only remind her of the bitterness of waiting and the evanescence of life and love.

There are two, often interlocking, major thematic concerns associated with the boudoir setting—female lamentation and the appreciation of feminine beauty. Each has its major formulaic modes of expression. Through their literary practice in the Palace Style and their anthologizing efforts in compiling *New Songs from a Jade Terrace*,

Figure 2.1 "Longing Woman in Autumn Boudoir" (Qiugui sifu tu) by Cui Wei (fl. in 18th c.). Here the painter portrays a woman resting in a pavilion in a garden and lost in her thoughts (presumably of her absent lover). This painting visualizes the typical theme of the boudoir plaint established in the poetic tradition. With the clues provided by the title, those familiar with the poetic tradition can understand what is on the woman's mind. The Palace Museum, Beijing.

Xiao Gang and his courtiers established the aesthetic space of the women's chambers in the Chinese poetic tradition. The anthology represents a significant moment in the founding of the subgenre of boudoir poetry.

The fact that they distanced themselves from the orthodox view of poetry while devoting themselves to the depiction of women's bodies and bedrooms made the court poets a target of attack by many critics from the Sui (581–618) onward. Palace-Style poetry became a synonym for "decadence" and "the tone of a lost dynasty."[42] The aesthetic site of the women's boudoir it helped craft, however, rooted itself, if only marginally, in the poetic imagination of later ages. It left behind a rich discourse that influenced later poets on boudoir themes for centuries, even when they adapted the language to other interests.

Although Palace-Style poetry gradually declined in the early Tang, it never really died out; later generations carried on the tradition in various ways. As scholars have noted, a widely recognized renewal of Palace-Style themes and technique was occurring in the hands of late Tang poets such as Li He (791–817), Wen Tingyun (ca. 812–ca. 866) and Li Shangyin (813?–858).[43] What these three hold in common is their unconventional use of Palace-Style conventions, which suggests that they were acutely conscious of such conventions. Paradoxically, they wrote both within and beyond the tradition. These late Tang poets mastered the Palace Style to the extent that they "could use palace poetry to comment on the genre itself or to point consciously to the historical circumstances that produced it."[44]

AMONG THE FLOWERS: THE DEVELOPMENT OF BOUDOIR AESTHETICS IN THE LYRIC

Unlike Palace-Style poetry, the *ci,* an alternative approach deviating from the orthodox *shi* poetics, arose from the very beginning as a popular form exploring love themes. Inspired by their involvement in the courtesans' and singing girls' quarters, literati authors developed the *ci* as a genre expressing private love and sentiment.[45] *The Anthology of Poems Written among the Flowers* (Huajian ji), generally recognized as the first major *ci* anthology, marked another founding moment for boudoir poetics, demonstrating how the boudoir topos established in *shi* poetry resurfaces in another important genre. The significance of this anthology should not be underestimated, considering the role it played in establishing the generic conventions of the *ci*. Like *New Songs from a Jade Terrace*, it was also compiled with well-defined boundaries. It consists of five hundred *ci* divided into ten chapters, a collection of lyrics written mostly during the Five Dynasties (907–60).[46] The authors are exclusively male literati who were either natives of Shu or had fled there from Chang'an, the capital of the fallen Tang.[47] The lyrics included in this anthology also fashion a world of women and love with sensual beauty and tender pathos. They bear a strong resemblance to Palace-Style verses in their thematic scope and descriptive imagery. In fact, the depiction of the boudoir setting in early *ci* is largely indebted to its stylistic and thematic precedents such as palace and boudoir lament poetry of the Southern Dynasties.[48]

Ironically, it is because of this obvious similarity to earlier love songs and poems such as Palace-Style poetry that the author of the preface to *Anthology of Poems Written among the Flowers*, Ouyang Jiong (896–971), feels compelled to distinguish the lyrics in his anthology from those of former works. He singles out Palace-Style poetry as the target of his criticism: "The Palace-Style poetry of the Southern Dynasties has revived the music of the prostitutes' quarters. Not only was its language uncultured; it was superficially elegant without substance."[49] His critique of Palace-Style poetry is somewhat ironic. The charge of being "superficially elegant without substance" can also be used against the style of the poems in the *Flowers* anthology. In his postscript to a Song edition of the anthology, Chao Qianzhi makes a similar critique within an overall positive comment: "Even though its language is decadent and useless in saving the world, it can be called crafted."[50] Ouyang Jiong's excessively ornate yet ambiguous preface cannot be taken at face value. His real concern is to elevate the literati's *ci* to a more respectable status.[51]

The central message conveyed in Ouyang's preface is that the literati should feel proud of composing and enjoying the *ci* form as a high art. Lavish private and official banquets are often mentioned in the preface, revealing the social setting and entertainment function of the *ci*. Ouyang feels no shame in talking about this function, but he is concerned about the literary quality of the form. He is right in pointing out the high craftsmanship of the lyrics in *Anthology of Poems Written among the Flowers*. The lyrics are indeed more sophisticated in their descriptive artifices and more evocative in expressing the moods of love, even though they are still in the process of development and far from the more elevated poetic genre that *ci* was to become in the Song period.

Due to its musical association, the *ci* has special linguistic demands and has thus generated more varied forms of expression.

The major thematic concerns associated with the boudoir setting in *Anthology of Poems Written among the Flowers* are still the expression of nostalgia for lost loves (most often from a woman's point of view) and appreciation of feminine beauty and the erotic.[52] However, the *ci* form added more lyrical qualities to the love stories. In general, the poetics and aesthetics of the boudoir are further developed in three correlated dimensions. First, the central setting is more consistently constructed as the private chambers of women. The imperial harem, a typical setting in Southern Dynasties and Tang palace verses, disappears from the *Flowers* anthology lyrics, as this group of authors was made up not of courtiers but of scholar-officials writing about their private pursuit of love and pleasure. While the setting is identified at certain times as the courtesans' quarters, the boudoir is more often depicted as a homogeneous and essentialized feminine setting rather than socially and historically differentiated women's lived spaces. In referring to the women's chambers, the authors use a variety of terms graced by aesthetic elegance, such as "the fragrant boudoir" (*xianggui*), "the red window" (*hongchuang*), "the green window" (*lüchuang*), and "the pavilion of embroidery" (*xiuge*). Among them, the "green window," a window with a green-gauze screen, is the most popular. A synecdochic reference to the boudoir, it had already been used in Tang poetry, but it was through the particular construction of the poets in *Anthology of Poems Written among the Flowers* that the term acquired its aesthetic quality and gained its popularity in later ages. Both Wen Tingyun and Wei Zhuang (ca. 836–910), the most prominent of the authors in the anthology, frequently use "the green window" as a central image in their lyrics. For example, Wen Tingyun's oft-cited lyric to the tune "Bodhisattva Barbarian" reads:

玉樓明月長相憶，	Jade tower, bright moon, I always remember;
柳絲裊娜春無力。	The willow branches were long and graceful in a languorous spring.
門外草萋萋，	Outside the gate grasses grew luxuriantly.
送君聞馬嘶。	While seeing you off, I heard the horse's neigh.
畫羅金翡翠，	On patterned silk, golden kingfishers;
香燭銷成淚。	Fragrant candles melt into tears.
花落子規啼，	Flowers fall, the cuckoo cries;
綠窗殘夢迷。	At the green window, the remnant of a dream dims.[53]

This two-stanza lyric constructs an indistinct world of memory, reality, and dream. While the first stanza deals with a scenario that is fresh in memory, the second depicts a real scene that blurs into a dream. The sorrow of separation, the bitterness of waiting, and confusion between reality and dream (there may also be the happiness of a brief reunion in the dream followed by pain upon awakening to lonely reality) are all framed by "the green window."

Second, the songs in the anthology employ more imagistic language than propositional statement, and more connotative than direct expression. Rather than offering an overview of the woman's image and her space, the poet selects isolated, dense imagery that intensifies the sensual impression of the scenario. Wen Tingyun has been hailed by *ci* critics as a master of coded imagery. His lines "Stitched in the silk of her bright new coat / Golden-threaded partridges fly pair by pair" are frequently quoted to show the intense aesthetic and connotative effect created by the image of the golden partridges flying in tandem: superficial beauty is combined with the deeper longing for love.

Another of Wen's lyrics to the tune "Bodhisattva Barbarian" shows more fully his typical approach to the depiction of a woman in the boudoir:

水晶簾裏玻璃枕，	Within a crystal curtain, a pillow of crystal;
暖香惹夢鴛鴦錦。	Warm fragrances rouse dreams in mandarinduck brocade.
江上柳如煙，	Along the river, willows like mist.
雁飛殘月天。	Geese fly beneath a sky of waning moon.
藕絲秋色淺，	Her lotus threads are a light autumn tint,
人勝參差剪。	Cloth-doll ribbons cut unevenly.
雙鬢隔香紅，	Side curls concealed by fragrant red,
玉釵頭上風。	Jade hairpins—a breeze in her hair.[54]

This *ci* is composed of two stanzas and three scenarios. The first stanza establishes the boudoir setting by juxtaposing two separate scenes. It begins with a close-up of the bed, drawing our attention to three images: the crystal curtain, the crystal pillow, and the mandarin duck brocade. The contrasting qualities of these images, carefully selected by the poet, strengthen our sensual impression of the setting. They not only are material elements of the bedroom but also reveal the love theme of this lyric. There is no mention of any human presence at this moment, but the dream roused by the mandarin ducks suggests an atmosphere of love. The poet's gaze then shifts from the bed to a broader view of the riverbank. This second scene, often suggestive of traveling, implies either the departure of the woman's lover or her expectation of his return. Both possibilities, however, point to his absence. Finally, the poet devotes the whole second stanza to the one left behind in the boudoir. She is described as if void of emotion. Only the movement of her hairpins leaves the reader to imagine what may have disturbed her.

Rather than asserting the female persona's concerns and emotions, the poem hints at her state of mind through objects. This approach, which is common in *Anthology of Poems Written among the Flowers*, resembles the celebrating-object mode but with a different agenda: it neither celebrates the object itself nor explores the symbolic meaning of the object but uses the object as a vehicle for conveying the subjective feelings of the persona.

Centered on a single image of wutong, or plane, trees on a rainy night, another lyric by Wen Tingyun illustrates this artistic effect:

玉爐香，	Incense in the jade burner,
紅蠟淚。	Tears of the red candle
偏照畫堂秋思，	Just shine on autumn grief in the painted hall.
眉翠薄，	Brow-kohl pales,
鬢雲殘。	Side-curl clouds thin:
夜長衾枕寒。	The night is long, coverlet and pillow cold.
梧桐樹，	Wutong trees
三更雨。	In the midnight rain
不道離情正苦。	Don't need to say the grief felt right now at parting.
一葉葉，	Leaf by leaf,
一聲聲，	Sound by sound,
空階滴到明。	They drop on empty stairs till dawn.[55]

Having revealed the theme of love-longing in the first stanza, the lyric devotes the second stanza to a depiction of the woman's feelings. However, the poet does not directly approach her emotion but turns to a description of the external world in order to reflect her internal emotional state. The central image is the large-leafed wutong trees, a kind of tree associated in legend with the nest of the phoenix. It is supposed to be a symbol of love's reunion, but here, ironically, the trees are witnesses to the pain of separation. It is a rainy night in autumn, and raindrops are splashing on wutong leaves. Unable to sleep, the female persona is alert to every noise the rain makes throughout the long night. The three-character line facilitated by the *ci* form provides a rhythm that vividly conveys the pitter-patter of raindrops falling on the leaves. The poet does not need to tell how painful the lonely night is for the woman; each drop of rain on the trees measures the intensification of her suffering.

Third, the poets in *Anthology of Poems Written among the Flowers* pay particular attention to creating a sensuous world in the boudoir. The sensuous tone also typifies the Palace-Style verses of the Southern Dynasties, but it is elevated here because of the special properties of the *ci* form and the lyrical writers' imagistic approach. With their particular attention to sensual details and delicate diction, the poets greatly expanded and enriched the vocabulary for describing images of women and the boudoir. Recent studies of the *Flowers* anthology have provided statistics on the *ci* writers' word use.[56] More than twenty of the nouns and terms used most frequently in the anthology relate to the boudoir furnishings and environment. Many emphasize the sensual aspects of a woman's image and boudoir such as color, scent, sound, touch, and other material qualities.[57] As statistical study shows, the poets tended to use the green-blue color series, such as azure (*bi*) and green (*qing*) for color, gold (*jin*) and jade (*yu*) for materials, and scented (*xiang*) for smell.[58] These are natural choices resulting largely from the actual living conditions and lifestyles of the women about whom the poets write. Emphasis on these aspects, however, also suggests the poets' interest and approach. The following lyrical piece to the tune "Telling Innermost Feelings" by Wei Chengban further shows how the sensual aspects of the boudoir setting are specially highlighted in the poet's imagination:

銀漢雲晴玉漏長,	Clouds pass from the Milky Way, the jade clock runs on.
蛩聲悄畫堂。	The chirp of a cricket fills the quiet hall.
筠簟冷,	The bamboo mats are frosty.
碧窗涼,	The green window is chilly.
紅蠟淚飄香。	The red candle splashes its perfumed tears.
皓月瀉寒光,	A chilled light seeps from the bright moon.
割人腸。	It cuts at one's own heart.
那堪獨自步池塘,	How can one bear to be so alone and walk beside the pond,
對鴛鴦。	And see the mandarin ducks![59]

This lyric is very short yet extremely rich in sensuous details as perceived by the female persona: the sound of the jade clock, the chirp of a cricket, the chill of the bamboo mats, the cold outside the green window, the redness and scent of the candle, the pain brought on by the brightness of the moonlight and paired mandarin ducks. In seeing what she sees, hearing what she hears, smelling what she smells, and feeling what she feels, readers are led to experience, though paradoxically, the subjective world of a woman in the boudoir as perceived by a male author.

In sum, the poets of *Anthology of Poems Written among the Flowers* were able to craft an evocative and emotive world of the boudoir. Furthermore, they reinforced the boudoir as a topos of feminine beauty, sexuality, and love. If the practice of palace poetry brought the boudoir to the front of the poetic agenda, the poets refined it in the poetics of *ci*. The male lover is still absent from the boudoir, but indirect suggestion replaces the direct remark found in palace verses, such as the voice complaining about "the empty bed." The emptiness of the space is depicted through the woman's sense of ennui and melancholy. A few poems also adopt a frank and explicit tone in asserting sexual desire and love, but the language in general is allusive and connotative. The anthologized lyrics are replete with erotic elements, but they are more often suggested through images and metaphors. Although the *Flowers* anthology represents an early stage in *ci* practice, its collection of lyrics paved the way for the feminine, "gentle and restrained" (*wanyue*) aesthetics of the *ci* genre recognized in later ages. The anthologized lyrics as a whole came to function as a repertory of the subjects, themes, and language that influenced practitioners of the lyric in subsequent periods. As Yeh Chia-ying claims, "It was only with the appearance of [the *Flowers* anthology] that [*ci*] achieved widespread recognition as a new genre with its own special characteristics and began to exert an influence that continued well after [it] had developed into other channels."[60]

CONVENTION AND TRANSFORMATION: THE NEW AESTHETICS OF THE BOUDOIR IN SONG *CI*

Palace-Style poetry and the lyrics in *Anthology of Poems Written among the Flowers* each represents a crucial stage of development in boudoir poetics and aesthetics. In the period that followed, no other anthologies achieved the canonical status of *New Songs from a Jade Terrace* and the *Anthology of Poems Written among the Flowers*.[61] With highly conventionalized themes, sentiments, settings, and imagery, boudoir poetry left only limited margins for further development.

For example, the subjects and themes of the songwriters of Ouyang Xiu's (1007–1072) generation were still largely confined to those of the *Flowers* anthology poems.[62] First, consider his *ci* to the tune "Immortal by the River,"[63] a song with an erotic theme:

柳外輕雷池上雨，	Faint thunder beyond the willows, rain in the pool;
雨聲滴碎荷聲。	Rain, the sound of it hitting and shattering lotus.
小樓西角斷虹明，	Over the western corner of the building, a fragment of rainbow glows.
闌干倚處，	They lean against the banister
待得月華生。	And wait for the moon to rise.
燕子飛來窺畫棟，	Swallows come to spy under painted beams;
玉鉤垂下簾旌。	The curtain hangs down from its jade hook.
涼波不動簟紋平，	The cool waves subside, and the bamboo mat is still.
水精雙枕，	Beside the two crystal pillows,
傍有墮釵橫。	A fallen hairpin lies.[64]

This poem tells a story through cinematic shifts of scene. It begins with a broader view of the surroundings and moves gradually from outdoor scenes and events to indoor ones as time passes. Once indoors, the reader is held at a distance. Only the inquisitive gaze of swallows is allowed. Finally, however, the poet invites the reader to focus on the lovers' bed—the bamboo mat woven with wavelike patterns, paired crystal pillows, and a fallen hairpin—a scene after lovemaking. Although these coded images are also repeatedly employed in the *Anthology of Poems Written among the Flowers*, Ouyang Xiu's description of the scene is obviously inspired by the Tang poet Li Shangyin's lines "The amber pillow on the wave-patterned bamboo mat, / Beside it is a fallen hairpin with kingfisher feathers."[65] His opening lines are also derived from Li Shangyin's "Faint thunder sounds beyond the lotus pond."[66] Borrowing phrases and lines from earlier works is not a personal tendency of Ouyang Xiu but a common textual strategy of songwriters of his time.[67] The practice of borrowing or adapting well-known lines, especially from late Tang verse, was encouraged by *ci* critics in order to add a quality of elegance to the *ci* writing. Shen Yifu (fl. 1247), for example, advised that "in seeking [material for] diction, one should look for fine and unvulgar lines from the poetry of Wen Tingyun, Li He and Li Shangyin."[68] Whether it is conscious borrowing or unconscious intertextual influences, a basis of recognized idioms showed the writer's familiarity with the tradition.

Of course, Ouyang Xiu, a writer with great creativity, can go further than borrowing lines; he is limited only by generic convention. Another widely circulated work of his to the tune "Butterflies Lingering over Flowers,"⁶⁹ a lyric considered to be a masterpiece of the boudoir lament, illustrates the interplay between tradition and innovation:

庭院深深深幾許？	The inner courtyard deep, so deep, how deep is it?
楊柳堆煙，	Willows pile up mist;
簾幕無重數。	Blinds and curtains are of endless layers.
玉勒雕鞍遊冶處，	Where bridle of jade and carved saddle are seeking pleasure,
樓高不見章臺路。	From the high tower, the road to Zhang Terrace cannot be seen.
雨橫風狂三月暮，	The rain rages and the wind blusters on an evening in the third month;
門掩黃昏，	The door closes twilight in—
無計留春住。	No way to induce spring to stay.
淚眼問花花不語，	Tearful eyes ask the flowers, but the flowers are silent;
亂紅飛過鞦韆去。	Confused red petals fly over the swing.⁷⁰

Ouyang Xiu is telling an old story: the abandoned woman longing for her absent lover. The allusion to the male wanderer frequenting the pleasure quarters ("Where bridle of jade and carved saddle are seeking pleasure, / From the high tower, the road to Zhang Tower cannot be seen") is a cliché. However, the poet explores the feminine world of the boudoir to a greater depth than did his predecessors. He begins by questioning how deep the inner courtyard is, which points to more than its physical depth. It is so immeasurable that even the writer seems lost in it. This immeasurable depth, however, paradoxically serves to convey the confinement of the woman within her boudoir (in this case, through its extension, the courtyard). The boudoir, by convention so readily open to voyeurism, is no longer available for easy connoisseurship in this lyric; readers must measure out its boundaries through an act of imagination. The poet ends his lyric in a way that is also craftily plotted, letting the fall of fragile blossoms speak for the destiny of the woman. Like Wen Tingyun, Ouyang Xiu relies heavily on evocative images; however, he does not merely juxtapose isolated images but begins with an image and then goes on to elaborate it as part of an event. This lyric has been widely hailed for its high literary quality. Several lyrics in the collection of the high songstress Li Qingzhao (1081–1155) not only thematically echo the above-mentioned lyric but also begin with its same opening line, "The inner courtyard deep, so deep, how deep is it?"[71] Whether or not these are forgeries attributed to Li, they are considered works of high caliber.

The representation of women and love surrounded by the boudoir environment prevailed in *ci* poetics from the late Tang through the Five Dynasties and early Song and remained a time-honored aspect of the feminized poetics and aesthetics of the genre in later ages. The lyrics by Ouyang Xiu discussed above are two classical models representing the themes of amorous and sensual feelings and the grief of separation. Along with the general developments of the *ci*, however, even as the old convention was reinforced, the ground of the boudoir topos was also expanded. As the *ci* matured into a sophisticated literary art in the Song period, its compositional scope was largely expanded thematically and stylistically. The most widely recognized trend is the rise of masculine (*haofang*) lyrics from the Northern Song (1127–1279) expressing male poets' political and heroic sentiments. Within the feminine style, however, lyricists also began to explore the breadth and depth of their inner, private worlds.

The lyrics by the prominent *ci* writer Li Qingzhao illustrate this remarkable change, by suggesting that this genre, shaped by the voice and feelings of women (though to a large extent constructed by male literati authors), provided women with "a 'natural' mode of expression."[72] Her lyrics fully embrace the generic conventions in expressing her sentiments as a woman (within de-eroticized, "clean" boundaries, as Grace S. Fong suggests).[73] Yet she also pushed the generic conventions to their limits in order to accommodate the depth, intensity, and complexity of her inner feelings. The major themes of Li Qingzhao's lyrics centered on the boudoir setting may still be the depressed feelings of the lovelorn woman, but the moods and sentiments expressed are expansive and complex. The following lyric to the tune "Flute Playing Recalled on Phoenix Terrace" is an example of Li Qingzhao's approach to the conventional theme of sorrow over separation:

香冷金猊，	The incense chilled in golden lions,
被翻紅浪，	The coverlet rumpled like red waves:
起來慵自梳頭。	I get up but am too lazy to comb my hair.
任寶奩塵滿，	Let the precious mirror be covered with dust,
日上簾鉤。	And the sun climbs as high as the curtain hook.
生怕閒愁暗恨，	So afraid of rootless sorrow and smoldering resentment,

多少事、	There are so many things
欲說还休。	That I would like to say but don't.
今年瘦,	The reason I have grown so skinny lately
非干病酒,	Is not because of too much wine,
不是悲秋。	Nor is it due to autumn sadness.
休休,	Over! It's all over!
這回去也,	When you left this last time,
千萬遍陽關,	Not even a thousand, ten thousand "Yang Pass" songs
也則難留。	Could keep you here.
念武陵人遠,	Remembering my Wuling fisherman now so far away,
雲鎖秦樓,	Mist locks in the tower.
惟有樓前流水,	None but the flowing stream in front of the tower
應念我、	Seems to remember me
終日凝眸。	Gazing upon it all day.
凝眸處,	Where the gaze is frozen
從今又添,	From now on there should add
一段新愁。[74]	A new sorrow.

Like Ouyang Xiu, Li Qingzhao often borrowed others' lines. The first two lines of her lyric are adaptations of famous lines by two of her contemporary male lyricists: "Incense is finished and chilled in golden lions," by Xie Yi (d. 1113), and "The coverlet embroidered with mandarin ducks rumpled like red waves," by Liu Yong (987?–1053?).[75] Playing with these famous lines, the woman poet sketches a typical boudoir setting. What follows is also a typical image of a woman listlessly dwelling in her boudoir. However, as the first-person persona projected in the rest of the lyric begins to voice what she feels about her situation, the story seems less familiar. The theme is revealed in the second stanza as sorrow over separation, but her expression of sorrow seems to have other implications. Instead of explicitly identifying these other reasons for sorrow, she indicates only that her emotional trouble is not caused by obvious reasons. This withholding of "truth" may be an aesthetic effect of the author's desire for indirectness, but it could also be the result of a conventional language that is too limited to describe the complicated feelings within her persona. The female voice presented in this lyric is different from the outcry of grief over abandonment expressed in early works on the boudoir plaint. As lines 6–11 ("There are so many things / That I would like to say but don't. / The reason I have grown so skinny lately / Is not because of too much wine, / Nor is it due to autumn sadness") suggest, it is more interested in exploring how to express sorrow than in voicing the sorrow itself. It reads like the writing subject self-consciously searching for a better mode of expression.

The availability of solid historical evidence related to Li Qingzhao's life and literary practice makes an autobiographical reading of her lyrics more credible. Although her texts may not simply mirror her actual life experience, the poet's subjective experience and perspective as a woman dwelling in the boudoir are likely to be a major source for the personal touches she adds to the boudoir stories in her lyrics. Consider the following lyric to the tune "Joy of Eternal Union":

落日鎔金，	The setting sun melts into gold,
暮雲合璧，	The evening clouds merge into a disk of jade,
人在何處。	But where on earth is he?
染柳煙濃。	The mist that dyes the willows is so heavy,
吹梅笛怨，	The flute that plays "The Plum Tree" sounds resentful—
春意知幾許。	God knows how many, many thoughts of spring!
元宵佳節，	The festival of the First Night,
融和天氣，	A weather that is nice and pleasant—
次第豈無風雨。	But later there is bound to be some wind and rain.
來相召，	People come to fetch me—
香車寶馬，	Fragrant carts and finest horses—
謝他酒朋詩侶。	But I decline the invitations of those companions of poetry and wine.
中州盛日，	In those glory days of Kaifeng,
閨門多暇，	Leisure reigned in the inner quarters,
記得偏重三五。	And I remember how we relished the Three Times Five:[76]
鋪翠冠兒，	Kingfisher-feather little chaplets,
捻金雪柳，	Snow-willow hairpins rolled of gold,
簇帶爭济楚。	As each tried to outdo the other with her headdress!
如今憔悴，	But now I am a bag of bones,
风鬟霜鬢，	My hair disheveled and turning gray—
怕見夜間出去。	I'm afraid to be seen when going out at night.
不如向、	Far better I should from
帘兒底下，	Behind a lowered blind
聽人笑語。	Just listen to other people's laughter.[77]

This lyric presents the perspective of an aged woman. Although earlier poets had sometimes invoked the image of old women such as elderly palace women in their poems, young and attractive female personae were predominant. The perspective and voice of the old woman elaborated in this lyric is not seen in earlier works. It is generally held that Li Qingzhao wrote this lyric in her later years after she moved to the south. Whether or not it is necessary to read this lyric against the background of the author's life, Li Qingzhao was definitely inspired by her widowed life in constructing the boudoir story in this lyric. It embraces several major motifs, such as separation (by death), loneliness, nostalgia for youthful years, and sorrow over aging. These motifs are not new, but the poet weaves them together, yielding a fresh perspective on the old theme of a lonely woman in her boudoir. Importantly, the loneliness in the boudoir is a choice, a choice of refusing company and public attention in order to guard self-esteem. This gesture is unconventional, yet it echoes the idiosyncratic voice she adopts in many of her poems.

Li Qingzhao individualized her boudoir stories with personal touches. However, the unconventional stamp she places on her boudoir lyrics are not always personal traits. She also introduced other literati conventions into her depiction of boudoir life by infusing rich details such as drinking, admiring flowers, and spending moments of leisure and meditation in fashioning her own lifestyle as a literata. For example, in a lyric to the tune "Telling Innermost Feelings," she writes:

夜來沈醉卸妝遲。	Last night I was so tipsy that I removed my headdress late;
梅萼插殘枝。	In my hair I still wear a branch of withered plum blossoms.
酒醒熏破春睡，	When I wake, its fragrance shatters my spring dream,
夢遠不成歸。	In which the one far away cannot return home.
人悄悄，	Everyone's quiet,
月依依。	The moon still lingers,
翠簾垂。	The kingfisher screens hang down.
更挼殘蕊，	Once again I rub the plum's remaining petals,
更捻餘香，	Once again I press out its leftover fragrance,
更得些時。	Once again I enjoy it for a moment more.[78]

The line "In which the one far away cannot return home" still suggests the theme of a woman missing her absent man. But with the elaborate motif on appreciating the fragrance of plum blossoms, the lyric reads more as a serene moment of solitude in the boudoir. The return to sobriety after being slightly drunk interrupts her dream of reunion with her beloved, but the moon is still her companion, and the plum blossoms comfort her with their fragrance. Interestingly, while her persona is awakened by the fragrant plum blossoms in this lyric, in another lyric she proposes to drink until intoxicated in order to celebrate the blossoming of the plum tree in the courtyard.[79] As an unconventional woman poet, Li Qingzhao likes to represent her idiosyncrasy with drinking motifs. Admiring plum blossoms, an image of nobility and integrity in literati culture, is also a gesture that demonstrates her cultured taste and unusual spirit. These rich details of the poet's daily life subtly change the sentiments associated with the boudoir setting.

As *ci* writers, including male authors, increasingly began to explore their perception of self or emotions in relation to the boudoir or inner space, they expanded and enriched boudoir thematics and sentiments. The boudoir setting came to be associated not only with explicit love sentiments between men and women but also with other categories of mood, including joy and sorrow. These associated moods may seem to derive from the ancient theme of an abandoned woman's grief, such as loneliness, ennui, depression, and languor, but their cause is no longer limited to separation from one's love, nor do the moods necessarily belong to female personae. Along with the expansion and subtle change of feminine sentiments in general, the boudoir topos also becomes subtle and ambiguous. In many cases, it is indistinguishable from a general interior, domestic setting. Due to the poet's gender, Li Qingzhao's lyrics can be read autobiographically as a woman's expression of her boudoir sentiments. However, the sentiments embodied in the following lyric by the male poet Yan Shu (991–1055), to the tune "Joy of Soaring Orioles," are less identifiable:

燭飄花，	The flame of the candle flickers;
香掩燼。	The incense tapers to ashes.
中夜酒初醒。	At midnight I just wake from my intoxication.
畫樓殘點兩三聲，	In the painted tower, the faint sounds of the second or third night-watch.
窗外月朧明。	The moon shines softly outside the window.
曉帘垂，	Dawn curtains hang down;
驚鵲去。	The startled magpie is gone.
好夢不知何處。	Where is the sweet dream?
南園春色已歸來，	Spring has come back to the southern garden.
庭樹有寒梅。	In the courtyard is a chilled plum tree.[80]

Yan Shu's *ci*, like Li Qingzhao's, captures a moment of sobriety in the midst of intoxication. The two lyrics share many elements: the moon, a screen, a dream, and plum blossoms. It is not surprising that both poets focus on these images, for they are describing a view at night seen from within the inner, domestic space.[81] Only Li Qingzhao's piece suggests that the setting is vaguely related to the female gender by the detail of removing her headdress. Although the persona in Yan Shu's *ci* can well be read as gendered feminine, there is no specific information in that regard. The theme of Yan Shu's poem is also elusive: it addresses the interruption of a sweet dream, as does Li Qingzhao's lyric, but does not indicate the dream's content. Nor does the mention of the return of spring help in clarifying the theme. On the one hand, it can be understood that although spring, the season of youth, love, and hope, has returned, the persona's pleasant dream is gone. On the other hand, it seems to suggest that while human life contains no good news, Nature offers something hopeful: spring has come back, causing a chilled plum tree to blossom. This poem, if not over-read, depicts a perception of a domestic environment tinted with a mood of light sorrow, which is not necessarily understood as the old theme of the boudoir plaint.

Another Yan Shu lyric to the tune "Washing Creek Sands," similar in style yet expressing a slightly more cheerful mood, reinforces this point:

宿酒纔醒厭玉卮。	Tired of jade goblets after I wake from my hangover.
水沈香冷懶薰衣。	The incense gets cold, but I am too lazy to scent my clothes.
早梅先綻日邊枝。	The early plum blossoms are bursting from sun-drenched branches.
寒雪寂寥初散後，	As loneliness has gone with the chilly snow,
春風悠悠欲來時。	Spring wind is loitering on its way.
小屏閒放畫帘垂。	The small screens are idly placed; painted curtains hang down.[82]

Yan Shu is believed to have been greatly influenced by the lyrics of the Southern Tang emperor and poet Li Yu (937–78). As many scholars have noted, Li Yu was one of a few pioneering lyricists in articulating the male subjective voice and perspective in *ci*. He is acknowledged particularly for his manipulation of the abandoned-woman convention in order to express his nostalgia for his lost kingdom.[83] Yan Shu seems also to have found an emotional outlet for his subjective feelings in projecting a boudoir-like setting, but his way of engaging with this domestic setting is different from Li Yu's. While Li Yu constructs the extraordinary personal perspective of the ruler of a fallen kingdom through references to his lost country and palaces, the voice in Yan Shu's lyrics quoted above is ambiguous, and the subtle moods it expresses befit the domestic setting and everyday life. In this way, Yan Shu transforms the conventional boudoir setting from within and constructs a new domestic space in the lyric for accommodating private feelings.[84]

Ronald Egan has observed that from the Five Dynasties to the Song, poets increasingly produced songs whose voice is ambiguous in terms of gender identity.[85] The gender indeterminacy results partly from the ambiguity of traditional Chinese poetic language and partly from the fact that Song male lyricists preferred to represent themselves and their inner states directly from their subjective perspective without employing the female persona. This subjective perspective is paradoxically constructed through impersonal, objective description. In other words, the lyric is seemingly objective yet is in fact a "soliloquy" by the author. In describing his or her perceptions, the poet does not need to always provide information regarding gender.

Based on the boudoir and by extension the domestic setting, *ci* writers in the Song period constructed a feminine world in a broader and more fluid sense. The sentiments appear to be womanly but not necessarily of women. As Fong has noted: "[T]he ideal program of a song lyric of the mainstream feminine style was to articulate subtle and elusive moods, perceptions, and states of feeling and emotion by means of feminized, 'domesticated' imagery and diction."[86] In this way, Song lyricists extended the territory of the boudoir topos by including subtle, delicate, and fluid feminine beauty and pathos. It became a locus of several sets of correlative themes and expressions: the boudoir plaint, amorous and erotic feelings, and tender pathos related to daily, domestic life. As the third category itself is elusive, it might not be easily recognized as a standard area of expression but would certainly affect poets of later ages who engaged in the genre. With the construction of an ambivalent feminine space in the lyric, Song *ci* writers constructed a poetics of "interiority" on two levels: an expression of one's inner state of mind framed by perceptions of an inner space. This poetics both accommodates old conventions and allows more latitude for the poet to explore his or her inner world within its stylistic limits.

PERFORMING THE LITERARY PAST: THE BOUDOIR CONVENTION IN MING-QING POETRY

In terms of the classical poetic tradition, writers in the Ming-Qing era lived in the shadow of previous ages. Confronting the formidable legacy of earlier ages, Ming-Qing poets often felt compelled to manage and reflect on the poetic tradition. In other words, it was impossible to write their own poetry without meditating on the relationship between their practice and the tradition. Time-honored boudoir poetry continued to hold an important place not only in critical discourse but also in writing practice by poets of both genders.

Boudoir poetry in its conventional sense was already overdeveloped by the Ming-Qing era. To sum up, traditional boudoir poetry, including both *shi* and *ci* genres, serves three correlative or overlapping interests: an aesthetic and erotic appreciation of feminine beauty and the feminine psyche, an expression of love sentiments and other tender moods related to daily, domestic life, and the metaphoric articulation of political messages through the tropes of women and love.

The third dimension has been schematically ignored in this chapter until now, because, on the surface, all the poems can be read as re-flections on women and love; the political meaning of the poem on a deeper level is derived from a contextualized historical reading. However, traditional Chinese hermeneutics indeed complicated the production and reception of male-authored boudoir poetry, especially the subgenre of the boudoir plaint.[87] The method of allegorical reading originates from the Han period exegeses of the Confucian classics *Book of Songs* and *Songs of the South*. The sexual desire expressed and relationships described in the texts are read as public and political: the relationship between the female persona and her lover or husband stands for that between minister and ruler. The typical poetic situation of unfulfilled desire and lamentation as depicted in the boudoir plaint is understood as the expression of the minister's or poet's frustrations with political reality. Due to their unique history of development, love lyrics were not subject to allegorical readings until very late in the eighteenth century. A group of *ci* writers and critics, known as the Changzhou school, made efforts to ascribe the reading and writing of *ci* to the allegorical tradition originating in the *shi* genre.[88] The founder, Zhang Huiyan (1761–1802), through compiling the *Anthology of Ci* (Ci xuan), proposed applying the allegorical approach to the practice of *ci*, not only in interpreting earlier works such as Wen Tingyun's lyrics, but also in consciously writing *ci* with allegorical intent. Although his idea and interpretations were criticized as rigid and far-fetched, the school had lasting influence on *ci* writers into the late Qing and the early twentieth century. The allegorical manipulation of the trope of female lament by male writers composing poetry as well as by critics who were interpreting it reveals the sociopolitical implications of literature in literati culture.

In dealing with the boudoir convention, Ming-Qing poetic practice recognized and demonstrated critical discernment between the two major branches of conventional boudoir poetics, the boudoir plaint and the erotic. In the *shi* genre, erotic poetry elicited more critical attention because, from the very beginning, it posed a challenge to the orthodox view of poetics. Some poets, especially in the liberal cultural ambience of the late Ming, indeed pursued erotic-style boudoir poetry for its own sake. The late Ming and early Qing saw a wave of interest in late Tang aesthetics based on sensual beauty. Scholars such as Wu Zhaoyi reprinted and annotated the collections of Li Shangyin and Han Wo (844–923) as well as *New Songs from a Jade Terrace*.[89] Derived from Han Wo's *Collection of the Scented Dress-Case* (Xianglian ji), the term "scented dress-case style" (*xianglian ti*) referred to poetry devoted to the aesthetic and erotic appreciation of woman's image and the boudoir scene. The late Ming poet Wang Yanhong (courtesy name Cihui) (1493–1642) was known as an avid practitioner in this regard. He left behind volumes of poems with sensual and erotic representations of women and the boudoir.[90] As the orthodox poetic movement gained more and more currency in the Qing, however, sensual and erotic poetry became more marginalized than in earlier periods. In stating his editing principles in his *Anthology of Qing Poetry* (Qingshi biecai ji), Shen Deqian (1673–1764) criticizes Wang's poems as "the most harmful to people's minds."[91] Shen's critique of Wang's erotic poems is not surprising, for he insisted on the Confucian view of poetics, that "poetry should express one's moral intent."

The subgenre of the boudoir plaint, however, enjoyed a respectable place in Ming-Qing mainstream poetic practice. Major anthologies are replete with poems with titles such as "The Boudoir Plaint" or "The Boudoir Lyrics." Shen Deqian's anthology, for example, includes a poem by Dong Yining titled "The Boudoir Plaint":

流蘇空繫合歡床，	Silk sash is tied on the joint-pleasure bed in vain;
夫婿長征妾斷腸。	As my husband is on his long march, my heart is broken.
留得當時臨別淚，	Since it preserves my tear stains at the time of parting,
經年不忍浣衣裳。	I could not bear to wash my robe for more than a year.[92]

This poem expresses the plaint of a soldier's wife. The first line makes use of stock images from *New Songs from a Jade Terrace*, such as "joint-pleasure bed," an erotic element. But this minor detail is subsumed within the sad story of the female persona's extreme sorrow. Presumably touched by this poem, Shen Deqian cannot help but note at the bottom of the text that "no one surpasses this poet's skillfulness in invoking the image of tears."[93] He reads the poem as a conventional boudoir plaint with an excellent artistic touch. Whether entrusting their own emotional experience to the boudoir plaint or simply writing as a literary exercise, Ming-Qing poets continued to create various versions of the lovelorn woman in the boudoir. A perfect version, whether by a man or a woman, would be appreciated for its own virtue in representing the classic situation and sentiments. The inclusion of boudoir poetry in mainstream anthologies suggests that even orthodox poetic practice valued this long-standing literary tradition as long as there was no particular attempt to evoke the erotic. The potential of the boudoir plaint for political allegory also made poems with this theme more acceptable in orthodox poetic practice.

As time-honored subjects and themes sanctioned by the *ci* form, women and the boudoir seem to have always assumed a central place in the genre from the late Tang onward. As generally held, the *ci* genre declined during the Yuan and Ming periods but was revived by some important late Ming and early Qing poets in the seventeenth century.[94] Modern scholars have attributed the seventeenth-century *ci* revival to the achievements of a few prominent poets such as Chen Weisong (1625–1682), Zhu Yizun, Chen Zilong (1608–1647), and Nalan Xingde (1655–1685). They are recognized for their broadening of the thematic scope of *ci*, their new emphasis on the quality of sincerity, and their injection of a poet's individuality into the work.[95] Although they turned to different earlier models for inspiration, these poets all reaffirmed the function of the *ci* as a vehicle of self-expression.[96] The *ci*'s generic convention allowed the poet to explore private emotions in more depth—not only love and desire, but also other sentiments. They continued to invoke the inner, boudoir space in representing these themes. While they engaged in the conventional mode of the boudoir plaint, they tended to produce love lyrics from their own perspectives as male lover or husband.

Of these poets, Chen Zilong and Zhu Yizun deserve special attention. A heroic Ming loyalist and romantic lover of the famous courtesan Liu Rushi, Chen Zilong has been particularly noted for his love songs. His patriotic intent and love affair imbue these poems with more political and historical implications,[97] although the political meaning of his love poems relies more on an allegorical reading. On the surface, however, his expressions of love are refreshed through his poetic exchanges with Liu Rushi, in which descriptions of her appearance and the boudoir setting are not as important as the subtle emotional communication with the addressee. Zhu Yizun, in his *Amusements on the Lute in Stilling-Ambition Dwelling* (Jingzhiju qinqu), a collection of his love lyrics and erotic songs, simultaneously follows generic conventions and pushes against their limits in inscribing his private feelings about and memories of his secret love affair.[98] The convention of the boudoir as a site of public eroticism is turned into a "forbidden space of illicit passion" in his autobiographical context.[99]

Generally speaking, the Ming-Qing male poets indeed continued to explore their "interiority" in more depth in the private, domestic setting, a fluid dimension already opened up by Tang and Song poets, but their engagement with boudoir themes in both the *shi* and *ci* genres did not exceed that of their predecessors in terms of broader thematic categories. Their boudoir poetry is primarily a performance of conventionalized themes and codes with more or fewer personal touches.

Despite its ambivalent status in Chinese poetic history, traditional boudoir poetics had a tremendous influence on Ming-Qing women's poetic production. It is evident that women not only had access to classical sources of boudoir poetry such as *New Songs from a Jade Terrace* but also consciously modeled their writing on conventional boudoir poetry, including Palace-Style poems. Poems that excessively evoke glamorous and erotic feelings, whether by men or women, were not acceptable by the standards of orthodox poetics; however, conventional expressions of feminine beauty and the tender pathos associated with the boudoir setting are commonplace in Ming-Qing women's poetry. In reading this type of poetry, it is often difficult to tell whether a poem is merely an exercise in the artistic conventions of the genre or a perception of boudoir life shaped by the author's textual experience of the literary past.

CHAPTER 2

A New Feminine Ideal

The Case of The Anthology of Correct Beginnings

Under the shadow of crimson clouds and deep behind the painted blind,
She refuses the visits of wandering bees and wanton butterflies.
She does not complain to the east wind about scattering;
In light rouge, she accompanies me idly singing by the secluded window.

絳霞掩映畫簾深,謝絕游蜂浪蝶尋。不向東風怨零落,幽窗紅粉伴閒吟。

—GUO JIE 郭矴

Women's writing was connected not only with the literary past but also more directly and substantially with the authors' contemporary world and society. The ideological prescription of the *gui* was not merely an ungrounded discourse; it was actually embodied in an institution that defined women's place and gender roles in society. As social subjects who were supposed to live in the *gui*, how did women poets depict this space that was supposedly their own? How did their social status and perspective influence their writing? How did their lives in the *gui* inform their writing, if at all? *The Anthology of Correct Beginnings by Inner-Chamber Talents of the Present Dynasty* and its sequel offer evidence of how Qing women poets refashioned the boudoir convention in order to project their cultural taste and lifestyle as *guixiu*, or the talented of the inner chambers. This new feminine ideal reflects the general development of women's literary culture from the late Ming onward as well as historical trends particular to the Qing period.

Boudoir poetry, a genre centered on the images and lives of women, both influenced and was influenced by women's subject positions and by representations that were constantly under construction. As women's literary culture developed, their poetic production increasingly reflected the literary tastes they had cultivated. Women's boudoir writing, understood as a product of this historical and cultural ambience, enlarged the parameters of and set up new limits of representation. The most typical scenario thematized by literati writers in the various versions of the boudoir is one in which lonely women are sadly waiting for absent lovers in an empty space. These narrow thematics and imageries of conventional boudoir poetry were inadequate for the expressive needs of women writers reacting to their society and culture. Furthermore, the erotic tint that colors some literati versions made it problematic for women to simply take up the female persona and voice. Women's boudoir writing was also shaped by the fact that a woman not only had to deal with already established conventions of the genre but also was expected to internalize moral propriety appropriate to her gender (of course on the condition that her act of writing was approved).[1] The conventional subject positions—the abandoned woman or the objectified beautiful woman—were rendered outdated or marginalized as women attempted to explore more meaningful subjectivities within their society.

The Anthology of Correct Beginnings marks a significant historical juncture. Through its retrospective selection of women's poetic production ranging from the beginning of the Qing to its own time (including poets who lived during the late Ming and Qing), the anthology was intended to establish a normative poetics of women's poetry in light of dominant ideological and literary discourses. The representation of women's lives in the inner chambers in this anthology reflects some commonly valued aesthetic qualities of femininity in the late imperial era as well as new trends emphasized in the late eighteenth century and the first half of the nineteenth century, a high point in late imperial Chinese women's literary culture, as many scholars have noted.[2] Important anthologies were instrumental in the establishment of the boudoir topos. This monumental anthology of women's poetry provides a rich source for examining the new normative boudoir poetics and aesthetics established by Qing women poets.

The Anthology of Correct Beginnings is a collection of *shi* poetry, a genre that is generally more directly involved than *ci* in the sociopolitical arena. Yun Zhu's anthologizing project, supported by a number of women poets and scholars, also reveals the textual politics of a female literary community. Seeking general approval from their social and literary authorities, women writers reformed the conventional parameters of boudoir poetics in order to align themselves with dominant social and ideological values. As their own "poet-autobiographers," these women poets were careful to consider how others might interpret the self-images presented in their poetry.³ While men could afford to discount the boudoir because it was marginal to their public domain, women, whose lives revolved around this space, were sensitive to its significance in their textual production.

THE ANTHOLOGY AND ITS AGENDA

In order to historicize the relationship of Qing women to literary discourse and authority at the historical juncture of *The Anthology of Correct Beginnings*, it is necessary to examine the context in which the anthology was compiled and the work's agenda.⁴ The volume was compiled by the woman scholar Yun Zhu (1771–1833) and published in the Daoguang reign (1821–50). By this time, the collection of Qing women's writings had reached an unprecedented level. With a first edition consisting of 1,736 poems by 933 poets and a sequel containing 1,229 poems by 593 poets, the anthology was a crystallization of contemporary women's literary culture. It was intended to be a summation of women's poetry from the beginning of the Qing (1644) through 1836. It was not the largest collection of Qing women's poetry, but it was perhaps the most widely circulated.⁵

Yun Zhu's anthologizing agenda was closely connected to two general trends in Qing poetics. The first is an interest among anthologizers in collecting poetic works of the current dynasty, a practice that can be traced back to the Tang dynasty but did not flourish until the first half of the Qing, especially from the Kangxi reign (1662–1722) onward.⁶ With the exception of a few anthologists who collected poetry by Ming "loyalists" (*yimin*), many, especially those who grew up in the new dynasty, aimed to celebrate the poetic culture of the Qing. Almost every anthology that honored the literary achievement of the Qing era, even the most famous and influential, considered women's writing indispensable. Some anthologists who did not include women authors felt compelled to offer explanations for the exclusion, which suggests that it was becoming standard practice to include women's poetry. In addition to including women's poetry in male-dominated anthologies, some Qing anthologists devoted their collections exclusively to the women poets of their own dynasty. This significant phenomenon occurred only in the Qing period.

The second trend, the effort to promote a "correct" or "orthodox" (*zheng*) poetics in light of the principle of "being earnest and gentle" (*wenrou dunhou*), was situated in the broad movement to revive classical learning.⁷ The term "being earnest and gentle" originally appeared in the *Book of Rites*, where it describes an ideal for poetics as well as personal character. Although it was emphasized differently by each poetic school, it generally referred to earnestness and morality in intention, and restraint and gentleness in expression. Despite changing social and historical conditions, the orthodox, Confucian poetics assumed a dominant place in Qing literary practice, from its revival in the late Ming through the Qianlong reign (1746–95), and "being earnest and gentle" became a catchphrase in poetic criticism. Shen Deqian was the central leader in this poetic movement.⁸ For him, the correctness of poetry is embodied in the principle of being earnest and gentle, which can be used to evaluate three aspects of poetry: an author's moral quality and cultivation, the poem's approach to indirect admonishment of the ruler by his ministers, and a poem's overall aesthetic standard.⁹ In general, he believed that a good poem should express a poet's authentic moral intent or convey social and political didacticism: it should be substantial in content yet gentle in style, written in elegant yet unembellished language. Shen's insistence on integrating moral and aesthetic values represents a summation of the literary trend of returning to the poetic orthodoxy that had been set forth in the Han exegesis of the *Book of Songs*.¹⁰ His collection, *The Anthology of Qing Poetry* known in his time as *The Anthology of Poetry of the Present Dynasty* (Guochao shi biecai ji), is a selection of works that embody his poetics.

Meanwhile, the poetic orthodoxy increasingly demanded that women's writing reflect moral values, forcing anthologists to be discriminating about the social status of female authors. Although Shen Deqian claimed that he was following the principle of selecting authors based on their poetry, he privileged a woman author's virtue over the elegance of her poetry.¹¹ Shen Deqian was perhaps the first person to unambiguously reject courtesan authors. Labeling them "fallen women of the green bower" (*qinglou shixing funü*), he completely excluded their writings from his anthology. Instead, he selected only poetry by "worthy women" (*xianyuan*).¹² Many Qing anthologists adopted Shen's critical stance against courtesans.

Yun Zhu's anthologizing project echoes orthodox literary trends of her time. Her ambitious agenda is epitomized by the title of her anthology, which combines three key terms: "the present dynasty" (*guochao*), "the talented of the inner chambers" (*guixiu*), and "correct beginnings" (*zhengshi*). Identifying with the present dynasty, Yun

Zhu not only embraces the mainstream fashion of anthologizing contemporary poets but also demonstrates her intention to incorporate Qing women's poetry into the ongoing imperial cultural enterprise. By aligning her project with similarly titled authoritative anthologies such as Shen Deqian's *The Anthology of Poetry of the Present Dynasty*, this woman editor was astutely attempting to elevate the status of women's writing. She particularly recognized the authority and significance of Shen's anthology and meticulously modeled her own collection after it. She aspired to make the *The Anthology of Correct Beginnings* a female counterpart to Shen's authoritative achievement in terms of both poetic and moral standards.

Yun Zhu's adoption of the term *guixiu* indicates not only the gender orientation of the project but also the exclusivity of the authors' social and cultural standing. The conception of *guixiu* changed over time. It could be used to refer to women with artistic talents in general (including courtesans) in the late Ming, but Yun Zhu followed the orthodox trend represented by Shen Deqian, excluding courtesans and other marginal groups from the category of *guixiu*. She phrased her explanation for excluding poems by courtesans in almost exactly the same terms as used by Shen Deqian: "Fallen women of the green bower often write poems about sexual love and romance. While earlier anthologies find their writings enjoyable, this anthology does not include them."[13] Shen Deqian selected a total of sixty-four women poets for *The Anthology of Poetry of the Present Dynasty*; of these sixty-four, fifty-nine were also chosen by Yun Zhu along with almost the same poems. However, she also enlists a few exceptional cases, such as the courtesan Liu Shi. In Yun Zhu's view, women could transcend their social status by marrying famous literati and performing virtuous acts in their later years. Likewise, although she explicitly claimed that nuns do not belong to the category of *guixiu*, Yun Zhu included several nuns who, she thought, took religious vows only as an expedient strategy for preserving their chastity.[14] Nevertheless, Yun Zhu's exclusion of courtesans and nuns was almost absolute. She also placed them at the end of her anthology, just as many male anthologists did with women and monks.[15]

The biographical notes for the authors represented in *The Anthology of Correct Beginnings* make it evident that these *guixiu* poets were mostly the wives or concubines and daughters of members of the gentry class, although the anthology also includes women from lower classes, such as poor commoners, and exceptional cases such as Liu Shi. This demonstrates that Yun Zhu's definition of *guixiu* identity is concerned with moral and cultural cultivation rather than class background exclusively. In order to celebrate "the sagely influence of our dynasty," Yun Zhu also selected poems by Korean women. She envisioned a *guixiu* culture that could go beyond boundaries of class, region, and ethnicity.[16] But the culture itself had to have a high degree of homogeneity. As Yun Zhu summarized the matter in her "Editorial Principles" (Liyan), *guixiu* poets should express "chaste and virtuous nature and emotion" in the "harmonious sound" of their poetry.[17]

Having brought forth a well-defined notion of *guixiu*, Yun Zhu attempts to construct a discursive arena for women based on "properly" defined gender boundaries as suggested by the third term, "correct beginnings." This term originally appeared in the hermeneutics of the *Book of Songs* to illustrate the moral didacticism of the songs in "The South of Zhou" (Zhou nan) and "The South of Shao" (Shao nan), the first two sections of "Airs of the States (Guo feng). Recognizing the influence of wifely virtue on affairs of state, the Great Preface states, "'The South of Zhou' and 'The South of Shao' are seen to illustrate correct beginnings, the basis of the process of kingly transformation."[18] More specifically, "Correct beginnings refer to the women's apartments (i.e., the domestic realm, women's realm) as the starting point for the process of kingly transformation that ordered the imperium."[19] Educated women had a good understanding of this commentarial tradition. For example, one author represented in *The Anthology of Correct Beginnings*, Wang Nairong, writes in her poem, "Reading the 'Zhou nan' and 'Shao nan,' / I understand the women's chambers is the beginning of the kingly transformation."[20] This is a point of departure from which Yun Zhu and her supporters attempted to bring forth a *guixiu* poetics.

Yun Zhu's elevation of women's writing and attempt to establish an explicit poetic for women set her apart from the women editors and male anthologists of previous collections of women's poetry. Yun Zhu's major strategy was to integrate female virtue with literary elegance, establishing a poetics of women's poetry within the bounds of propriety. In introducing the poems in her "Editor's Words" (Bianyan), Yun Zhu claims that "[t]he genres and their contents vary, but the sentiment and tone of each is correct. Pure beauty, chaste emotion, conjugal harmony, limpid verse—none would shame the woman scribe's admonitions, and all conform to the standards required of a poet."[21] This poetics is unique in its gender-specific orientation. It does not merely consider the sex of the author but also evaluates her poetry according to the prescriptions placed upon the female gender by orthodox discourses. In other words, the poetics represented by *The Anthology of Correct Beginnings* constitutes women's participation in the revival of the Confucian view of poetics. Although there is some degree of inconsistency involved in the anthology's corpus—not every poem conforms to Yun Zhu's standard—the gendered poetics articulated in her editorial writings does account for the main currents of expressions represented by the collection. This explicit poetics provides important clues for understanding the major forces that influenced Qing women's representations of themselves and their place in society.

The most obvious change that took place at the hands of female authors is the great expansion of boudoir thematics. Poems written on conventional themes are greatly outnumbered by those depicting new boudoir scenarios. Maureen Robertson has delineated a long list of the activities associated with the boudoir setting in Ming-Qing women's poetry, including "sewing, study, chess, writing, playing and listening to music, teaching (children and other women), conversing, religious activities (meditating, chanting sutras, reading religious works), painting, dinner parties, resting, and sleeping."[22] In *The Anthology of Correct Beginnings*, the boudoir as a space of women's self-representation accommodates such a broad topical range that even Robertson's rather comprehensive list does not cover it.

The pictures of daily life that women authors depict in their poetry, however, do not deal with every aspect of their lives but present what they think is proper for poetic topics and appropriate to their social and cultural status as *guixiu*. The construction of an ideal *guixiu* identity was a major force underlying the transformation of boudoir poetics. While the poets included in the anthology do not have an identical understanding of *guixiu* attributes, their self-representations do share common values and ideas. They adopted two correlative approaches: the revision of conventional boudoir themes and motifs, such as the erotic and the boudoir plaint, and the reconceptualization of the boudoir space with new cultural ideals. These poets established a distinctive boudoir aesthetics and poetics that corroborate Yun Zhu's vision of a women's poetics.

RECODING FEMININE IMAGES

In representing themselves, women poets encounter a poignant irony: while they are called on to be virtuous subjects and moral guardians in orthodox gender ideology, their images and the boudoir space are portrayed as objects of sexual desire and erotic pleasure in the sensual, erotic mode of boudoir poetry. Even though women writers of boudoir poetry found their emotional world in many ways connected with traditional boudoir sentiments, many realized that it would be problematic if they used the available sources without discriminating among them. De-eroticization was the first and foremost stylistic consideration for a woman who intended to embrace orthodox ideology and poetics. Filtered through Yun Zhu's censorship, *The Anthology of Correct Beginnings* had no place for the erotic. This was not only articulated in Yun Zhu's anthologizing agenda; individual women authors were also conscious of the potential harm that sensual, erotic poetics might do to their moral images. As Tang Jingxian urges her peers in her poem "Stirred by Feelings after Reading Poems by Guixiu": "Earnestly I tell friends of powder and rouge / Cultivate moral character to avoid being criticized."[23] "Powder and rouge," women's makeup, is a term male critics often used to characterize trivial feminine qualities, including women's writing of poetry. Tang Jingxian uses it to refer to other women poets as she cautions them to avoid becoming targets of critique.

In *The Anthology of Correct Beginnings*, a few poems evoke neutral tender feelings such as lamenting the passing of spring, but the evocation of erotic feelings is entirely absent. The boudoir is used to depict more serious themes than the appreciation of feminine beauty. Many Ming-Qing women poets, including the authors in *The Anthology of Correct Beginnings*, were familiar with the tradition of Palace-Style poetry. For example, a poem by Gao Jingfang (fl. 1718), "Composed on 'Looking at a Dropped Hairpin Reflected in the River's Flow,'" in her collection *Drafts from the Snow-Geese Tower* (Hongxuexuan gao), is modeled exactly on Xiao Gang's poem "Looking at a Dropped Hairpin Reflected in the River's Flow." Xiao's poem reads:

相隨照綠水,	One by one reflected in green water,
意欲重涼風。	They seem to crave a cooling breeze.
流搖妝影壞,	The flow trembles, painted image ravaged.
釵落鬢華空。	A hairpin drops; coiffure flowers vanish.
佳期在何許,	Where is her beloved so long?
徒傷心不同。	She suffers in vain for hearts no longer one.[24]

Xiao Gang's poem consists of only six lines, but Gao's poem is lengthy, containing twenty-six lines, including:

出簾容灼灼,	Coming out from behind the bamboo screen, her appearance glistens;
拂檻步徐徐。	Hand gliding over railings, her pace is elegantly slow.
直度白花架,	Straight, she crosses under the trellis of white blossoms
橫過紫竹廬。	And turns to pass by the Purple-Bamboo Hut.
戲停文石岸,	To play, she stops at the patterned rock bank,
微漾合歡裾。	The joint-love pleats of her skirt slightly swaying.
露濕愁苔滑,	Dew moist, she is worried about slippery lichens;
波澄慶檻虛。	Waves clear, she is happy that railings are open.
影搖同藻荇,	Her reflection sways with the water weeds;
臉媚並芙蕖。	Her lovely face is next to a lotus.
顧盼聊相向,	Exchanging glances as they idly face each other,
低徊怪儼如。	Lowering and turning her head, she marvels at their likeness.
整襟嫌釧重,	Arranging her lapel, she finds her gold bracelets too heavy;
攏鬢惜釵除。	Touching up her coiffure, she regrets that her hairpin has dropped.
墮水金猶亮,	Fallen in the water, the gold still glitters;
臨深玉怯舒。	Facing the depths, she is afraid to stretch out her jade arms.
鬢空羞更照,	Hairdo bare (of ornaments), she's embarrassed to look again at her reflection;
髮薄擬重梳。	Hair flattened—she intends to have it redone.
惆悵歸來晚,	Sorrowful, returning late,
憑軒態有餘。	Leaning against the pavilion, her manner is more than charming.[25]

Focusing on the detail of a woman dropping her hairpin into a pond, Xiao Gang's poem repeats the abandoned woman's tale. As the title suggests, Gao Jingfang's poem is most likely a poetic exercise, working on precisely the same theme, except that the woman poet devotes a lengthy section to the description of the female persona's appearance, activities, and surroundings before giving a thematic remark in the final two lines. Her approach differs from Xiao Gang's, but it is an approach influenced by the Palace Style in general. In this poem of twenty-six lines, all the couplets, except for the first and last, are structured by parallelism. They are meticulously arranged to show the beauty and elegance of the persona, as well as her harmonious relationship with the environment. The parallel between the persona's image and the garden scene—both are beautiful and cultivated—is especially emphasized in the poem. The woman author's elaboration on her model demonstrates not only familiarity with but also skillful mastery of the Palace Style.

Gao Jingfang was one of Yun Zhu's favorite authors. In addition to including Gao in *The Anthology of Correct Beginnings*, Yun Zhu also included the poet in her *Precious Records from the Orchid Boudoir* (Langui baolu), a much smaller but not less significant collection of biographies of female paragons in categories such as virtue and talent.[26] Although the entry for Gao consists only of a brief biographical note that is almost exactly the same as the note in *The Anthology of Correct Beginnings*, the inclusion of Gao in *Precious Records from the Orchid Boudoir* shows Yun Zhu's special recognition of Gao's artistic talent:

> Gao Jingfang belongs to the Han banner: She is the wife of the first-rank Marquis Zhang Zongren. Specializing in both the seal and clerk scripts in calligraphy, she is capable at composing poetry and rhapsody, and she is also good at parallel-style prose. She has produced the collection *Drafts from the Snow-Geese Tower* in thirty-six *juan*.[27]

In spite of the fact that Yun Zhu mistakenly notes that Gao Jingfang's collection contains thirty-six *juan* (it is actually six *juan*), the biographical note suggests that she might have consulted Gao Jingfang's individual collection.[28] Yun Zhu includes eight poems by Gao Jingfang in *The Anthology of Correct Beginnings*, but the long poem written on the dropped hairpin is not among them. Among the eight poems, only one is on the boudoir theme. It reveals some of the concerns that shaped Yun Zhu's anthologizing agenda:

晨妝	MY MORNING MAKEUP
妝閣開清曉，	I open up my dressing room in the clear dawn;
晨光上畫欄。	Morning sunshine lights up the painted railings.
未曾梳寶髻，	As my chignon isn't done up yet,
不敢問親安。	I dare not pay respects to my parents.
妥貼加釵鳳，	I properly add a phoenix hairpin;
低徊插佩蘭。	Lowering my head, I pin on an orchid blossom.
隔簾呼侍婢，	Behind the bamboo blind, I call the maid
背後與重看。	To take a second look from the back.[29]

This poem captures a moment in which a woman meticulously dresses herself after rising in the morning, a familiar boudoir scenario depicted in palace verses such as Xiao Gang's "A Lovely Woman's Morning Makeup" (quoted in chapter 1). Gao Jingfang seems to have been inspired by Xiao Gang's poem in plotting the scenario of her poem. Although she focuses on a different detail, hairstyling, the scenario progresses in a way similar to Xiao Gang's. Like Xiao Gang's persona, who is "[s]weet, shy, unwilling to come out" because "her makeup isn't done," Gao Jingfang's is also afraid to step out of the boudoir until she makes sure that her hair is perfectly done. The only significant difference lies in the reasons these two women are making themselves up. While Xiao Gang asserts for his persona that "No doubt with all this she's sensational; / She deserves to be called 'Adorable'!" Gao Jingfang claims that "As my chignon isn't done up yet, / I dare not pay respects to my parents." Dressing up in Gao's poem thus becomes a ritualized aspect of paying respects to parents; the female persona's meticulous attention to her appearance reveals the degree of a daughter's or daughter-in-law's filial piety.[30] The woman author sets up a new, "serious" context for the reader in which to locate the meaning of a typical boudoir activity.

In the two poems by Gao Jingfang and the one by Xiao Gang cited above, the image of the "hairpin" (*chai*) plays a crucial role in the boudoir scenario. A staple in the boudoir convention, a hairpin functions not only as a signifier of female gender and feminine adornment but also as an object suggesting sexuality and desire.[31] It is often used, especially when linked with the image of the pillow, as a cue for a scene of lovemaking as exemplified in Ouyang Xiu's lyric and Li Shangyin's poems. Writing on an occasion in which a hairpin was dropped for a reason other than lovemaking, Xiao Gang plays with the image on a different level in order to reveal the theme of unfulfilled passion: the dropped hairpin reminds the female persona of her absent lover. But the evocation of the image still falls into the thematic category of love between a man and a woman. Following poetic convention in her "Composed on 'Looking at a Dropped Hairpin Reflected in the River's Flow,'" Gao Jingfang also writes a narrative in which a hairpin has dropped. However, she morally rescues the image in "My Morning Makeup," a self-referential poem, by "properly" using it for the occasion of paying respects to her parents. The poet must have understood in her historical and cultural context that a woman's loose hair suggests improper etiquette and lax morality.

Echoing Gao's manner of rescuing a "fallen" hairpin, Zhu Zhongmei (1521–1661) also creatively transforms this image steeped in eroticism into a "proper" element in her poem "Spring Night":

瑟瑟湘簾裊裊垂，　The silk curtain gracefully drops, rustling in the breeze;

A New Feminine Ideal 63

嬌鶯初囀最高枝。	Lovely orioles begin to chirp on the highest branches.
枕棱畫得金釵響，	I draw on the edges of the pillow with my tingling gold hairpin,
為記深宵夢裏詩。	To remember the poem I dreamed of last night.[32]

The opening couplet consists of clichés describing the scene as a woman awakens in her boudoir. If the poet were to have followed the boudoir convention, in the second couplet, the female persona would likely have stated her dream of a reunion with her lover, often with sexual innuendoes. The female poet, however, suddenly changes the tone of the poem by making clever use of the hairpin: it helps the female persona remember the poetic lines she had composed in her dream. This subtle yet significant change demonstrates a *guixiu*'s "pure" imagination and taste as well as her literary skill.

Image coding is essential in shaping the boudoir topos. Sets of recognizable expressions and coded images establish the boudoir as a sensual, erotic, and sentimental setting. Although the authors in *The Anthology of Correct Beginnings* to a large extent inherit the conventional lexicon, in many cases, women authors felt compelled to reinscribe established image codes that were not suitable for their expressive needs. Unlike what scholars have observed, that women's rewriting of coded images is not conducted in "any programmatic way,"[33] many women authors in this anthology consciously modify conventions that conflict with their interests

If the above examples are not explicit enough to show the authors' innovative intent, the following poem, "Peach Blossoms in a Vase" by Guo Jie assertively demonstrates the poet's plan to alter conventional, negative associations with the images of women and the boudoir.

絳霞掩映畫簾深，	Under the shadow of crimson clouds and deep behind the painted blind,
謝絕游蜂浪蝶尋。	She refuses the visits of wandering bees and wanton butterflies.
不向東風怨零落，	She does not complain to the east wind about scattering;
幽窗紅粉伴閒吟。	In light rouge, she accompanies me idly singing by the secluded window.[34]

In this poem, the female author unveils to the reader a secluded corner of her room sheltered by elegant blinds. Although the title indicates that the poem is written about peach blossoms arranged in a vase, the flower is an obvious metaphor for her self. The peach blossom conventionally symbolizes a sexually attractive woman and can also stand for a woman of lax virtue. It attracts "wandering bees and wanton butterflies," metaphors for philandering males. The famous lines by the Tang poet Du Fu (712–770), "Wanton willow catkins dance with the wind; / Frivolous peach blossoms flow with the stream," represent this point of view.[35] In Guo Jie's depiction, however, the peach blossom adopts an explicit moral gesture: she positively declines any frivolous wooing. The peach blossom is well guarded, impermeable to any gaze or invasion. Guo's poem contrasts sharply with the voyeur's gaze in Xiao Gang's poem "Her Late Boudoir":

> Her hidden room in cold sun grows late,
> Declining rays cross the window sill.
> Red blinds far do not prevent my view,
> Light drapes hang half rolled up.
> . . .

Arranged in a vase and well sheltered in the boudoir, the peach blossom feels both secure and confident in her ability to control her destiny: kept indoors, she is saved from withering and scattering in the wind. She also finds something meaningful to do in this inner world, enjoying the pure pleasure of poetry. By making use of the flower metaphor, the woman poet portrays the self-image of a chaste and talented woman enjoying her boudoir life.

If Guo Jie enjoys her boudoir as a sacrosanct space, Tong Feng's poem "Writing about My Feelings" describes a woman who wants to open up the space of her boudoir for homosociality:

排悶拓窗紗，	To release my boredom, I push open my window screen:
春亭竹影遮。	The shadows of bamboo obscure the spring pavilion.
渴蜂窺硯水，	A thirsty bee is peeping at the water in the ink slab;
閒蝶息瓶花。	An idle butterfly rests on the flowers in the vase.
弄笛聲全澀，	I try to play the flute, yet its trill is rather jarring.
題箋字半斜。	I inscribe a poem on letter paper, but the characters fall aslant.
相招鄰女至，	The girl next door just arrived at my invitation;
一笑啜新茶。	With a smile, we sip this year's new tea.[36]

The boudoir in this poem is represented as an open house. Some guests are invited, and some guests come in unexpectedly, such as the bee and the butterfly, conventional symbols of philandering males that are rejected in Guo Jie's "Peach Blossoms in a Vase." But the poet places these unwelcome "guests" in a different setting. The bee is usually linked with nectar by convention, a metaphoric description of a sexual consummation. As Han Wo suggests in his poem "Amorous," love occurs "at the place where the bee just tastes the wild nectar it steals."[37] The woman poet intends to break with this formulaic expression. In her depiction, what the thirsty bee attempts to drink is not nectar but the poet's ink; the butterfly lands not on wild flowers but on those carefully arranged in a vase. Having opened her window, the poet intends to display her artistic engagements, although she appears to be a novice in these arts in her humble self-representation. What is more precious to the poet, however, appears to be the carefree moment shared with female company, which dispels the state of boredom and ennui with which the poem began.

In recoding the established images, the common strategy these women authors adopt is recontextualization. By introducing "a new frame of reference" in their poetry, they attempt to direct the reader toward a different understanding of the conventional codes.[38] Although such examples appear to be sporadic, the changes these women authors made are crucial in being clearly conscious efforts to alter conventional associations with women and the boudoir while adhering to the aesthetic taste of their own time. Late Ming women's texts increasingly emphasize physical attractiveness and the compatibility of beauty with virtue and talent in shaping a new womanhood.[39] Within the poetic tradition, however, the change occurring in Yun Zhu's era is the emphasis on morality rather than beauty: as reflected in *The Anthology of Correct Beginnings*, women authors' inscription of female beauty with moral values was the new trend against the conventional construction of women's images as aesthetic and sexual objects.

Weng Guangzhu's "Poem on Making Up" goes further, linking the issue of women's appearance and propriety with poetic expression and thus shedding light on the new trend of women's textual transformation in rewriting conventional feminine aesthetics:

孟光歸伯鸞，	When Meng Guang was married to Boluan,
遷流歌五噫。	They were banished because Boluan sang the "Five Sighs."[40]
道路隨傭夫，	Following laborers on the road,
聊挽髻如椎。	She simply knotted her hair in a cone shape.
堂堂士人室，	For the wife of a dignified scholar,
閨範自有宜。	There are naturally fitting models for the boudoir.

儀容不修飾，	If you don't adorn yourself and beware of your manner,
尊嫜且詰之。	Your venerable parents-in-law will criticize you.
始知學古人，	Now I know if we want to learn from the ancients,
學之須適時。	We should do so in a way suited to our times.
鄰女竟靚妝，	The girl next door competes to make herself pretty;
如為徐庾辭。	It's like adopting Xu's and Yu's rhetoric.
我亦何所擬，	What I would like to imitate is
澹素陶韋詩。	The plain simplicity of Tao's and Wei's poetry.[41]

The poet cautions against two extreme tendencies: a woman not paying attention to her appearance and one obsessed with it. She begins by analyzing the case of Meng Guang, a recognized virtuous wife who possesses more inner than outer beauty. Many authors in *The Anthology of Correct Beginnings* identify Meng Guang as a role model, claiming for their own the image of a wife wearing a "thorn hairpin and plain skirt." Weng Guangzhu, however, opposes an undiscerning imitation of Meng Guang that does not first consider Meng's historical situation. For Weng, a gentry wife should be dressed properly for performing her gender roles and in accord with her social status. But the poet also frowns upon women's excessive concern with beauty and glamour. At this point, she begins to draw parallels between women's dressing and poetic styles. In the lines "The girl next door competes to make herself pretty; / It's like adopting Xu's and Yu's rhetoric," she links as negative examples a woman's elaborate makeup and Palace-Style poetry, referred to here as "Xu's and Yu's rhetoric" (*Xu Yu ci*), as practiced by Xu Ling and Yu Xin (513–581). In this way, she articulates her critique of the aesthetics of shallow beauty and ornamentation in general.[42] What she prefers, she goes on to say, is naturalness, simplicity, and elegance as represented by the poetic style of Tao Qian (365?–427) and Wei Yingwu (737–792?). Although the poet is discussing the issue of women's dress, she perceives it as an aesthetic issue intimately related to poetics. The naming of Tao and Wei as role models and the denigration of Palace-Style poetry reveal an orthodox poetics that values the substance of poetry over its formal properties. Though this is the only extant poem by Weng, it seems certain that she would have kept a critical distance from the boudoir convention in representing herself. Her assertive poem makes explicit the intention of those women authors who attempted to rewrite conventional feminine images in light of orthodox poetics and aesthetics.

"SENT TO MY HUSBAND": REWRITING THE BOUDOIR PLAINT

The boudoir plaint in the narrow sense of the deserted woman's lament seems to constitute an inconsequential portion of *The Anthology of Correct Beginnings*. There are only fourteen poems explicitly titled "Boudoir Plaint." However, a wife separated from her husband remains a common poetic situation explicitly or implicitly conveyed in the texts. The anthology includes more than one hundred poems with titles that indicate they were written to husbands who were away from home. Titles such as "Sent to My Husband" and "To the One Faraway" explicitly mark this topical territory. Poems claiming to be written by historical women to their (absent) husbands can be traced back to the Han period, as recorded in *New Songs from a Jade Terrace*. But only with the emergence of the sizable group of writing women in the late imperial period and solid evidence of their textual production can it be shown that wives writing to their husbands in poetry had become a significant practice. This is consistent to a remarkable degree with the lived situations of these authors, who were gentry wives. Although the separation of men's and women's spheres was not a monolithic and fixed social practice, it was not merely constructed on an ideological level; it had an institutional basis. Women were barred from civil examinations. While men could go outside to pursue education and official careers, women were supposed to remain inside and shoulder domestic responsibilities. Because Ming-Qing officials could be appointed only to posts that were not in their native places, travel away from home was an obligation.[43] Although gentry wives did have opportunities to follow their husbands to their official posts, staying home to take care of their families was also a responsibility they often had to assume.[44]

The Anthology of Correct Beginnings was not the only source for poems written by wives to their husbands, but it was the first anthology to collect a considerable number of poems by contemporary authors. For Yun Zhu, this was clearly an important site of poetic production. In the anthology, these works compose a topical subgenre resulting from the women authors' innovations with the boudoir plaint. Although there are specifically wifely images and voices in early boudoir plaint poems, the emotions and sentiments of the "longing wife" (*sifu*) are more often than not indistinguishable from those expressed in the voices of courtesans or singing girls. While the authors in this anthology speak from a textual position similar to that of the longing wife and rely heavily on old vocabulary, the emotions and sentiments expressed are distinctively those of the wives, mothers, and women of their society. Consider the poem "Sent to My Husband," by Zhou Yao (fl. 1799):

香撥金猊冷，	Stirring the incense in a cold gilt lion censer,
春深子夜中。	Spring is deep at midnight.
一襟楊柳月，	A lapel full of moonlight through willow boughs
雙鬢杏花風。	Brushing the hair on my temples, an apricot-blossom breeze.
鴛繡此時倦，	Too tired at this moment to embroider mandarin ducks;
魚箋幾日通。	For several days I've been writing letters to him.[45]
嬌兒方睡穩，	Our lovely child having just fallen soundly asleep,
緘意託飛鴻。	Sealing my thoughts, I entrust them to the flying geese.[46]

The cluster of familiar, sensuous images, such as the chilled lion censer, the fragrance of spring blossoms, and the embroidered mandarin ducks, immediately reveals the degree to which the poet was inspired by the boudoir convention. But the detail of "our lovely child" stands out against the familiar background. The presence of the sleeping child changes the tone of the conventional boudoir setting. The female persona is not so much a lonely wife longing for her absent husband as a loving mother who is thinking of the father of her child. The juxtaposition of the mother identity with that of the wife distinguishes the persona in this poem from the conventional abandoned-woman persona. In order to articulate their sexual fantasies, literati authors in *New Songs from a Jade Terrace* create "an iconic image of woman" that bears no "referentiality to actual women."[47] The mention of the child in the above poem, however, provides much information regarding the dynamics of the poet's communication with her husband and potential readers. The detail of the sleeping child may be intended for the father, and it may also be intended to assure the reader that the woman's yearning for her husband comes only after the fulfillment of her responsibilities as a mother. The sequential order in which the poet arranges the last couplet is crucial to conveying the latter sense: she puts the child to sleep before finishing the letter and sealing it to be sent. While the poet relies on the boudoir topos in this poem, the moment of life presented is much more than a performance of the literary past; it is a wife's self-representation informed by both her actual situation as a mother and awareness of her motherly role.

A New Feminine Ideal

The following poem, "Stirred by Feelings on a Spring Day," shows that women poets such as Qin Puzhen went even further in rewriting the boudoir plaint. The poem demonstrates that women were not only aware of poetic conventions but also consciously wrote against the tradition if they deemed it improper for their self-representations:

不嫌夫婿覓封侯，	I don't complain about my husband's seeking for noble rank;
我輩情鍾語亦羞。	Feelings are concentrated on our kind, yet we are too shy to express them.
未免難忘緣底事，	But it is hard to forget matters in our destiny—
清吟花下待誰酬。	I await the one who harmonizes with my pure poems under the flowers.[48]

The first line speaks directly to the famous poem "Boudoir Plaint" by the Tang poet Wang Changling (698?–756?):

閨中少婦不知愁，	The young wife in the boudoir doesn't know what sorrow is;
春日凝妝上翠樓。	On a spring day, dressed up well, she climbs up the green tower.
忽見陌頭楊柳色，	All of a sudden, she sees the color of willows on the road;
悔教夫婿覓封侯。	She regrets letting her husband go to seek noble rank.[49]

The last line of Wang Changling's poem, "She regrets letting her husband go to seek noble rank," has become a cliché that epitomizes the boudoir plaint. Qin Puzhen's direct challenge to this line asserts her opposite opinion: she is not the conventional "young wife in the boudoir" but a woman of a new generation who supports her husband's pursuit of an official career and knows how to contain her private feelings. She is not without passion, but she understands how to express it in a proper manner. Poetry, as she states in the last line, becomes a medium to which she entrusts her emotions. Only at this point does she suggest how she misses her husband: "I await the one who harmonizes with my pure poems under the flowers." What is significant is that she has transformed her relationship with her husband from a merely sexual or emotional one to one based on literary sharing.

It is also noteworthy that in addition to the boudoir plaint cliché, Qin Puzhen modifies another literati idiom, "feelings are concentrated on our kind" (*wo bei qing zhong*), which is derived from "the place where feelings are most concentrated is precisely on our kind," from *A New Account of Tales of the World* (Shishuo xinyu).⁵⁰ Situated in the context of the cult of *qing* (feelings and emotions) in the late Ming and Qing, this phrase became a slogan for the literati's promotion of *qing* and their identity construction.⁵¹ In her poem, Qin identifies with "our kind" yet distinguishes herself as one who is "too shy to express them [her feelings]."

Qin Puzhen was not exceptional in rewriting the boudoir plaint cliché. The second couplet in the quatrain "Boudoir Sentiments," by Yang Sushu (b. 1741), also challenges and negotiates Wang Changling's lines "The wonderful scene of the willow road is boundless, / Yet my fragrant heart has never regretted his pursuit of nobility."⁵² These examples demonstrate that women such as Qin and Yang were consciously keeping their distance from the conventional boudoir representations of women and attempting to present new female images that conformed to their contemporary aesthetic and moral standards.

Chen Shulan's poem "Sent to My Husband" provides an example in which a woman carefully constructs an ideal self-image:

小院清香撲面來，	In the small courtyard, pure fragrance blows on my face;
拋針幾度立蒼苔。	Several times I put aside my needlework and stand on green lichens.
幽蘭亦有懷人意，	The secluded orchid seems also to be thinking of someone;
素蕊微含不放開。	Lightly holding in its white pistils, it would not bloom.⁵³

The orchid, which often grows in secluded areas and has an unusual appearance and fragrance, is a generally recognized symbol of superior purity, loftiness, and virtue in the Chinese cultural context. These positive meanings were particularly acknowledged in the literary tradition after the canonical poet Qu Yuan's frequent association of the image with his virtuous self, a gentleman (*junzi*). The woman author's first name, Shulan (literally "virtuous orchid"), is obviously derived from this culturally assumed meaning, and she is playing with this symbolic dimension of her name in portraying her self-image. The first couplet is still much indebted to the conventional descriptive formulas, which establish a typical boudoir setting. The second couplet, however, introduces an image that is not normally associated with the scenario: a pure, virtuous orchid. Through personifying the orchid, the poet both claims a self-image with lofty attributes and expresses her love for her husband in a reserved and elegant manner.

A New Feminine Ideal

According with the status of a loving and virtuous wife, this way of expression would be deemed highly admirable in her cultural context.

Writing to their husbands was not merely an artistic activity but also an important means through which women poets communicated with their husbands as cultured wives. Some felt more compelled to report on matters of "rice and salt" than to express love sentiments. For example, Mao Shuzhen wrote the following poem to her husband:

臥起敲冰歲已闌，	Knocking on ice as I get up, the year has come to an end;
破裙難敵朔風寒。	My worn-out skirt cannot keep out the chill of the north wind.
君前不獨兒衣薄，	Responsibilities facing you, not only that your son's clothes are thin,
知否中廚缺晨餐。	Do you know our kitchen is also short of breakfast?[54]

Each line of this quatrain is devoted to depicting a difficult situation the wife or the family encounters. Insofar as the speaking voice of the wife is complaining, the poem can also be characterized as a boudoir plaint. The difference is that her complaints are all about poverty and the hardships she faces in managing the household. The poem does not explain why the husband is away from home and where he is, but it is clear that the wife has been left behind to take care of their needy family, and she is calling his attention to the situation through the poem. The realistic description of the family's straitened circumstances suggests that life in the inner chambers was not always composed of tender, romantic moments.

While Mao Shuzhen is outspoken about her difficult life, not surprisingly many more women poets in *The Anthology of Correct Beginnings* present the self-image of an understanding and contented wife. Consider the following poem by Li Yingzhou:

消受春光祇素餐，	While enjoying the spring scene, I eat only vegetarian food;
阿郎小阮各平安。	A Lang and Xiaoruan are both doing fine.
圖書整暇清無事，	At this moment of leisure after sorting out books,
特為裁詩報伯鸞。	I especially compose a poem to send news to Boluan.[55]

A Lang is an ancient term for one's father. "Xiaoruan," the nickname of Ruan Xian (234–305), the nephew of Ruan Ji (210–263), became an affectionate term referring to a nephew in poetic convention. By these terms, the poet refers generally to the family. The language of this poem is plain and simple, and the line mentioning the family members is especially colloquial. The poem reads as though the wife is chatting with her husband. She tells him how the family fares, what she eats, and how she spends the day, all everyday matters. Her tone is easy, or she intends her tone to be easing and soothing in order to allay her husband's worries about the family as she writes to him with news from home. In the last line, Li Yingzhou refers to her husband as Boluan, the husband of Meng Guang, revealing both her respect for her husband and her self-definition as a virtuous wife. As Pan Suxin, another author in *The Anthology of Correct Beginnings*, suggests, "Because I am afraid to hinder your ambition / I dare not tell you my sorrow over our separation."[56] These wives understood the ideal wifely role they were supposed to perform.

As writing wives, these women are conscious of how to present themselves to their husbands and society. In their poems, they demonstrate not only their efforts and capabilities in household management but also their artistic talents as cultured wives. Sheng shi's (née Sheng) poem "I Chatted with My Children on a Moonlit Night" manages to exemplify almost all the important features of poems by writing wives discussed above:

江上霜鴻叫二更,	Over the frosty river geese announce the second watch;[57]
窗前兒女話平生。	Beside the window I talk about my life with my children.
月明簾命奚童捲,	Because the moon is bright, I order the servant boy to roll up the blind;
鐺沸茶看小婢烹。	When the water boils in the pot, I watch the maid make tea.
髮為愁貧容易白,	My hair easily turns gray due to worries about poverty;
詩因懷遠忽然成。	A poem is suddenly completed because I miss the one who is far away.
閨中不省都門路,	Living in the boudoir, I don't know the way to the capital gate.
昨夜何緣夢到京。	How did I arrive in the capital in my dreams last night?[58]

This poem, as Sheng shi proudly claims, is inspired by her thoughts of "the one who is far away." It begins by projecting the image of a loving mother and, at the end, shifts to that of a loving wife. The major theme of this poem is the ability of a wife and mother to live a contented and harmonious life with her family while her husband is away in his office in the capital. The poetic form adopted by the author is "regulated verse" (*lüshi*). In the regulated parallelism of the middle couplets, the second describes a symmetrical picture of the arrangement of the servants' labor, and the third presents a contrast between the difficulty of managing the household and the ease of composing poetry. Her complaint about poverty in the third couplet may be contradicted by her earlier mention of servants, but what is important is that by this detail the author attempts to emphasize her efforts in fulfilling her domestic responsibilities. Moreover, the contrast between the meanings in this couplet may also have been created in order to conform to the conventions of parallelism. They cannot be taken absolutely at face value. However, linking the two motifs in conceiving this couplet is certainly the author's conscious choice, the choice to consider the two essential attributes of a cultured wife. She would like to be seen as coping with the hardships of life as mother and wife while maintaining her artistic sensibility. The final couplet continues to play on another level of contrast: the poet indicates her social and physical location, the inner chambers, and the distance from her husband, but she can move beyond these boundaries in her dreams and meet him. The poet herself seems to be amazed by both her strong feelings for her husband and her imaginative power.

Just as the term "correct beginnings" was originally related to wifely virtue in the hermeneutics of the *Book of Songs*, wifely virtue is especially celebrated in *The Anthology of Correct Beginnings*.[59] In commenting on "Guanju," Confucius states: "The tone of 'Guanju' is joyful yet not lewd; sad yet not wounded in spirit."[60] These women authors indeed attempt to portray ideal images of the wife in light of the teaching in the *Book of Songs*. The voice of the wife in their poetry is chaste and often positive. However, these writing wives, in communicating with their husbands and society, modified the conventional wifely voice and image with insights informed by their own age. They opened up a distinctive topical territory alongside the ancient boudoir plaint tradition.

VALORIZING DOMESTIC LIFE WITH NEW CULTURAL IDEALS

Although Yun Zhu and her editing team rhetorically claim a discursive space for women based on the socio-symbolic space of the inner chambers, women's literary imagination, as reflected in their rich corpus, goes far beyond its boundaries. Their re-vision of the boudoir life is not only informed by their socially gendered experiences but also inspired by broader cultural and literary visions that could lead them to transcend gender boundaries.

Androgyny is a useful concept in the study of Ming-Qing women's literary culture.[61] Originating from a Western cultural context, the term describes an ideal state in which female and male elements are synthesized. Coining the term "cultural androgyny," Kang-i Sun Chang uses this concept to characterize the commonalities shared by the cultural spheres of both genders. While the marginalized Ming-Qing male literati engaged in "a kind of self-feminization," talented women developed "a lifestyle typical of the educated male" in engaging in artistic pursuits such as writing poetry.[62] "Cultural androgyny" thus created a common ground in poetics that erased the female-male opposition. Although using a Western term to define a complex cultural phenomenon in the Chinese context is always problematic, it is a productive way to think about the cultural interests shared by both genders in the late imperial era.[63] The notion of cultural androgyny may be used to explore in more depth how the cultural ideals and expressions developed in literati self-cultivation influenced women's self-perceptions and created an idealization of their lived space.

Concepts related to femininity were undergoing significant changes in late imperial China's social and cultural life. Specifically, the emphasis on women's learning and artistic talent was a major trend in the rewriting of traditional womanhood. The new identification of women with letters was instrumental in Ming-Qing women poets' transformation of boudoir poetics. Participation in artistic, especially literary, activities constitutes a striking feature in women authors' self-representations. The self-image of a devoted poet in the boudoir setting was rare in earlier poetry. She is knowledgeable, talented, and diligent in reading and writing, in sharp contrast to the passive and lovelorn female of conventional boudoir poetry. As Huang Youqin argues in her preface to *The Anthology of Correct Beginnings*, writing poetry indeed became one of the Qing *guixiu*'s vocations.[64]

Though still confined within the frame of the boudoir, the female persona presented in *The Anthology of Correct Beginnings* no longer feels only listlessness and ennui. She often finds something meaningful with which to busy herself, as shown in Tang Qingyun's poem "A Night in Early Summer":

A New Feminine Ideal 75

夜坐樓前思悄然，	At night sitting in front of my tower, I meditate in silence;
清和時候二更天。	It is a pure and peaceful time at the moment of the second watch.
風從嫩竹梢頭軟，	Brushing over tender tips of bamboo, the wind becomes soft;
月向新桐葉底圓。	Approaching new leaves of the wutong tree, the moon is round.
覓句心閒拈句寫，	My heart is at leisure in conceiving lines, writing them down as they come;
看書眼倦抱書眠。	As my eyes become tired from reading, I fall asleep holding a book.
偶然一夢如仙境，	In a fleeting dream, it seems that I entered an immortal realm;
醒後香煙滿袖邊。	Waking up, I find incense wafting next to my sleeves.[65]

It is late at night, but the poet is still awake, sitting thoughtfully outside her tower. She is preoccupied with composing poems and reading books. She falls asleep for some time, exhausted from reading for so long, but feels refreshed after a dream of the immortals' land. She is alone in the boudoir, but she has her books to hold. Robertson points out that the association of the self with books in this poem de-eroticizes the sleeping and dreaming motifs as represented in literati poetry. Indeed, the image of books marks a distinct change from the sensual, erotic tone of conventional boudoir sentiments. More important, the activity of learning has transformative power for the poet here, not only providing her with a serene mood in which to enjoy the quiet night in the boudoir, but also suggesting that she has found a way to transcend her life through the immortality of her verse.

Tang Qingyun's poem is representative of numerous similarly themed poems. As Robertson and Chang note, Ming-Qing women poets tend to portray their boudoir as a study and themselves as bookworms.[66] Their association of themselves with artistic activities had already become a convention of women's self-representation, as exemplified by numerous poems included in *The Anthology of Correct Beginnings*. Books both physically and spiritually fill the void in the boudoir, as suggested by Wang Yaofang's lines "What accompany me are thousands of books; / What is peeping at me is the moon shining through the curtain."[67] With the company of thousands of books, the poet enjoys her exposure to the moon. She reinscribes the moon, the "voyeur" of lonely women's restlessness in traditional boudoir poetry, into a witness of her knowledge.

Poems portraying women enjoying more meaningful cultural activities in the boudoir consequently changed the plaintive or sentimental tone associated with the boudoir setting. A comparison between a *yuefu*, or Music Bureau song, by Cao Rui (204–239) from *New Songs from a Jade Terrace* and a poem by Zhang Lingyi (ca. 1671–ca. 1724) will help clarify this important transformation. Cao Rui's poem reads:

昭昭素明月，	Shine, shine, white moon bright,
輝光燭我床。	Let gleaming rays lighten my bed.
憂人不能寐，	One in despair cannot sleep,
耿耿夜何長。	Dull, dull nights so long.
微風衝閨闥，	Soft breeze blows the bedroom door,
羅帷自飄颺。	Silk curtains unmoved flare and drift.
攬衣曳長帶，	I take my robe trailing its long sash,
縱履下高堂。	Put on slippers, leave the high hall.
東西安所之，	East, west, which way to turn?
徘徊以彷徨。	I hesitate and falter.
春鳥向南飛，	A spring bird southward flies,
翩翩獨翱翔。	Soars and soars fluttering alone.
悲聲命儔匹，	Sad its voice calling to its mate,
哀鳴傷我腸。	Mournful cries that wound my breast.
感物懷所思，	Moved by nature I long for my lover,
泣涕忽沾裳。	Suddenly spilling tears drench my coat.[68]
佇立吐高吟，	I have stood long, singing my song loudly
舒憤訴穹蒼。	To express my anger to Heaven.[69]

This poem is voiced by a female persona, expressing her sorrow over being left alone in the boudoir (*guida*). We do not know whether her lover deserted her or passed away, but she is deeply troubled by his absence. She cannot sleep while the moon lights up her empty bed. As the wind shakes her door and her bed curtains flutter, she might believe, mistakenly, that somebody is coming. She goes outside but is unsure where to go. Spring birds flying in pairs again remind her that she is without a companion. Heartbroken, she bursts into tears and laments her misfortune to Heaven. This earlier *yuefu* poem included in *New Songs from a Jade Terrace* presents a strong representation of the forceful voice of the female lament.

Zhang Lingyi's poem "Facing the Moon by the Bookworm's Window" reads:

徘徊愛良夜，	Pacing to and fro, I love this beautiful night;
吾廬有佳趣。	There is so much enjoyment in my hut.
星稀月轉明，	Stars thin out, as the moon increases in brightness;

A New Feminine Ideal

Figure 3.1 "Composing Poetry on a Stormy Day" (Fengyu weiyin) is one of a group of paintings depicting elite women's activities in the inner chambers by Jiao Bingzhen (17–18th c.), a prominent portrait painter in the Qing. Writing poetry was one of the typical activities featured along with other themes such as embroidering and playing musical instruments. National Palace Museum, Taipei.

冷侵階前樹。	Chill invades the trees in front of the steps.
疏影自橫斜,	Sparse shadows of branches naturally aslant
正對簾鉤處。	Cast onto my hooked curtains.
藻荇散庭除,	Water weeds here and there on the outer veranda,
水光還四布。	Water shimmers on all four sides.
曲檻好尋詩,	Balustrades meandering, good for finding poetry;
修廊宜緩步。	Corridor narrow, I'd better slow down.

寒花浮酒盞,	Chilled petals float in the wine cup;
落葉添茶具。	Fallen leaves decorate the tea set.
鸛巢松樹顛,	Storks nest on the tops of pines;
靜夜如人嗽。	The night quiet, somebody is coughing.
高天鴻雁鳴,	Wild geese cry high in the sky,
唳入秋雲去。	Gone with the autumn clouds.
坐久欲忘眠,	Sitting long, I almost forget to go to sleep;
煩襟感涼露。	The world-weary mind is cooled by dews.
欲寫此時景,	I want to describe the scene at this moment,
誰能展毫素。	But who can pick up paper and brush?[70]

The female persona's restless night in the boudoir, an emotional sign of her missing the lover, is a common motif in the boudoir-plaint tradition. However, the scenario is remarkably transformed in Zhang Lingyi's poem, which also depicts a sleepless night but with the female poet is finding "so much enjoyment." She appears to be alone, but she is not missing anybody. She takes pleasure in every moment of the night's beauty. In this poem, the female persona is emphatically not a lovelorn woman isolated in the boudoir but an inspired poet indulging in her perceptions of the world around her. Everything is poetry for her, and she is so enchanted with her vision of beauty that she protests that she cannot stop to write it down. Of course, she writes it down anyway. The irony is only to suggest the intensity of the poet's sense perception. The poetic form adopted by Zhang Lingyi is the pentasyllabic "ancient style" (*gushi*), the same form used by Cao Rui, but the female author constructs a completely different world.

The joy and pleasure Tang Qingyun and Zhang Lingyi find in their everyday lives are not the exclusive prerogative of women in the inner chambers. As Chang points out, the sixteenth century began to see the emergence of the culture of the "marginalized literati," a group who withdrew from the public domains of examinations and officialdom and indulged in artistic pursuits such as poetry.[71] The ideal of withdrawal and pursuit of the meaningfulness of private life had long existed in the literati tradition.[72] With more sources of inspiration and opportunities for self-cultivation, the Ming-Qing literati simply brought this culture to an unprecedented level. Particularly relevant here is that literati poetry also depicts the home as a place of retreat.[73] The valorization of leisure or disengagement itself not only was a luxury the gentry class could afford but also could be useful in protecting individual integrity from political corruption.[74] Consider the poem "Sitting Alone" by the Ming poet Yuan Hongdao (1568–1610):

胸臆知難盡，	I know my heart but find it is difficult
行藏未可陳。	To express whether I should work or withdraw.
攤書嫌字小，	Opening books, I find the characters too small,
烹水試茶新。	So I boil water in order to taste the new tea.
撥悶占茅卜，	To release boredom, I cast lots to divine;
祁歸拜土神。	Praying for a return home, I pay respect to the earth god.
閒雲與倦鳥，	Idle clouds and tired birds,
終是一流人。	They are in the end the foremost among men.[75]

A poetic leader of the Gong'an school, Yuan Hongdao not only valued individualism and honest expression in his poetic theory but also followed his heart in his life decisions.[76] He had served as magistrate in Wu County for less than two years when he retired from office for the rest of his life. The allusion to the proverbial "idle clouds" and "tired birds" expresses a scholar-official's disenchantment with officialdom and desire to return to nature. The details of daily life in the home setting are central in this poem. Many of these details, such as reading books and tasting new tea, are also common in the poems in *The Anthology of Correct Beginnings*. These shared details in texts by authors of both genders reveal some common interests and tastes that were valued in late imperial Chinese culture. Both men and women not only took delight in everyday life in the domestic setting but also took pride in doing so.

Read in this light, one can understand better why the Manchu woman poet Bing Yue enjoys her life in the boudoir. Her pleasure is clearly indebted to the literati's ideal of self-cultivation:

暮春感懷用陸放翁韻	MOVED BY FEELINGS IN LATE SPRING, USING LU FANGWENG'S RHYMES[77]
春歸無計遣長天，	When spring is leaving, I don't know how to send away the long day;
幾卷殘編醒晝眠。	Several tattered scrolls keep me from my daily nap.
世淡自知心似水，	Being indifferent to worldly affairs, my heart is like still water.
身閑始信日如年。	Being at leisure, I begin to know a day is as long as a year.
漫言詩懶無佳句，	You may just say that I'm lazy, not composing fine lines,
卻喜囊空少奉錢。	But I'm happy that my bag is short of official salary.
此味近來頗自適，	Recently this flavor rather suits me;
空閨兀坐趣幽然。	Sitting absorbed in the empty boudoir, my enjoyment is profound.[78]

The poet refers to the space in which she lives as "the empty boudoir," a term derived from the boudoir convention, yet the meaning of emptiness in this poem is profoundly different. It may still point to the absence of a husband, but it definitely takes on philosophical depth as the poet's persona develops a new perspective on her life within the confines of the boudoir: the day is long in the boudoir, yet this allows her time to pursue her interests; she does not have a salaried job, but she does not have worldly concerns either; in her leisure, she can listen more to her heart. As the line "Recently this flavor rather suits me" suggests, she may not have thought about her life in this way before. Inspired by the ideal of withdrawal, she also finds that her appreciation of her boudoir life is "profound." The boudoir has thus become a sanctum to her.

Once she finds a way to transcend her worldly concerns, Bing Yue also becomes detached from the material world. In "My Humble Residence," she writes:

敝宅當窮巷,	My humble residence is located at the end of the alley;
幽然可適歟。	Secluded, it is suited to my taste.
人因難住棄,	Uninhabitable, it is discarded by other people,
我作寄居看。	But I take it as a place to lodge.
門靜可羅雀,	The gate is unfrequented; only sparrows come to rest;
牆危若累丸。	The walls are as unstable as piled balls.
敗窗繩繫穩,	Rickety windows are held up with ropes;
朽柱木支安。	Decayed pillars are buttressed with wooden sticks.
雁齒階難備,	Goose-teeth steps are hard to fix;
魚鱗瓦不全。	Fish-scale tiles are incomplete.
榻緣風數徙,	My bed has to be moved frequently to avoid wind;
書為蛀重攤。	My books need to be aired because of bookworms.
客至愁堂窄,	When guests come, I'm worried about the narrowness of the hall;
花開喜院寬。	Flowers in blossom, I like the breadth of my backyard.
植蒿聊當竹,	I plant wormwoods as if they were bamboo
蓺草且為蘭。	And grasses as orchids.
夜檻蟾光白,	At night, the moonlight brightens the threshold;
朝簷日色丹。	In the morning, the sunshine reddens the eaves.
高軒即此是,	This is my high studio,
何必置雕欄。	Why is it necessary to build carved rails?[79]

This long, elaborate poem is constructed through a striking contrast between the shabby condition of the dwelling and the inhabitant's high spirits. The inspirational forces that keep her spirits high come from two sources popular in her historical and cultural context. First, as the term "lodging" (*jiju*) suggests, the poet holds the Buddhist view of human life as transitory; no matter how luxurious a house may be, for her it is just a place in which to pass a short life. Second, in highlighting images encoded with cultural values such as books, bamboo, and orchids, the poet suggests that she pursues learning, purity, and strength even in extremely difficult situations. This poem can be literally summed up in the line by the Tang poet and prose writer Liu Yuxi (772–842): "My hut may be mean, but the fragrance of Virtue is diffused around."[80] The concept of virtue with regard to the female gender has different meanings, but the woman poet can still empower herself by placing a high value on transcending harsh living conditions.

In contrast to the refined and decorous setting represented in the boudoir convention, Bing Yue's "My Humble Residence" introduces a completely different aesthetic modality, which represents an alternative mode adopted by Qing women poets in depicting their lived space. They tend to portray a bleak space (whether based on real conditions or not) as a background against which to emphasize the spiritual quality of their daily lives. In many cases of this kind of representation, the female authors claim that they do not have the luxury of a boudoir, whether due to poverty or misfortune. A curtain or blind is an essential component that defines the boundary of a woman's room and controls the reader's gaze or the persona's vision. However, Yuan Hanhuang presents her family's poor abode as not having walls:

療饑自有忘憂處，	To ease hunger, I certainly have a place to forget sorrow—
樂此衡門水一灣。	I delight in the bay in front of Hengmen!
漫訝家貧無四壁，	Don't be surprised that my poor home lacks even four walls;
家無四壁好看山。	Without walls, it is easier to appreciate the mountain view.[81]

As Yun Zhu notes in Yuan's biographical sketch, Yuan remained unmarried in order to take care of her widowed and sonless father. Her father was a commoner, and the family was in straitened circumstances.[82] The impoverished condition of her life as implied by the poem is consistent with this background. However, what she intends to show is not her destitution but her positive attitude and sense of humor in dealing with the problem: she still finds pleasure in simple nature. Even though she does not have the luxury of an upper-class boudoir, she is able to preserve her integrity along with her spiritual power. She is proud to be who she is and content to live the life that she lives.

Similarly, Mao Huifang writes in her poem "My Wall Was Damaged by a Storm":

我本清貧者，	I'm originally a pure and poor person;
三間蔀屋斜。	I have only three crooked rooms as a shelter.
莫愁風雨甚，	Don't grieve that the wind and rain are too harsh;
補壁有梅花。	There are plum blossoms to mend my broken wall.[83]

The poet begins by claiming to be a person who is poor yet pure in spirit, or *qingpin zhe*. It is because of this spirit that she is not stricken down after the storm ruins her house. Instead, she comforts herself that a blooming plum tree survived the storm and can be seen through the broken wall. In the Chinese cultural lexicon, the plum blossom stands for integrity, purity, and strength in confronting difficult circumstances. In this poem, the image of the plum blossom suggests an unyielding spirit, echoing the poet's strength of character.

The principle of "maintaining firmness in adversity" (*gu qiong*) is upheld in the *Analects* and applied specifically to the male literati's self-cultivation.[84] The subject who upholds this principle was considered a gentleman. In poetic history, the Eastern Jin poet and hermit Tao Qian is celebrated as an exemplar of this principle.[85] He chose to withdraw from his official career in order to preserve his integrity when it was threatened by the dark politics of his time. Returning to life in the country, a life of "farms and fields" (*tianyuan*), he sought pleasure and inspiration in nature. He died poor but never relented. Tao Qian wrote a group of poems expressing admiration for seven "poor gentlemen" (*pinshi*) in Chinese history, his role models.[86] In his poems, hunger and cold are recurrent factors that challenge the choice of personal principle, but they testify to his iron will to hold onto what he perceives as the "Way":

豈不實辛苦，	Isn't it hard enough in reality?
所懼非飢寒。	But what I fear is not hunger or cold.
貧富常交戰，	Poverty and affluence are ever at war,
道勝無戚顏。	But when the Way prevails there is no sad face.[87]

Although Tao Qian was a role model more relevant to men faced with political choices, many Qing *guixiu* drew inspiration and strength from his image and poetic legacy. There are quite a number of poems written about Tao Qian in *The Anthology of Correct Beginnings*. The self-image of "a pure and poor person" claimed by Mao Huifang reveals her intent to be such a virtuous "gentleman." Strengthened by the belief that they also hold the Way, women like Yuan Hanhuang and Mao Huifang have "no sad face" even when facing extreme difficulties. However, while women appreciate Tao Qian's personal integrity and free spirit, they also find gender barriers between his world and their own, as Wang Wei's lines suggest:

我本巾幗儔，	I'm from the rank of women,
曠達亦自喜。	But I myself also like being broad-minded and carefree.
安得似陶公，	How can I be like Sir Tao
優游樂餘齡？	And enjoy the rest of my life in worry-free wandering?[88]

Presumably, she means that a woman's household responsibilities restrain her from pursuing a lifestyle like Tao's.

Xu Zaipu informs us, however, that although she could not afford the ideal life of a hermit, she has managed to live in a carefree world by relying on her inner forces:

偶吟	A POEM OF IMPROVISATION
保養餘生絕外緣，	To protect and nourish my remaining life, I withdraw from external relations;
畫閣獨掩自恬然。	Shutting the door of my painted pavilion, I am naturally at peace.
結廬欲遠人間世，	I had wanted to build a hut far from the human world,
何處青山不要錢。	But in what place does a green mountain not charge you money?[89]

By shutting the door of her boudoir to external human society, Xu Zaipu establishes an unperturbed world for herself. She does not even bother to take refuge in secluded mountains. She adopts instead the way of "reclusion in the city" (*yin yu shi*), an ideal inspired by Daoism: one can find refuge in society as long as one can protect oneself from the vulgar and profane.[90] The third line of this poem, "I had wanted to build a hut far from the human world," is derived from Tao Qian's lines "Building my hut in the human realm, / But there is no noise of wagons and horses."[91] With similar wit, the female poet creates a protective, nurturing, and relaxing space for herself within the boundaries of the boudoir.

Despite gender boundaries, these women authors internalize various cultural factors regarding self-cultivation and attempt to craft an ideal space not in terms of their gender roles but with respect to their personal qualities. The space depicted in their poems appears to be distinct from the traditional feminized boudoir, and in most poems, there are no explicit terms specifying their gender identity (except for Bing Yue's first poem). In the sense of cultivating a literary style that transcends gender, these women adopt an androgynous stance in depicting their lived space.[92]

In general, the women poets included in *The Anthology of Correct Beginnings* adopt two approaches to depicting the confines of their domestic lives. First, they use the boudoir convention critically in their self-representation. On the one hand, they adopt descriptive skills and vocabulary derived from the tradition, but on the other hand, they rewrite conventional images to express proper, meaningful activities in the boudoir. The physical setting of the boudoir is similar to that in poetic convention—ornamented and elegant—yet it is filled with completely different personae and activities. They de-eroticize the space of the boudoir and change the tone of traditional boudoir sentiments from plaintive to positive and joyful. The women represented in the poems have the leisure time and autonomy to pursue their cultural interests and enjoy themselves with or without companions. The boudoir is consequently re-encoded as a space within which a talented daughter, a cultured woman, or a capable wife can take pleasure in her daily life. Second, these women authors project a broader cultural perspective that transcends gender. They do not limit themselves to representation of their gendered experiences but valorize their everyday, domestic life with values derived from literati cultural ideals. In doing so, they neither necessarily frame their living space with the symbolic, gendered *gui* nor represent it as a feminized space even in a loose sense. Whether based on their real life experiences or a product of their literary creativity, the alternative space these women authors craft enables them to explore further dimensions of their personal lives.

These are two different kinds of self-representation, but both serve a common goal in emphasizing the positive aspects of the authors' everyday lives. As most of the life vignettes examined in this chapter have shown, these women poets attempted to capture what they perceived to be an ideal life in the inner chambers. No matter whether they are within or outside the physical space of the *gui*, and whether rich or poor, they emphasize self-contentment and individual integrity as the ideal qualities of the interior self. These positive attitudes are not only required by the moral principles of female virtue but also valued by the orthodox, didactic poetics of the age.

As Yun Zhu claims, *The Anthology of Correct Beginnings* is intended to present voices of "gentleness and meekness." Specifically in keeping with this principle, most of the poems she selected conform to the standard of "no resentment and lewdness" derived from the hermeneutic tradition of the *Book of Songs*. Although "to voice grievance" (*yuan*) is considered by Confucius to be one of the major functions of poetry, along with "to stimulate" (*xing*), "to observe" (*guan*), and "to socialize" (*qun*), it is not a desirable poetic mood or aesthetic in orthodox poetics.[93] As the Great Preface states, "The tones of a well-managed age are at rest and happy; its government is balanced. The tones of an age of turmoil are bitter and full of anger; its government is perverse."[94] The revival of the Confucian view of poetics from the early Qing onward, which was firmly supported by the court, was intended to reflect the glory of the new age and consolidate the Qing empire. As stated in her editing principles, Yun Zhu seriously incorporates her anthologizing project into this ongoing imperial enterprise. Coordinating women's writing with authoritative discourses on both female gender and poetics is the major strategy the anthology editors and authors use to elevate women's poetic voice. Whether their appropriation of dominant discourses was merely a tactic or based on their genuine belief in the values espoused by their society, Yun Zhu's anthologizing strategies and rhetorical remarks make explicit the underlying value system.

The women authors in *The Anthology of Correct Beginnings* crafted a meaningful space out of the boudoir and beyond, and this space not only demonstrates the distinctive features of women's culture but also reveals that this culture was evolving within a larger historical and cultural context.

CHAPTER 3

Convention and Intervention
The Lyrical World of Gu Zhenli

Hairdo resembling after falling from a horse, makeup imitating weeping,
I just won't learn these manners of the boudoir.
I'm used to being careless and lazy,
Chewing petals and blowing leaves,
Discarding powder and rouge.
I have too many illnesses to be able to manage household chores;
Although I'm not talented, I dare dislike my husband who is not my match.

墮馬啼妝、學不就、閨中模樣。疏慵慣、嚼花吹葉,粉拋脂漾。
多病不堪操井臼,無才敢去嫌天壤。

—GU ZHENLI 顧貞立

The women poets anthologized in *The Anthology of Correct Beginnings by Inner-Chamber Talents of the Present Dynasty* represented a new literary force and collectively reinscribed the space of the boudoir with their own sociohistorical experiences and perspectives. As an effect of Yun Zhu's selective representation in the anthology, the *gui* became a sort of "public" sphere in which to display women's shared experiences. Even if Yun Zhu had intended to include *ci* poems in her anthology, she would not have chosen the above song lyric by Gu Zhenli (1623–1699).[1] The four *shi* poems by Gu Zhenli in the anthology are indistinguishable from the poems of other authors. Indeed, these four poems that accord with Yun Zhu's standard do little justice to Gu's complex poetics.[2] A woman poet like Gu deliberately adopts an "individualist" or "nonconformist" approach in order to represent a self-identity that she perceives as different from socially recognized models. As she searches for alternative modes of self-representation, her lyrics create a heterogeneous poetics of the boudoir, revealing complex interrelations between her conceptions of self and other and cultural codes of femininity. Her various textual strategies in representing the boudoir illustrate her engagement of the poetic tradition and her literary agency in attempting to carve out an alternative discursive space for her self-expression. Above all, with its combination of conventionality and unconventionality, Gu Zhenli's boudoir poetics provides an illuminating case that can be set against the larger background outlined in the preceding chapters. As such, it can deepen our understanding of the ways in which Ming-Qing women poets participated in the meaning production associated with their gendered identity and location.

With her transgressive voice and idiosyncratic self-image, Gu Zhenli stands out among Ming-Qing writing women. Scholars claim that her lyrics represent a "breakthrough" in the conventional aesthetics of the lyric; they neither "carry on the tradition of the boudoir plaint" nor "follow the teaching of being earnest and gentle [*wenrou dunhou*]." They compose a "heterodoxy" (*yishu*) in the realm of Qing women's poetry.³ Indeed, Gu Zhenli's lyrical voice poses a challenge to both gender-based social etiquette and conventional feminine poetics. Furthermore, her lyrical world provides a fruitful view of the relationship between the poet's subjectivity, individual literary agency, poetic discourse, and, in particular, the *gui* topos. The transgressiveness of her mode of representation is relevant to others adopted in her lyrics. The continuum between her performance of the modes of boudoir poetics prevalent in her time and her deliberate disruption of these modes reveals her complicated interaction with the conventions of femininity as she struggled for self-understanding and representational space within the limitations of the existing symbolic order.

Gu Zhenli was active as a poet in the early Qing. Her achievements in both *shi* and *ci* poetry were acknowledged by the famous early Qing scholar Chen Weisong (1628–1682) in his *Collection of Women's Writing* (Furen ji).⁴ However, her unconventional lyrical voice gained broad recognition only later.⁵ Gu Zhenli's earliest collection of *shi* and *ci* poetry, *Shi and Ci Poetry from the Fragrance-Nesting Pavilion* (Qixiangge shi ci), seems to have never been published.⁶ While a male relative, Gu Xiangquan, selectively published her *shi* poetry later in *The Records of Poetry from Liang Creek* (Liangxi shichao),⁷ her *Collection of Ci from the Fragrance-Nesting Pavilion* (Qixiangge ci), the more widely circulated and still extant collection of her *ci*, was not published until 1823 by Li Zhiling.⁸

In her *ci*, Gu's reflections upon her self and her place in society as a woman emerge clearly in her negotiations with the symbolic space of the boudoir, whether as subversions of gender conventions associated with this space or as explorations of alternative representations for articulating her idiosyncratic sense of self. Her lyrics reveal a range of different modes of representing the boudoir. Unlike many other women's poetry collections, the sequence of poems in Gu Zhenli's *ci* collection does not chronologically mirror the phases of her life and poetic practice. However, these lyrics reveal a number of transformations through which one can trace the author's adaptation of textual strategies for different expressive needs. Several contrasting and even contradictory depictions of the boudoir space are prominent in her lyrics. These can be roughly related to her life course as a woman and may reveal some development of self-identity. However, there is by no means a linear, progressive evolution through these modes. Rather, there is a struggle between different identities and sets of meanings. The author's positioning in relation to the boudoir is not unitary, nor is there consistency in her ways of dealing with the associated conventional feminine codes. Instead, the boudoir in her lyrics is rendered ambivalent, heterogeneous, and multifaceted.

EMULATING THE BOUDOIR CONVENTION

Gu Zhenli mastered the conventional mode of boudoir poetics. A number of lyrics in this category are interspersed throughout her collection. Emulating classical models of boudoir poetry was an important stage in her practice of *ci* writing. The following lyric to the tune "Washing Creek Sands" exemplifies her way of synthesizing elements from well-known boudoir poems:

好夢留人悔卻醒。	Lingering in a sweet dream, I regret being awoken.
誰教鶯語弄新晴。	Who let orioles twitter, playing in this new clear weather?
乍寒還暖又清明。	Suddenly chilly, then turning warm, it is the Clear-Bright Festival again.
門掩落花春寂寂,	Behind closed gates flowers fall, spring so quiet,
香消睡鴨晝沈沈。	Incense consumed in the sleeping-duck burner, the day so dreary.
日長閒自理瑤琴。	On this long day I idly pluck the jade zither.[9]

Convention and Intervention

This lyric is laden with a familiar lexicon and imagery that can be easily traced back to their sources of inspiration. The opening of the first lyric is indebted to the well-known poem "Spring Plaint" by the Tang poet Jin Changxu, a classic in the boudoir plaint tradition:

打起黃鶯兒，	I hit and startle the oriole,
莫教枝上啼。	Not to let it cry on the branch.
啼時驚妾夢，	When it cries, my dream is interrupted;
不得到遼西。	I cannot then reach Liaoxi.[10]

Liaoxi was the frontier where soldiers stood guard. By presenting a brief drama in simple and colloquial language, Jin's poem poignantly illustrates the theme of the boudoir plaint in the voice of a soldier's wife. Being awoken from sleep by the chirping of birds is a common poetic motif, but the specific elements "dream" and "orioles" and the syntactic structure (compare the phrases "who let" and "not to let") used by Gu Zhenli in conveying the birds' disturbance of the persona's dream obviously echo those in Jin's poem.[11] Gu Zhenli's lyric is unclear on the content of the persona's dream, but the inspiration of Jin's poem is clear. The succeeding lines depict a scenario in the spring boudoir and courtyard that we have encountered in Li Qingzhao's lines, also to the tune "Washing Creek Sands":

小院閒窗春已深。	Beside the quiet window, spring in the small courtyard is deep.
重簾未卷影沈沈。	Layered curtains are not hooked up; shadows are heavy.
倚樓無語理瑤琴。	Leaning against the tower, speechless, I pluck the jade zither.[12]

Although Gu Zhenli does not directly adopt the diction of these lines, each line in her lyric is a faithful translation of the boudoir scene and sentiment presented in Li Qingzhao's work, not to mention her borrowing of the central image of the persona plucking the zither.[13] In brief, Gu's lyric presents a generic depiction of the boudoir in which intertextual links with poetic predecessors constitute the very fabric of textuality.

Qin Guan, an important poet in the feminine style, is another model for Gu Zhenli's *ci* writing. In the following example, the similarity between Gu's and Qin's lyric to the tune "Washing Creek Sands" is particularly striking:

盡日簾垂嬾上鉤，	All day long the curtain droops, too lazy to hook it up;

無端春思在眉頭。	For no reason a spring thought appears on the eyebrows.
絮飛花落夢悠悠。	Catkins flying and flowers falling, the dream lingers on and on.
蠆蠆輕寒朱戶寂，	Waves of light chill—the vermilion door is quiet;
絲絲細雨小窗幽。	Strands of drizzling rain—the small window is dim.
東風腸斷不堪留。	The east wind, hard to retain, breaks the heart.[14]

Qin Guan's lyric reads:

漠漠輕寒上小樓。	An expanse of light chill rises up to the small tower.
曉陰無賴似窮秋。	This cloudy morning is listless as the end of autumn.
淡煙流水畫屏幽。	Light smoke and flowing water are dim in the painted screens.
自在飛花輕似夢，	Free-flying catkins are light as a dream,
無邊絲雨細如愁。	Boundless threads of rain fine as sorrow.
寶簾閒掛小銀鉤。	The ornamented curtain idly hangs on a small silver hook.

Not only do the two works adopt the same rhyme but from imagery to diction, from motifs to the major theme, Gu Zhenli's lyric is a closely rephrased version of Qin Guan's work. The only significant difference is that Gu is more explicit in revealing the boudoir theme. In the term "spring thought" (*chunsi*), a conventional suggestion of romantic love usually associated with a woman subject, Gu's poem presents the gender of the persona more explicitly.

The lyrics by Gu Zhenli cited above appear to be simply the utilization of established compositional codes and subject positions. Without contextual information, we cannot determine whether they were merely literary exercises or written for self-representation. However, her extension of the boudoir convention into the context of her personal life is apparent in two lyrics written in relation to her husband, "To the Tune 'Song of the South County': Thinking of the One Far Away":

POEM NO. I

鸞鏡掩清光，	The phoenix mirror is covered from clear light.
莫向簾前試淺妝。	Don't try on light makeup in front of the bamboo blind.
翠嶺春雲都付與，	Spring clouds in the green mountains have all been consigned to—

秋霜。	Autumn frost.
驗取多愁掩鬢傍。	If you want to examine my many sorrows, they cover the hair on my temples.
殘夢倦堪傷。	In a lingering dream I'm tired and heartbroken.
不待秋陰釀嫩涼。	Not waiting for autumn shades to brew a tender cool,
自撥爐熏垂繡幌，	I light up the brazier and drop down the embroidered curtain—
留香。	Keeping the fragrance within.
一縷柔煙伴夜長。	A strand of gentle smoke keeps me company in the long night.¹⁵

POEM NO. 2

花影伴淒然。	The shadow of flowers accompanies my loneliness.
辜負濃香桂子天。	The season of thick cassia fragrance is wasted.
彈指韶光如夢也，	Prime years pass by in the snap of fingers like a dream—
嬋娟。	The beautiful moon,
能得窗前幾個圓。	How many times will it be full in front of my window?
移過博山煙。	After moving the Boshan incense burner
屏掩瀟湘獨自眠。	With the screen blocking the Xiang River, I sleep alone.
冷透重幃吟未就，	Chill penetrating layers of bed curtains, my poem is not finished—
濤箋。	On Xue Tao's paper.¹⁶
總有新詞莫浪傳。	I will always have new lyrics—don't pass them around recklessly.¹⁷

As the subtitle of these two lyrics indicates, they are written as the woman thinks about her husband who is traveling away from home. The speaking voice expresses primarily the sentiments of a longing wife in the boudoir, lamenting her loneliness and her ephemeral youth and beauty. The images that convey these meanings are also borrowed from the repertoire of conventional signifiers. She encloses the interior of the boudoir with embroidered curtains and painted screens, the mirror reflects her aging, flowers contrast with her fading beauty, and the bright moon witnesses the passing of her youth. However, the time-honored themes and sentimental tone are refreshed with the insertion of unexpected elements. For example, in the second stanza of the first lyric, Gu writes: "Not waiting for autumn shades to brew a tender cool, / I light up the brazier and drop down the embroidered curtain." Unlike the typical abandoned-woman persona, who tends to be obsessed with her emotional trouble and unconcerned for her own welfare, this gesture signifies action taken by the persona to alleviate loneliness and take care of herself. Also noteworthy is Gu's self-designation as the writing subject projected in the second lyric. In claiming that she can always come up with new lyrics and urging the intended reader (her husband) not to "pass them around recklessly," the voice is authorial, self-conscious, and proud.

Although these poems cannot be dated, judging from the larger body of Gu's song lyrics, they are suggestive of an early stage of her lyric writing. Gu Zhenli was self-reflexive about her poetic practice. In her lyrics, she often comments on the style or nature of her previous writing not only from the perspective of poetic criticism but also in terms of Buddhism. A lyric to the tune "Washing Creek Sands," which recollects some memorable moments of her earlier years, sheds some light on her poetic pursuit at the time:

卻愛流鶯喚曉眠。	But I loved flying orioles to wake me up in the dawn.
一簾新月漾窗前。	Through the bamboo blind, the new moon shimmered in front of the window.
杏花開也記當年。	The apricot blossoms were blooming—I recall that year.
怨綠愁紅銷慧業。	Poems lamenting green leaves and grieving over red flowers consumed my natural intelligence.
青谿白石浣衣天。	Beside the blue creek and white rocks, the season of washing clothes.
南唐佳句寫裙邊。	I wrote wonderful lines of the Southern Tang style on the hem of my skirt.[18]

The phrase "I recall that year" indicates that the poet is writing of her past. As the lyric continues, the poet recalls primarily both her devotion to and enlightenment by poetry. The first line alludes to the poetic cliché of orioles waking up the lonely wife in the boudoir, but it endows the allusion with a different attitude. In contrast with the complaint of the wife persona, Gu's line displays a cheerful mood more typical of a young, carefree girl excited about getting up early to embrace a new day. The image of blooming apricot trees then emerges from memory, leading to the next motif in this lyric—"lamenting green leaves and grieving over red flowers"—sorrow over the passing of spring and, by extension, youth and beauty. The poet has rewritten these images, which characterize the conventional boudoir lifestyle and sentiments, as a critical summary of her own poetic engagement at the time. Her reference in the last line to the lyrics of the Southern Tang, an important period in the development of boudoir-plaint lyrics, echoes this characterization. However, these lines reveal an ambivalent attitude. In mentioning her improvisation on "wonderful lines of the Southern Tang style" on her skirt, the poet conveys her pride in her own talent and the poetic inspirations that emerge from everyday life. But as she views her writing as "consuming her natural intelligence," she may also be suggesting the negative force of her devotion to poetry in terms of the Buddhist view of artistic speech, and especially embellished feminine language, as harmful to one's nature.[19] In any case, those "wonderful" lines written on her skirt would eventually be washed away. Although the author may not necessarily use the motif of washing clothes in order to suggest this meaning, her later poetic practice indicates that she attempted to move beyond the poetry she perceived as belonging to the Southern Tang style.

In sum, whether imitating classical models or recording experiences resonant with literary tradition, the lyrics in this category to a large extent reiterate conventional, feminine textual positions and voices. From imitating classical models of representation to trying to insert her consciousness as a writing subject, these lyrics illustrate one way in which Gu Zhenli entered into the tradition of boudoir poetics. The stylistic categories of feminine and masculine were well established by Gu Zhenli's time. However, Gu's collection does not contain any lyric that coherently or systematically emulates the established models of the masculine style, although the appropriation of masculine rhetoric and style plays an instrumental role in her transformative boudoir poetics.[20] Gu Zhenli's entry into *ci* writing, which began with conventional feminine language, was very much determined by her gender status. Although these lyrics occupy only a small portion of her collection, they represent a crucial stage in her poetic training and expression.

THE "EMPTY BOUDOIR": REPRESENTATIONS
OF CONFINEMENT

Most of Gu Zhenli's lyrics appear to have been written after her marriage. The examples examined here focus on feelings about marital and widowed life in the boudoir. As indicated by the lyrics' titles or ways of addressing the named reader, the textual subject is marked as the poet speaking in her own voice. While these lyrics should not be treated simply as records of Gu Zhenli's lived experience, they also cannot be read as merely textual expressions unrelated to her personal life, and so it is sometimes necessary to contextualize these poetic expressions with her historical experiences. Only in this way can the significance of Gu's lyrics be fully appreciated as they were written and received in their historical context.

Gu Zhenli was married to Hou Jin (courtesy name Rongbin), a minor official from her native region of Wuxi.[21] In one lyric examined below, Gu Zhenli claims that she and her husband were mismatched.[22] This assertion is likely a gesture through which the poet shows her unusual personality; thus, it cannot be taken at face value as a summary of Gu Zhenli's relationship with Hou Jin. However, in both her direct assertions and her evident nostalgia for her former life as an unmarried daughter, her lyrics portray marriage as a downturn in her life. Marriage, the ultimate social institution defining a woman's role, was a specific source of unhappiness for her. In her lyrics in this thematic category, she depicts the boudoir as the enclosure of a bitter self, a self trapped in the role of wife (and perhaps a widow in later years) and forced to deal with various hardships.

Poetic exchange with husbands was a productive channel of communication for Ming-Qing women poets. In Gu Zhenli's 160 lyrics, however, only 3 relate explicitly to her husband. This fact supports Gu Zhenli's claim that she and her husband were not intellectually compatible. In addition to the two lyrics in "Thinking of the One Far Away," discussed earlier, there is the following lyric to the tune "Full River Red," subtitled "Thinking of the One Far Away; While Rongbin Is Traveling in the North." In it, the torrent of emotions cannot be adequately characterized as the usual "sorrow over separation" (*li chou*):

雁泣西樓,	Wild geese weep over the west tower;
天亦瘦、	Heaven also appears wasted away,
慘黃愁翠。	With the wretched yellow and sad green.
難消受,	Unable to bear it,
長歌當哭,	I sing long as I cry;
孤燈瀉淚。	Beside the lonely lamp, my tears flow like torrents.
典盡難留嫁日衣,	Having pawned everything, it's hard to keep my wedding robes;
醉來卻喜書空字。	When drunk, I like to write the character "empty."
問斷腸、	If you ask what breaks my heart:
吟就是何題,	Whatever topic I compose,

長門句。	It's lines of the "Long Gate."
屏山靜,	Hills on the screens still,
鑪煙細。	The incense smoke fine.
聽不了,	I can't bear to listen to—
寒蛩砌。	Chilled crickets chirring on the steps.
數離愁多少,	If you measure my sorrow over separation,
撐天塞地。	It adds up to the sky and fills the earth.
故國迷漫殘照外,	The homeland is indistinct beyond the setting sun;
美人宛在瀟湘裡。	The fair one seems to be somewhere along the Xiang River.
坐閨中、	Sitting in the boudoir
對此可憐宵,	On this pitiful night,
人憔悴。	Haggard is this person.[23]

This lyric brings forth two major motifs. First, the detail that the poet has to pawn her dowry indicates the straitened circumstances under which she lives. The struggle to make ends meet is a compelling and recurrent theme in Gu Zhenli's lyrics. Elsewhere, in another lyric to the tune "Full River Red," she describes selling her needlework in order to feed the family:

剪綵為花,	Cutting colored silk into flowers,
曾譜出空中金屋。	I've patterned an imaginary golden chamber
翻花樣龍飛鳳舞,	And unfolded the shapes of flying dragon and dancing phoenix,
碧梧修竹。	Blue paulownia and tall bamboo.
閉戶再添今夜綫,	Behind closed doors I'll add tonight's strands again;
停鍼便換明朝粟。	Laying down the needle, I'll exchange my work for millet for tomorrow.
到如今袖手任長貧,	By now I have surrendered to eternal poverty.
真堪哭。	It could indeed make me cry.[24]

Although half of the lines are devoted to demonstrating her craft, any sense of pride is shattered by her bitterness that all these beautiful things are created only to barter for food. The clothes she wore or brought to her husband's home on the wedding day must have been made by her at her natal home in preparation for her trousseau. As such, they would have been symbolically important to her as witnesses to her passage from unmarried daughter to wife. The loss of her wedding clothes would have made the condition of poverty even more emotionally difficult. As "a female form of property that stood outside orthodox Confucian beliefs about joint family ownership," the dowry was primarily at the wife's disposal.[25] There are cases of women voluntarily and proudly contributing their dowries during times of financial difficulty in their married lives and writing poetry to show their "virtuous" action.[26] Gu Zhenli, however, viewed the exhaustion of her dowry as a sign of her failing marital life.

Her bitterness over using up her dowry is related to the second motif. In writing "Whatever topic I compose, / It's lines of the 'Long Gate,'" alluding to the "Rhapsody on the Long Gate" (Changmen fu) by Sima Xiangru (179–117BCE), Gu Zhenli brings up the issue of her problematic relationship with her husband.[27] Long Gate Palace was the residence of the estranged imperial consort Chen (Chen Huanghou), Emperor Wudi of the Han dynasty having turned his amorous attention to another consort. Hoping to regain the emperor's favor, she commissioned the famous writer Sima Xiangru to write "Rhapsody on the Long Gate." The rhapsody moved the emperor and helped restore her to favor.[28] The allusion to this story in Gu Zhenli's lyric suggests a similar crisis in her marital relationship: her husband might have had other sexual or love interests. The significant difference, however, is that she, not a male ghost writer, is the lyric writer. Whether her purpose is to move her husband or to complain, Gu Zhenli's lyric again conveys a negative view of marriage.

The emotional intensity and instability evident in this lyric are striking. Eruptive, unrestrained, and forceful, the sentiments expressed in the first stanza exceed the decorum of the conventional boudoir plaint. Unlike the typical abandoned woman, who is represented as passive and listless, the persona is portrayed as energetic and active in managing her strong emotions. Her sorrows are released and complaints expressed through singing, weeping, drinking, and meditating. Far from fearing to reveal her inner feelings, the poetic persona confronts the intended reader (her husband) with her intense emotions. In describing the strength of her "sorrow over separation," Gu Zhenli adopts a grand gesture comparable to the masculine style: "If you measure my sorrow over separation, / It adds up to the sky and fills the earth." The sentiment engendered in the boudoir becomes so powerful that it cannot be contained within but breaks into the outside world, filling the universe.

By the end of the lyric, however, the poet's persona seems to be both emotionally and physically exhausted. While the lyric begins with a broad view of the depressing autumn scene, the enclosed surroundings of the boudoir gradually come to attract her attention: the screens are immobile, fine lines of incense smoke rise from the burner. But as the crying of autumn insects stirs her feelings, she projects her gaze afar once again: "The homeland is indistinct beyond the setting sun; / The fair one seems to be somewhere along the Xiang River." The meaning of these two lines is difficult to determine, as the terms "hometown" or "the former country" (*guguo*) and "fair one" or "beauty" (*meiren*) are rich in meaning and cultural significance. First, the "fair one" associated with the Xiang River (in present-day Hunan) may allude to the legend of the "the kingly concubines of the Xiang" (Xiang fei), the two loving and virtuous wives of the mythical ruler Shun who died of grief and became goddesses of the Xiang River after Shun's death. In a way, the lines can be read as the poet's attempt to see through the eyes of her husband, who is traveling far from home: he looks back to his hometown and to the fair one who longs for his return. This reading brings forth the conjugal love suggested by the story and thus complicates Gu Zhenli's earlier expression of resentment toward her marital life.

Another possibility is to read "hometown" as indicative of the poet's projection of her gaze upon her native place and former country. By "fair one" she may refer to herself, sadly trapped in an area far from her old home. Gu lived through the Ming-Qing transition, and nostalgia for her natal home and/or the fallen Ming is a recurring theme or motif in her lyrics. Here, Gu's feelings toward her husband and marriage as expressed in the first stanza may not be unrelated to loyalism. Moreover, her unsatisfactory marriage, when set against the broader background of national trauma, conveys a situation of greater complexity than was normal for a conventional boudoir persona. This makes the feelings expressed at the end of this lyric even more despondent.

Despite the ambiguity of these two lines, the lyric closes with the suggestion of a strong sense of confinement within the boudoir. Although the point of view shifts outward and inward in turn as the lyric progresses, it finally returns to the interior. Gu seems unable, ultimately, to surpass the confines of the boudoir, allowing herself to languish passively in sorrow. With this ending, all the cries and struggles presented earlier in the lyric appear to have been in vain.

The boudoir as represented in Palace-Style poetry is a metaphor for the emotional void caused by the absence of the male lover. Ming-Qing women poets often adopt the image of the empty boudoir in their poetry. But the term "empty boudoir" is infused with different meanings. Bing Yue, one of the authors included in *The Anthology of Correct Beginnings*, represents her empty boudoir as a spiritual retreat free of worldly concerns such as wealth and fame. As the line "When drunk, I like to write the character 'empty'" in "Thinking of the One Far Away; While Rongbin Is Traveling in the North" suggests, Gu Zhenli also attempts to engage with the Buddhist concept of emptiness in her perception of boudoir life. Her surrender to despondency at the end of the lyric, however, demonstrates the failure of Buddhist practice to bring transcendence. Unlike the authors represented in *The Anthology of Correct Beginnings*, who in general reconstruct the boudoir as a space in which women can enjoy domestic life, Gu Zhenli emphasizes the sense of confinement and bitterness that comes with dwelling in the boudoir. In the first of two lyrics to the tune "Longing for the Southland," subtitled "Thinking of My Sister-in-Law," she writes:

西窗月。	The moon beside the west window
邀人瘦影成三絕。	Invites me and my thin shadow to become the unique three,
成三絕。	To become the unique three
清愁虛冷，	In pure sorrow and empty coldness,
都無話說。	All having nothing to say.
金釵劃損闌干漆。	Inscribing with the golden hairpin, I scrape off the paint on the railing.
鑪煙裊篆屏山寂。	Smoke curling up from the incense burner, screen hills are still.
屏山寂。	Screen hills are still.
侍兒促睡，	The maid urges me to sleep,
單衾寒怯。	But I'm afraid of the coldness of the thin quilt.[29]

The opening lines of this lyric were conceived under the influence of Li Bai's lines in his poem "Drinking Alone by Moonlight," in which Li animates the moon and his own shadow as his companions in merrymaking:

花間一壺酒，	Here among flowers a single jug of wine;
獨酌無相親。	No close friends here, I pour alone
舉杯邀明月，	And lift cup to bright moon, ask it to join me,
對影成三人。	Then face my shadow and we become three.[30]
...	

A poet of great personality and creativity, Li Bai constructs an ironic world of "solitude"—himself and his imagined friends. The created companions prove to be useless for alleviating his loneliness.[31] In succeeding lines, the moon and his shadow fail to provide the sort of company he desires: "The moon never has known how to drink; /

Convention and Intervention

All my shadow does is follow my body." The poet's final dismissal of these companions makes the sense of loneliness poignant.³² Inspired by Li Bai's lines, Gu Zhenli also imagines the moon and her shadow as company, yet she makes them only witnesses of her loneliness within the boudoir. In mentioning "the unique three," she emphasizes their isolation from the rest of the world, an isolation that is only strengthened by their presence together. They are together yet unable to communicate. This is a moment of absolute loneliness. From the second stanza, Gu Zhenli's perspective focuses only on the enclosed world of the boudoir. The strokes of her hairpin on the railings record the degree of this bitter struggle. Moreover, as the subtitle of this lyric "Thinking of My Sister-in-Law" indicates, the expressed feelings are directed toward or intended to be shared with this female relative.

In the second lyric to the tune "Longing for Qin E," Gu Zhenli refers to her sister-in-law as Qin E, an abandoned-woman persona established in a lyric to the tune by this title,³³ attributed to Li Bai:

西窗月。	The moon beside the west window
照人夜夜如相識。	Throws light on me every night as if it knew me.
如相識。	As if it knew me,
穿簾入幕，	It shines through the blinds and enters the curtain,
故來尋覓。	Going out of its way to look for me.
空閨此際真愁絕！	At this moment, in the empty boudoir I'm truly extremely distressed!
遙知尚有秦娥泣。	I know far away Qin E is also weeping.
秦娥泣。	Qin E is weeping;
與君嘗盡，	You and I have suffered all kinds of sorrows
生離死別。	Over separations in life and death.³⁴

By alluding to the image of Qin E, Gu Zhenli perceives the three of them as sharing the same sorrowful situation. Deng Hongmei claims that Gu Zhenli was widowed when writing these two lyrics.³⁵ The phrase "separations in life and death" possibly suggests the loss of her husband. However, whether she was widowed or not at the time, Gu Zhenli inscribes the bitter feelings of entrapment in the space of the empty boudoir.

In this lyric, Gu begins again with the image of the moon. Although the moon is portrayed as a quiet companion in the first lyric, it is further personified here as an old friend who has come purposely to visit her. This can be read as a pathetic fallacy, underlying which may be the opposite fact that it is the poet who gazes upon the moon every night and persistently seeks its companionship. However, this imagined comfort immediately turns out to be a prelude to an emotional breakdown as the poet cries out her distress at the beginning of the second stanza. At this moment, she can no longer contain herself. The double usage of the adverb "truly" (*zhen*) and the complement "extremely" (*jue*) conveys the great intensity of her emotion: "I'm truly extremely distressed" (*zhen chou jue*). In particular, *zhen*, a colloquial word that responds directly to a certain condition confronting the speaker, interrupts the impersonal, picturesque effect produced by the primarily imagistic language of the first stanza. This rupture in stylistics marks the author's subjective assertion in reacting to her emotional entrapment in the boudoir.

In the lyric "To the Tune 'Bodhisattva Barbarian': I Cannot Sleep on an Autumn Night," she adopts a similar approach:

霜砧碎擣愁腸裂,	At the sound of pounding clothes on frosty rocks, my grieving heart breaks;
啼蛩絮語愁心切。	At the chirr of crying crickets, my sorrow is pressed on.
露葉墮空庭,	Dewy leaves fall in the empty courtyard;
窗穿月倍明。	Shining through the window, the moon is doubly bright.
朝衾隨便擁,	Just wrapping myself up in the morning quilt,
難續春前夢。	It is hard to continue the dream I had before the spring.
玉匣閣輕紈,	Light silks are stored in the jade box;
空閨一樣酸。	All the empty boudoirs are equally afflicted.[36]

Most of the lyric is constructed through a cluster of highly imagistic elements: "pounding clothes on frosty rocks," "crying crickets," "dewy leaves" falling in "the empty courtyard," a "doubly bright" moon shining through the window, and so on. Encountering these stock images one after another, a reader could easily conclude that this lyric reproduces another generic version of boudoir-plaint lyrics. The assertion in the last line, however, breaks with these formulaic descriptions, standing out with its direct discursiveness and unusual choice of the descriptive *suan* (literally "sour" or "acid," by extension meaning "afflicted" or "grieved"), a word not preferred in the poetics and aesthetics of femininity.[37] In this way, Gu Zhenli invests the voice with unconventional touches. Her concluding remark ends with gendered empathy, declaring the commonplace of women suffering in the empty boudoir, and her "strange" diction succeeds in giving her poem novelty.

In a number of lyrics, Gu Zhenli refers to her boudoir as an "empty boudoir." She may, following convention, mean the situation of a wife or widow without a husband's presence, but these lyrics do not simply fall into the category of conventional boudoir plaints. She emphasizes not the lovesickness of the persona but the pressures of specific domestic problems and struggles with conflicting emotions, articulating the space of the boudoir from a woman-centered perspective.

"I JUST WON'T LEARN / THESE MANNERS OF THE BOUDOIR": IN SEARCH OF AN ALTERNATIVE SPACE FOR SELF-REPRESENTATION

Whereas Gu Zhenli sees marriage as a downturn, her former life in the boudoir as an unmarried daughter appears to be a paradise to which she persistently returns in her dreams and memories. In a lyric to the tune "Treading the Sedge," she includes a relatively long preface articulating the feelings that stir her as she prepares to write:

> When I was not yet married, every year in the spring month all my aunts returned home to visit their parents. Our grandparents would bring several of us cousins together; we would give ourselves up to feasting and making merry. Since the year Wuyin [1638] and Jimou [1639], we all married like the Three Stars entering the door, bearing fruit to benefit the house. We can no longer get together but can only entrust our feelings to the evening clouds and spring trees. At this moment when the moon looks pale and the lamp is green, my feelings are difficult to dispel. Therefore, I compose this lyric.[38]

Using phrases derived from the *Book of Songs*, Gu briefly outlines the important events related to her and her cousins becoming wives and mothers.[39] For Gu, however, the transition to these roles also deprives them of the happiness and freedom they had enjoyed as unmarried girls. The preface is followed by the lyric, which enriches the above narrative with more recollections of a lost paradise:

暈掩青燈，	A halo surrounds the green lamp;
寒侵翠袖。	Chill invades my kingfisher-blue sleeves.
音書望斷重陽後。	Since the Double Ninth, I've waited in vain for news from letters.
昔年閨閣鬥新妝，	In past years we competed with new fashions in the boudoir;
而今追憶難回首。	Now recalling those days, it is impossible to return.
夜月聯床，	On moonlit nights we joined our beds side by side;
曉窗同繡。	In the morning we embroidered together beside the window.

踏燈挑菜頻攜手，	Going to view lanterns and pick vegetables, we often went hand in hand;
夢中依約聚難分，	Vaguely in dreams we reunited and felt the hardship of parting;
覺來贏得愁腸逗。	Waking up, I gain only sorrow, upsetting my heart.[40]

Gu juxtaposes two temporalities of the boudoir by shifting between the present and the past. Poignantly, she returns to where she begins, the moment of her emotional pain. The memory of the days when she enjoyed the company of her cousins temporarily removes her from this sad reality. What she recalls are typical "girly" activities. Nostalgia for her former boudoir life is a recurring theme in Gu Zhenli's lyrics and a significant way in which she tries to escape the unhappiness of her married life. However, this imaginative, temporary flight is not ultimately sufficient.

The poet's reflections on her writing make explicit the intentions underlying her textual transformation. In a lyric dated 1672, when she was forty-eight years old, Gu offers a commentary to her own *ci* writing in which she informs the reader of her wish to go beyond what she perceives as her limitations:

…	
羞說擅詞場，	I feel ashamed to say I'm good in the arena of the lyric;
總是愁香怨粉章。	What I've written are always verses lamenting fragrance and rouge.
安得長流俱化酒，千觴。	How can I transform the long river into wine— One thousand goblets
一洗英雄兒女腸？	To cleanse the hearts of heroic men and women once and for all?[41]

The middle-aged Gu Zhenli was already a recognized poet. The humble position she assumes here, however, is taken not out of modesty (other lyrics display a flamboyant style) but as a self-critique of her *ci* writing. She may exaggerate in characterizing her writing as always being "verses lamenting fragrance and rouge," an idiom related to the boudoir plaint and, by extension, feminine poetics in general. It may have been the case, however, that she had, up to this point, been mostly engaged in and famous for the feminine style. Her contemporary Chen Weisong, for example, records only three typical boudoir-plaint lyrics by her in *The Collection of Women's Writing*.[42] In any case, Gu's negative evaluation of her lyrical style reveals that she was dissatisfied with the "feminine" nature of her writing. While feminized song lyrics expressing private sentiments of love were also problematized in the male social and political domain, Gu Zhenli's self-critical attitude may suggest a deeper frustration with the fact that her engagement with the poetic feminine was greatly determined by her gendered status. Finally, setting forth her quest for the magical power to transform a river into wine, Gu allegorically expresses her dissatisfaction with the current feminine status of her lyrics (and maybe also of her life) and her desire to transcend her perceived limitations. The ability to drink prodigiously is a common trope manipulated by literati poets to express frustration over failed political pursuits or to demonstrate an unrestrained, heroic manner. In borrowing this masculine gesture, Gu Zhenli is literally making reference to the oppositional masculine style in order to transform the feminine-gendered conventions by which her writing is limited. Gu developed a mature, coherent self-representation inspired by the literati's masculine poetics.

Most of the lyrics examined here appear to have been written by Gu Zhenli in her old age. The voice is that of an elderly woman retrospectively examining her life and asserting an independent stance that she feels at ease to express. As an elderly woman, she feels free to be herself and do as she likes. This new textual position was one not of seeking escape from the condition of confinement but of speaking out against it from within that very condition. She developed a distinct mode of expression, which breaks free from social or symbolic systems restricting her personality and inclinations. She created an image of herself as a nonconformist, opposing what she perceived as vulgar feminine fashions as well as the orthodox meanings of womanhood. With her sweeping subversion of gender conventions, she made a significant move toward transcending the symbolic order associated with women and the boudoir.

This sense of subversion is clearly expressed in several of her long lyrics, which, with their similar organization and phrasing, reiterate alternative positions and ways of expression. In these long, two-stanza lyrics there is a recurring binary organization in which she begins by attacking conventional codes of femininity and concludes by portraying her alternative self-image. This typical structure is evident in the following lyric to the tune "Spring in the Garden of Qin":

掠鬢梳鬢,	Combing tresses into chignons,
弓鞋窄裏,	Bound feet squeezed into bow-shaped shoes—
不慣從來。	I have never gotten used to these.
但經營理料,	As for cooking and household management—

茶鐺茗盌，	Setting out teapot and cups,
親供灑掃，	And taking care of housecleaning—
職分當該。	These should be my duties.
還謝天公深有意，	Still I'm thankful to profound Providence
便生就、	For allowing me to be born
粗疏邱壑才。	A person of crude manner and grand talent.
將衰矣!	I am growing old!
短景頻催。	In the shadow of the setting sun,
斜陽日影，	Fleeting scenes urge one on.
閒身不妨多病，	Illness bears no harm for an idle body;
且憑他位置、	Just place it
廢苑荒臺。	In the ruined garden and deserted terrace,
伴香濃琴靜，	Accompanied by rich incense and a soothing zither,
百城南面，	Facing south to rule a hundred cities,
青編滿架，	Having a full shelf of books,[43]
湘軸成堆。	Silk scrolls in piles.
一縷茶煙和字煮，	A whiff of fragrance rises as I brew tea while writing,
只數點秋花手自栽。	Just a few spots of autumn flowers planted by my own hands.
都休也!	Forget about everything else!
蠅頭蝸角，	Flies' heads and snails' horns—
於我何哉!	What do they have to do with me![44]

In the first stanza, Gu Zhenli announces her disdain for feminine fashions. Few women in her time wrote about the bound foot, let alone openly attacked the culturally embedded practice.[45] In claiming "I have never gotten used to these," Gu Zhenli explicitly voices dissent, demonstrating the divergence of her position from culturally recognized feminine attributes. On the one hand, she appears to adopt a stance toward domestic duties that is less radical than that in many of her other lyrics. On the other hand, admitting these responsibilities does not necessarily mean that she is happy to play her prescribed part.

In fact, in the first stanza of the second lyric to the tune "Spring in the Garden of Qin" (in her collection placed right next to the lyric to the same tune quoted above), she clearly asserts her "natural" inclination against the process of becoming a woman:

嘯傲生成，	I was born unrestrained and haughty
薄游身世，	Into an unfortunate and floating life,
慘澹情懷。	Feeling numb and dispirited.
也曾經料理，	I once managed
繡床花樣，	Flowered patterns on the embroidery stand
回文機杼，	And the palindrome on the loom,

空裏樓臺。	Making towers and terraces in emptiness.
怕向鍼神稱弟子,	I'm afraid to call myself a disciple of the Goddess of Needlework,
但通國、	But all over the country,
閨娃受教來。	Girls in the boudoir have been taught this.
今難再,	Now I can no longer stand
看殘絲剩綫,	To look at the remnants of silk floss and thread.
意嬾心灰。	My mind lazy, heart turned to ashes.[46]

In this self-reflection, she focuses on her own socialization in womanly work such as weaving and embroidering, proper training for *guiwa*, or girls of the inner chambers. Some of Gu's other writings indicate that she became proficient in these traditional skills, and, indeed, she occasionally professed pride in her ability. Nevertheless, she confesses in this lyric a reluctance to be "a disciple of the Goddess of Needlework." Given this confession, her weariness in doing needlework is not due to the typical mood of ennui associated with the boudoir but demonstrates her personal stance against this womanly practice and the subjection of woman by society. While Gu's own preoccupations as represented in her lyrics indicate that engagement in either womanly work or other cultural activities did not necessarily mean the exclusion of the other, the discarding of needlework asserted in the context of this lyric is symbolically important in suggesting the intentionality of her transition from a traditional womanly role to one in which she would be free to pursue whatever she liked.

In a similar yet more radical textual move in the first stanza of a song lyric to the tune "Full River Red," Gu Zhenli launches into a wholesale rejection of traditional womanhood, including both feminine fashion and domestic roles, before proclaiming her own position:

墮馬啼妝,	Hairdo resembling after falling from a horse, makeup imitating weeping,
學不就、	I just won't learn
閨中模樣。	These manners of the boudoir.
疏慵慣、	I'm used to being careless and lazy,
嚼花吹葉,	Chewing petals and blowing leaves,
粉抛脂漾。	Discarding powder and rouge.
多病不堪操井臼,	I have too many illnesses to be able to manage household chores;
無才敢去嫌天壤。	Although I'm not talented, I dare dislike my husband who is not my match.
看絲絲、	Looking at every strand on my temples,

| 雙鬢幾時青， | How long can they remain black? |
| 空勞攘。 | Don't make vain attempts.⁴⁷ |

"Hairdo resembling after falling from a horse" and "makeup imitating weeping" were the feminine fashion and manner created by the Han dynasty woman Sun Shou 孫壽.⁴⁸ Shen Huiyu and other authors in *The Anthology of Correct Beginnings* often used similar terms as synecdoches for "vulgar" or "immoral" femininity as a way of critiquing feminine vanity and artificiality. In this lyric, Gu Zhenli also claims a critical distance from what she terms "these manners of the boudoir." However, she is not thereby joining Shen Huiyu in asserting a correct aesthetic standard. Rather, she attempts to show that she is not concerned with conforming to any feminine trait: she is idle and lax rather than diligent and observant, and she destroys and discards flowers and rouge instead of wearing them. She goes even further by challenging the basic moral requirements of womanly virtue. First, she excuses herself from household responsibility because of illness. Illness is a common theme or motif treated in Ming-Qing women's poetry.⁴⁹ As Fong insightfully points out, women poets not only represent illness as "an apt signifier of femininity" but also turn moments of illness into "an alternative temporality" in women's lives in which they can pursue self-reflection, meditation, and other creative and intellectual activities.⁵⁰ While Gu Zhenli may not actually have been exempted from household chores during illness, as were many women in more well-to-do families, her use of illness as an excuse to shun her domestic duties is an open challenge to the norms of womanhood.

Even more surprising is the bold condescension she expresses toward her mediocre husband. The line she uses is derived from the story recorded in *A New Account of Tales of the World* in which Xie Daoyun (fl. 376), the icon of young female talent, shows her displeasure at the intellectual inferiority of her husband compared to the talented men in her family: "In this one household, for uncles I have A Da, Zhonglang, and for cousins and brothers I have Feng, Hu, E and Mo. But I never thought that there could be such a [stupid] person as Wang Lang between heaven and earth."⁵¹ It appears that Xie Daoyun is comparing her husband to her male relatives, but in fact she is complaining that he is a mismatch for her.⁵² In claiming to have no talent in comparison with Xie Daoyun, yet still adopting an equally arrogant attitude toward her husband, Gu Zhenli portrays herself bluntly as a transgressive woman: she ignores the prescribed roles for women in the domestic sphere, slighting both household responsibility and her husband's authority.

Her self-indulgent pleasure in music, books, tea, and gardening echoes this resistance to the conventional roles and responsibilities of women. Gu often elaborates these pleasures in the second stanzas of her lyrics. These activities or signifiers are commonplaces in literati culture and are also alternative sources of inspiration for Ming-Qing women's literary culture. However, they are particularly significant for Gu Zhenli in helping her not only to escape from the women's concerns and activities she disdains but also to be positive in dealing with the impossibility of women pursuing public, political careers. Her lines "Facing south to rule a hundred cities, / Having a full shelf of books" are adapted from "The Biography of Li Mi," in which Li Mi claims, "If a great man owns ten thousand scrolls of books, why would he need to demonstrate his power by facing south to rule a hundred cities?"[53] Although, as a woman, Gu did not have the option of entering the political arena, she could achieve a kind of self-empowerment by turning to self-cultivation.

However, her denial of domestic responsibilities does not mean that she is entirely carefree. It is often followed by an effort to persuade herself not to be burdened with worldly concerns. In the second stanza of the lyric to the tune "Full River Red," the first stanza of which is quoted above, Gu goes on to show the specific strategies that she adopts in coping with the problems in her life:

應不作，	I should not think of
繁華想，	Richness and glory
收拾起，	But pull myself together
淒涼況。	In the wretched situation.
向牙籤境內，	In the realm of books,
自尋幽賞。	I seek deep enjoyment alone.
昨夜樓頭新夢好，	Last night in my tower my new dream is sweet—
清風吹送瑤臺上。	A clear wind sent me to Jasper Terrace.
散閒愁、	To dispel idle sorrows,
高枕是良方，	A high pillow is a magic remedy,
飛璚餉。	A treat provided by the Fairy Feiqiong.[54]

As the term "richness and glory" suggests, Gu's dream for her life may have included achievements that belonged to the world of men in addition to a better material situation. The decision not to dream of a life unattainable to her but to cheer herself up in the midst of adversity is a gesture of both resignation and affirmation. The poet tries to make peace with her destiny. Unable to extricate herself from these circumstances, she decides to appreciate her life in its own right. The changed perspective indeed takes her beyond the mundane to Jasper Terrace, the immortals' land. She thus concludes that her dreams can provide escape from sorrow and pain. The critical-turned-detached attitude expressed in this lyric contrasts sharply with the bitterness about her confinement in the lyrics examined in the previous section. They can be read as signposts of her spiritual transcendence.

In describing all the activities unbefitting the womanly role, Gu Zhenli intends to make them suit her "inborn" personality—"a person of crude manner and grand talents." This is an image whose masculine connotations make it unconventional as a woman's claim. In emphatically claiming that she was born to be such a person, Gu Zhenli attempts to maintain her differences from the conventional meanings attached to being a woman, thus emphasizing an alternative self-identity. In the above-mentioned second lyric to the tune "Spring in the Garden of Qin," she also characterizes herself with the term "unrestrained and haughty" (*xiao'ao*), which, by convention, describes a manner of spontaneous response to one's true feelings and freedom from social restrictions. Male literati authors often adopted this term to represent their free spirits and unconventional lifestyle, intentionally distanced from the dark realm of sociopolitics. Tao Qian, for example, writes in one of his famous "Drinking Wine Poems": "Being unrestrained and haughty under the east veranda, / Having somehow found my life again."[55] The "wild" (*kuang*) and "arrogant" (*ao*) poetic self was also well-established in masculine-styled lyrics.[56] Lu You composes the following lines, which could be the very inspiration for Gu's construction of self-image:

貪嘯傲，	I'm obsessed with being unrestrained and putting on a haughty air;
任衰殘，	Let the body grow old and waste away;
不妨隨处一開顏。	There's no harm in smiling wherever I go.
元知造物心腸別，	I always know that the Creator has a contrary mind:
老却英雄似等閒！	Letting a hero grow old seems to him an ordinary matter![57]

Disregarding external conditions and placing more confidence in the inner self, Lu You is gesturing a retreat from the pursuit of fame and success in the sociopolitical domain to which he belonged. Whether or not this self-transcendent gesture is successful (in fact, it is belied by his deeper frustration, as suggested in the last two lines), the term "unrestrained and haughty" has become a cliché that literati used to assert their nonconformity. Gu Zhenli's professed loyalty to a "true" self also evinces the continuing influence of late Ming trends that emphasized individualism and expressionism, such as Li Zhi's (1527–1602) notion of "innocence" (*tongxin*) and the Gong'an School's "nature and inspiration" (*xingling*).[58] Eccentricity had become an essential element in many areas of late Ming and early Qing literati culture, and being "true" to oneself often meant departing from conventions and norms.

The idea of being a rebellious eccentric was also inspirational to women. In addition to Gu, contemporaries such as Zhou Qiong[59] expressed their unwillingness to be ordinary women:

每憐俠骨慚紅粉，	I always admire the chivalrous bone and feel ashamed to be wearing powder and rouge.
肯學蛾眉理艷粧。	How can I be willing to learn from those with moth-like eyebrows to dress myself prettily?
風度曲欄閒種竹，	Wind crossing the meandering railings, I plant bamboo in idleness.
花迷小檻靜焚香。	Flowers hide the small baluster; I burn incense in serenity.
波瀾世路無青眼，	In this stormy world there are no sympathetic eyes.
誰識人間我獨狂？	Who recognizes my unique wildness in this world?[60]

Even though Zhou's poem is written in the *shi* form, it clearly echoes Gu Zhenli's discarding of conventional womanhood and embrace of the eccentric self. The "wild" and "arrogant" self-image Gu and Zhou adopt was not their invention but served as an inspiration for like-minded women who wished to escape their womanly roles and claim an eccentric self-identity in the poetic space of the boudoir.

In the second stanza of the second lyric to the tune "Spring in the Garden of Qin," Gu Zhenli uses eccentricity to establish her sense of subjectivity:

清神猶餘眼耳，	Clarity still remains in my eyes and ears.
便霜鬢雪鬢，	Even if my hair has turned to frost and snow,
任屬形骸。	Let the body be what it will.
與青谿小妹，	To my little sister by Green Creek,[61]
飛牋索賦。	I send hurried letters to ask for verses.
孀閨病嫂，	With my sickly sister-in-law in her widow's boudoir,
險韻同裁。	Together we compose poems with challenging rhymes.

痼癖煙霞誰得似，	By nature eccentric like mist and clouds—who would be like me?
有疏影、	There is the dappled shadow of
孤山一樹梅。	The plum tree on Lone Hill.[62]
江南夢，	In the dream of Jiangnan,
想群花未醒，	While many flowers are not yet awakened,
雪裏偏開。	She would bloom in the snow.[63]

In this stanza, Gu presents a deliberately strange self-image. While the young, attractive female body, well cared for in order to retain its youth and beauty, is the center of conventional boudoir poetics and aesthetics, Gu focuses instead on signs of her body's aging. Importantly, this aging does not concern her. Instead of dwelling on the external conditions of her life and body, she expresses appreciation that she is still able to actively engage in her poetic pursuits. She works hard to avoid mediocrity. In challenging herself with the composition of *xian yun*, an exceedingly difficult rhyme pattern, she is evidently convinced that only poetry of outstanding quality can match her exceptional personality.

Once again in this lyric, she accepts illness and prefers to situate the "sick" body in "the ruined garden and deserted terrace." This place likely refers to her ironically named boudoir-studio, Fragrance-Nesting Pavilion (Qixiangge). In another lyric, she writes "I laugh at the Qixiang, for its garden and terrace have always been ruins."[64] Her willing "sickness" and "marginality" reveal a poignant sense of self-displacement, an ironic demonstration of individual agency in resisting a normative subject position. The "sickly sister-in-law in her widow's boudoir," who has many experiences in common with Gu, as shown in other lyrics, is represented as one of only a few understanding companions. Gu concludes that she is an "eccentric" by nature. The details of "strangeness" in earlier lines are intended to illustrate this nature.

By posing a rhetorical question, "who would be like me?" and claiming "the plum tree on Lone Hill" as her double, Gu further elaborates on the cultural values behind her eccentricity. The image of the plum tree that Gu adopts here alludes to the Song poet and hermit Lin Bu (967–1028), a recluse on Lone Hill, close to Hangzhou. He is famous for his fondness for and poems written on plum trees. His poem, "The Small Plum Tree in the Mountain Garden," is recognized for its masterful characterization of the aesthetic and moral values of the plum tree.[65] The poet himself also became the icon of a lofty recluse purposefully disengaged from the vulgar world. Through embracing the pure and noble spirit as embodied in the image of the plum tree, Gu goes out of her way to choose a different path from that of her peers, those whom she refers to here as "many flowers" (*qun hua*).

The recurring binary structure of these lyrics shows that Gu Zhenli's nonconformist subject position evolves through two phases: disidentification from the womanly role assigned to her and self-invention of an eccentric personality. Transgression becomes a necessary way for Gu Zhenli to escape from her subjection. The claim "I just won't learn these manners of the boudoir" summarizes her radical stance against conventional gender ideology. Simultaneously, deconstructing the conventions of femininity paves a way for her self-invention. Ming-Qing women poets commonly adopted the approach of incorporating literati cultural ideals into their self-representations. However, Gu appropriates literati poetic discourses in a way that challenges the gender-based social and poetic conventions.

By means of the song lyric, she establishes a distinct subjectivity in the discursive space of the boudoir. The following lyric to the tune "Full River Red" illustrates the powerful effect of this textual transformation:

摘碎花魂,	The soul of the flowers picked to pieces
鄉夢杳,	Dream of the hometown remote;
擁衾還起。	Wrapped up in a quilt, I get up.
淒絕處,	At this moment of extreme sorrow,
燈昏香燼,	The lamp dims as incense turns to ashes;
重門深閉。	Double gates are deeply shut.
握管欲吟紅雨曲,	Holding the brush, I want to compose the melody of red rain,
啼痕先把青衫漬。	But tears already stain my black robe.
卸金釵、	Removing the golden hairpin,
閒自撥燈灰,	I idly stir the ashes of the lamp
書愁字。	And write the character "sorrow."
今古事,	Affairs of past and present,
醉而已。	I get drunk and forget about them.
死歸也,	Death is going home;
生如寄。	Life is a temporary lodge.
任旁人妒口,	Let the jealous mouths of others
或憐或鄙。	Pity or condemn me.
嘯傲久成衰鳳侶,	Unrestrained and putting on a haughty air, I've long been the aged Phoenix's companion;
粗疏好與頑仙似。	Rough and careless I like to act like an obtuse immortal.
問從來、	I ask, since the beginning of time,

淪落孰如予,	Who has sunk into a situation as wretched as mine?
應無二。	There shouldn't be another.[66]

This lyric includes a brief preface informing us of the circumstances under which it was written: "On a rainy night in the cold spring, I could not sleep. I got up to sit in front of the stove and asked for wine to be brought in. I drank happily till I finally became drunk and wrote this." In the first stanza, the poet employs the familiar strategy of drawing a parallel between the depressing interior of the boudoir and a troubled mind. The literal inscription of the character "sorrow" (*chou*) within the boudoir suggests that she may have sunk again into an emotional morass. However, as the second stanza goes on to reveal, the poet's perspective is suddenly elevated beyond her sorrow through drinking, and she begins to view even life and death with detachment. Armed with this attitude, she sees the hostile world as less threatening. She realizes that there may be attacks by those with "jealous mouths" (*du kou*), but she is ready to confront them. Things that others might consider undesirable—her unfortunate life experience and eccentric manners—are transformed into labels of the "unique" self-image she claims. In other words, she affirms her eccentricity or otherness as the very constituent of her self-identity.

In studying the poetics of Emily Dickinson and Marianne Moore, Sabine Sielke has observed the significance of eccentricity in the two poets' self-representation: "Eccentricity served both poets as a refuge, a sacrosanct space, a kind of magic hat under which to hide, write, and handle life as well as a strategy for self-presentation by self-dramatization."[67] In the case of Gu Zhenli, the claim of an eccentric personality provides her with an opportunity to "act out" her nonconformity to the conventions of femininity. The nonconformist approach, while not exclusive to Gu Zhenli, constructs a subject position outside or in excess of the socially and culturally recognized models of female identity because of its radical stance. Through deconstruction and construction, Gu Zhenli finds an alternative framework for her self-representation and, ultimately, transforms the boudoir poetics.[68]

A DISRUPTED POETICS OF THE BOUDOIR

The different, even contradictory, expressive modes in the corpus of Gu Zhenli's lyrics constitute both the richness and the heterogeneity of her poetics. Her inscriptions on the boudoir produced effects of poetic "disruption" on two levels. First, read in the continuum of Gu's different modes of depicting the boudoir, her subversive assertions against the gender conventions associated with the boudoir represent a breakthrough in traditional boudoir poetics. She deconstructs the feminine space of the boudoir and establishes an eccentric female subjectivity through her appropriation of masculine-style language and imagery. Second, the effect of disruption also takes place on a more concrete level. The utterances of the speaking subject within one text are shot through with stylistic incongruities: feminine discourse is often interrupted by masculine rhetoric, and imagistic, evocative language is interrupted by discursive statements or assertions in a direct, colloquial style. These stylistically incongruent insertions may be seen as traces of negotiation, marks of her subjective intervention in the poetic tradition.

Following Julia Kristeva's theory of poetic language and subjectivity formation, the Western feminist critic Sabine Sielke relates poetic disruption to the construction of female subjectivity in her study of Dickinson's and Rich's writing, reading ruptures of their texts as "traces of the processes of subject constitution and as subversions of the symbolic order."[69] Sielke argues, "Subjectivity—be it historical or fictional—involves selecting from a wide range of institutional frames, discourses, grammars, tones of voice, and imagery that allow for locally transgressive moves and may envision alternative positions, or "third event[s]."[70] Her analysis of the significance of Dickinson's, Moore's, and Rich's unorthodox poetic practice in relation to their literary agency is specifically illuminating in understanding Gu Zhenli's transformative poetics. As she points out, "[T]he unorthodoxy of their texts underlines that subject and subjectivity are never completely modeled according to prearranged fashions."[71]

Although coming from a different cultural context, Gu Zhenli's lyrics are a salient illustration of an individual woman's challenge to the limits of poetic language and the stereotypes of female subjects. The heterogeneous poetics of Gu's lyrics can ultimately be read as a negotiation with the gendered poetics particular to the *ci* genre. The impulse underlying her textual transformation has much to do with her consciousness of gender. She struggled not only with her sociocultural categorization as a woman versus her subversive subjectivity but also with the influence of feminine poetic conventions, which supposedly befit her gender status, versus the impulse to search for alternative modes of self-expression. "If woman escapes from her subjection, it is for her ability to shift position in discourse."[72] In her lyrics, Gu Zhenli demonstrates a complicated positioning vis-à-vis the boudoir, involving oppositional strategies of both identification with and dis-identification from conventions of femininity. While her shifting textual positions can be viewed as a destabilization of the subject position in literary texts, they can also be seen as symbolic moves deliberately chosen by Gu Zhenli as a historical agent.

CHAPTER 4

Inside Out

The Gui in Times of Chaos

Beacon fires leap across passes and mountains—suffering is not yet over;
Deep in the boudoir, she searches for poetic lines—stirred by autumn's lament.
Sweeping away powder and rouge, she intends to set aside the brush;
Reciting, she gazes upon winds and clouds, leaning against the tower.

烽火關山苦未休，深閨覓句動悲秋。掃除粉黛思投筆，吟眺風雲愛倚樓。

—HE GUOCHEN 何國琛

Consigned to the inner, domestic sphere, women were supposed to be not only circumscribed by gender-based conventions of etiquette but also physically protected from dangers and threats from the outside world. As shown by most of the poems included in *The Anthology of Correct Beginnings by Inner-Chamber Talents of the Present Dynasty*, peace and harmony are ideal qualities associated with life in the women's sphere. Compiled during the early decades of the nineteenth century, a time when social and political life was relatively stable, at least in Jiangnan, the anthology was intended to celebrate the prosperity of its age. But the larger picture of women's textual practices beyond the thematic scope and temporal frame of *The Anthology of Correct Beginnings* was far more complicated. The earlier Ming-Qing transition, the Opium War (1840), and the Taiping Rebellion (1850–64) were indeed tumultuous. During these times of social upheaval, even the sheltered women of the higher classes were thrust into the chaotic world beyond the inner quarters.

Women in the late Ming and Qing were not the first to witness tragic historical changes, but it was the first time that "a large number of women poets began to bear witness to war atrocities, apparently through a conscious process of emulation and creation."[1] Scholars have also noted that with the spread of literacy, personal records of witnessing and reflecting on social disorder became particularly prevalent and significant in late imperial individual lives.[2] Although most of these records were written by men, women also played active roles in constructing textual responses to historical crises and personal losses.[3]

Most of the records left by women are in the form of individual collections. Many of these collections are arranged in chronological order, allowing the reader to observe the author's life course or development of her poetic practice. Compared with anthologies, these individual collections provide an immensely rich source of information regarding the poets' personal lives and experiences.

The violent conquest of China by the Manchus and the Taiping Rebellion stand out as the two most turbulent moments in the cultural memory of late imperial China. Not surprisingly, these two events also received the most attention in women's poetic accounts. In delving into individual collections by women produced from the mid-nineteenth century through the late Qing, one frequently encounters poems written about "chaos caused by soldiers" (*bingluan*). Poems with titles such as "Escaping from the Disorder of War" or "Escaping from Bandits" stand in sharp contrast with the titles of poems by the same authors depicting the placid and sentimental boudoir scenarios of more peaceful times. Although many of the collections include only a few poems on these topics, the authors seem deeply traumatized by their experiences of war and chaos. For those who suffered great personal losses, their lives were changed forever, as were their perspectives on life and history and their approaches to the writing of poetry.

Although women's engagement in historical meditation often compelled them to go beyond the *gui*, or the inner chambers, as subject matter, as the normative location of female gender, it is still deeply implicated in their representation of their traumatic experiences of disorder. The fires of war may have ruined the physical space of the inner chambers along with their homes, but the image or concept of the *gui* still frequently appears in their poetry as a comforting shelter, a hub of memories, or a framework for negotiating gender boundaries. Social chaos seems to have opened up a perspective from which women poets could consider their place in society. Directly addressing the ways in which the *gui* confined women and hindered them from participating in military and political activities, some women poets went out of their way to protest gender restrictions. Their textual production under extraordinary circumstances illustrates how they understood the *gui* against the larger sociohistorical background of disorder. The broader social and historical experiences these poets brought to their writings further transformed conventional boudoir poetics and aesthetics, including the development of new conventions in contemporary women's literary culture.

GUIXIU IN DISPLACEMENT: ENCOUNTERING WAR AND CHAOS

The transition from the Ming to the Qing is considered by many historians to be one of the most socially disruptive dynastic successions in Chinese history.[4] The Manchu conquest of China and the subsequent consolidation of the Qing empire was a long, violent process that encompassed the nation and continued until the last decades of the seventeenth century.[5] The mid-nineteenth-century Taiping Rebellion, which lasted almost two decades, and several concurrent outbreaks such as the Nian Rebellion (1853–68), also brought "gigantic human catastrophes" to the Chinese people.[6] Twenty million people died as a direct result of the Taiping Rebellion alone.[7] When waves of social turmoil turned the larger world upside down, women found that the inner world of the *gui* changed, too, or even collapsed. In war-torn areas, people were forced to leave their homes and take refuge in remote areas or mountains. Countless women lost their lives during the turmoil. Writing women who survived these calamities left behind rich records of their agonizing experiences of war and violence.

Historical concerns and political sentiments were supposed to be in the male social sphere; in expressing these themes, Chinese literary history had canonized the perspectives and voices of male literati. In poems by women recording war and chaos in the Ming-Qing transition and later times, however, the authors tended to record what they personally saw and experienced *as women*. In other words, their poetry often expresses a woman's gendered point of view. It is important to note that in these gender-marked accounts of trauma, the concept of the *gui* is frequently invoked even when the actual space of the *gui* has been destroyed by war.

The poem "Escaping from the Red Turbans," by Dong Baohong (fl. 1853), a survivor of the Taiping Rebellion, exemplifies this characteristic:

四望烽煙如掌合，	Looking around, beacon smoke all around, like a palm closing up.
避凶趨吉身何往。	To escape misfortune and seek luck, where should I go?
抽身我固哭真州，	Turning around, I can only weep for Zhenzhou;
從此家山勞夢想。	From now on, I will be haunted by dreams about my homeland.
離家初記宿寒溪，	I remember I lodged beside a chill creek when I had just left home—
野店荒村入戶低。	An uninhabited inn in a deserted village with a low gate.
再宿忽訝臨小市，	The second night, I was surprised to come to a small market;
人地生疏難近視。	Both people and places are strange; I am afraid to take a close look.
可憐閨中身！	How pitiful—this body that used to belong to the inner chambers!
可憐亂世苦！	How pitiful—her bitterness of chaotic times!
羅敷有夫夫可依，	If Luofu had a husband, that husband could be relied on.
羅敷無夫誰代主。	Luofu without a husband, on whom can she count?[8]

By "the red turbans," the author means the Taiping army.[9] Dong Baohong was a native of Yizheng, Jiangsu, which the author refers to as Zhenzhou.[10] Presumably, this poem was written about her situation when Taiping troops attacked Yizheng in 1853.[11] The author narrates her experience of fleeing the war after catastrophe befell her hometown. Forced to abandon her home and plunged into a chaotic world, she is terrified and confused. She drifts from place to place, seeking shelter, but it seems that she can never settle down. Bewildered by this strange world that she has not seen before, she lets out her cry of sorrow at being torn from the place where she used to belong, the *gui*: "How pitiful—this body that used to belong to the inner chambers! / How pitiful—her bitterness of chaotic times!" Moreover, she identifies herself as Luofu, a beautiful and clever female persona portrayed in *yuefu*, or Music Bureau song, poems.[12] In one of these songs, Luofu succeeds in discouraging a man who intends to take her by claiming that she has a powerful husband.[13] However, the Luofu in this poem does not have a husband on whom to rely. As a poem mourning her late husband, also in the collection, suggests, Dong Baohong was already widowed at the time.[14] Through these details describing her encounter with the "alien" world as a widow, the poet depicts the powerless and helpless situation of a *guixiu*, or the talented of the inner chambers, who has become a refugee.

One of the poems Dong Baohong wrote on her life in the *gui* will provide a better understanding of what she means by claiming to belong to this space:

閨中雜詩	IN THE BOUDOIR: A MISCELLANEOUS POEM
靜處深閨裏，	Serenely, I dwell in the secluded boudoir,
閒情寓以詩。	Entrusting my idle feelings to poetry.
碧窗橫卷冊，	Beside the emerald window, volumes of books are spread out;
銀管架花枝。	A silver brush is hung on a flowering branch.
繡只春風覺，	Only the spring breeze is aware of my embroidering;
吟惟夜月知。	Only the moon knows when I compose poetry.
紅憐花點徑，	I cherish the red flowers that dot the path;
綠愛柳垂絲。	I love the green willow strands hanging.
得句期兄和，	Coming up with poetic lines, I hope my brother will harmonize with them;
添香怪婢遲。	Adding incense late, I complain to the maid.
幽居偏寂寞，	Living in seclusion, it tends to be solitary;
常分自操持。	As for ordinary matters, I can manage them.
描鳳初非志，	Drawing phoenixes is not my original intent;
塗鴉不點脂。	I can paint, but I do not wear rouge.
父書堆一案，	Father's books pile up on my desk;
母訓退三思。	I step back to reflect often on mother's instruction.
懷古崇芳烈，	Meditating on the past, I admire heroic women;
居今美孝慈。	Living at the present time, I value filial piety and compassion.
粉奩藏翰墨，	In my powder case, I store inkstones;
鏡檻疊文辭。	On my dressing table, my writings are folded.
近事還從俗，	In affairs of our time, I might follow custom as well;
新妝勉入時。	That's why my new makeup is slightly fashionable.
抽身渾一笑，	Turning round, I let out a smile,
洗硯亦臨池。	As I rinse my ink-slab "facing the pond."[15]

In this poem, the author's persona is secure within the inner chambers, enjoying her peaceful everyday life. She is free from household labor yet busy with reading, embroidering, and composing poetry. She is served by maidservants, inspired by her elder brother's and father's learning, and guided by her mother's moral instruction. She does not pay much attention to the fashions of her time but values moral and literary cultivation. With a cluster of parallel couplets, the author describes the typical lifestyle of a well-to-do gentry daughter, or a standard *guixiu*, in times of peace. In her later poems, she repeatedly invokes this scene in expressing her sorrow over the hardship of life as a widow in wartime. In addition to lines such as "In those years I wore light silk robes in my embroidered boudoir. / Who'd expected I would now suffer?"[16] she also composed "Rhapsody on My Life's Encounters," which expresses her bitterness over her suddenly reduced circumstances.[17] In it, she begins with a similar claim, "In the past I was living in my secluded boudoir," and goes on to contrast her previous comfortable life with what "the sudden emergence of the Red Turbans" has brought her.[18] Her marriage into a family plagued by ill fortune was a turning point. Both her mother-in-law and husband passed away after she was married.[19] The difficulties of her life as a widow were further exacerbated by the war. As she claims in another poem, "Recording My Feelings," she feels unable to cope with the harsh reality she faces: "My strength exhausted, there is no place to settle in this world." After this line, she explains in an interlinear note that this is "[d]ue to the disturbance of the Red Turbans."[20] Dong Baohong's repeated reference to her former life in the *gui* demonstrates her strong identification with the normative location of women, and her way of protesting the war is also a well-sheltered *guixiu*'s typical reaction to social upheaval.

The nostalgic memory of the peaceful *guixiu* lifestyle typifies women's textual responses to social disorder. Earlier in the Ming-Qing transition, Cai Runshi (1612–1694)[21] also presented a striking contrast between her old life in the inner chambers and the terrible experiences of war in a long poem, "While I Dwelled in Poverty in the Mountains, My Younger Sister Liansu Came By to Visit Me and Talked about the Difficulties of Wandering as Refugees":

. . .	
長安姚母學針繡，	We learned embroidery from Madam Yao of Chang'an;
餘暇共習詩與賦。	In our spare time we both studied the art of poetry.
武陵梅閣同硯席，	We shared desk and ink at Wuling's Plum Blossom Pavilion;
相攜踏遍桃源路。	Holding hands, we explored all the paths to the Peach Blossom Spring.
昔何歡娛今何苦！	How happy our life was, and how miserable it is now!
遭難流離更多故。	After the calamity, we've suffered more misfortunes as refugees;
河陽驛道二子失，	I lost two sons on Heyang's post station road
懷孟山坳雪中仆。	And collapsed in snow in the valley of Mount Huaimeng.
會逢舊僕得再生，	Running into an old servant, I was able to survive;
十旬破廟悲流寓。	Three months in an old shabby temple, I grieved at my homelessness.

風號時聞殺掠聲，	In the howling wind, I often heard noises of killing and plunder;
血腥觸鼻更憂怖。	Smelling the stench of blood, I felt more worried and afraid.
千言萬語說不盡，	Thousands of words cannot describe what I've suffered;
相對嘿嘿淚霑露。	Facing each other, we cried with tears like rain and dew.[22]

Cai Runshi was the wife of the Ming loyalist and martyr Huang Daozhou (1585–1646).[23] She became Huang's second wife in 1626, when she was only fifteen.[24] After the fall of the Ming in 1644, Huang Daozhou joined the Southern Ming regimes and actively participated in the restoration cause.[25] He was captured by Qing troops in 1646 and killed in the same year for refusing to surrender to the Qing.[26] While Huang devoted himself to his military campaigns, Cai stayed home in Fujian taking care of the household.[27] She wrote the above poem after Huang's death.[28] The "calamity" brought her tremendous loss and emotional trauma. She lost her husband, sons, and home and confronted bloody violence face-to-face. The ordeal she suffered is, in her words, beyond description.

The peaceful and joyful life in the *gui* that Cai Runshi once shared with her sister, Liansu, can be revisited only in memory. Given the traditional practice of referring to a female friend or relative of one's own generation as a sister, Liansu was not necessarily her biological sister; however, as suggested in the poem, they were very close and seem to have grown up together. The author recalls primarily activities typical of the *guixiu* lifestyle at that time, such as embroidering, composing poetry, and sightseeing. The pavilion mentioned in the line "We shared desk and ink at Wuling's Plum Blossom Pavilion" was likely a place in the family's garden that they frequented in the old days. The Peach Blossom Spring mentioned in the following line, "Holding hands, we explored all the paths to the Peach Blossom Spring," may refer to a place they had actually visited. Sightseeing was not unusual for women of their status. But the Peach Blossom Spring is also a literary allusion to an ideal world of peace and innocence hidden from the vulgar and chaotic world.[29] Recalling this imagined utopia would have helped the author escape in her imagination from the terrible circumstances she faced.[30]

The nostalgic sentiments expressed by Cai Runshi can be observed even in the writings of Huang Yuanjie (ca. 1620–ca. 1669), an early "professional" woman who challenged traditional gender boundaries.[31]

Huang lost her home after the Qing army occupied Yangzhou in 1645. She spent the remainder of her life wandering around Jiangsu and Zhejiang, relying on her artistic skills to support her family. She, rather than her husband, became the breadwinner of their household. In her poems she is often bitter about her wandering life and expresses a sense of powerlessness. Lines such as "There are one thousand poems in my bag to which I can entrust my feelings; / Although my home does not have any walls, I always think of returning" reveal a strong sense of nostalgia for home and stability.[32] In "Harmonizing with Meicun's Four Pieces on Mandarin Duck Lake," her four-poem reply to the male poet Wu Weiye (1609–1672), Huang Yuanjie writes, "Since like bramble flying with the wind, I've been seeking a hiding place. / Where can you send your poems to me when they're done?" and "I recall in the past in the gilded boudoir I used to match your tunes / By the bank of the small river outside No-Sorrow City."[33] These lines do not challenge the image of Huang Yuanjie as a boundary-crossing figure but rather show her strong sense of misfortune as a displaced woman.

However, women poets did not always represent themselves as powerless, dislocated victims of war. Even when war had led to the destruction of their homes, the boudoir could function as a spiritual site from which they drew both comfort and strength to empower themselves in adversity. Wu Chai's (1838–1874) boudoir and study, Pavilion of Autumn Sash (Peiqiuge), played just such a role in helping her survive the upheaval of the Taiping Rebellion. Wu Chai was a native of Wu County, Jiangsu. She was married in 1858, but her husband soon died from disease, and the son born shortly after succumbed to illness while Wu was fleeing the war.[34] The Pavilion of Autumn Sash was likely the name of Wu Chai's boudoir before she married and experienced all these misfortunes. Her collection, *Posthumous Manuscripts from the Pavilion of Autumn Sash*, was named after this place. As a significant location in her life and memory, it frequently appears in the poems, as in "At the Pavilion of Autumn Sash, I Sit at Night with My Sisters and Write This Poem for My Second Eldest Sister Who Is Married to a Family of Lujiang":

頻年蹤跡感難知，	Wandering all these years—it's hard to know how we feel;
殘竹哀絲又一時。	In the music of broken bamboo flutes and sad strings, another season passed.
斜月簾鉤風弄影，	The setting moon hangs by the curtain hook; the wind plays with the shadows;

小窗燈火夜填詞。	Beside lamplight by the small window, we compose song lyrics.
兵戈聚首良非易,	Indeed, getting together in the midst of soldiers and weapons is not easy,
涕淚餘生最可悲。	But the bitterest sorrow would be to weep the rest of our lives.
太息蘋蘩勞悴甚,	Sighing from all your chores, you're exhausted and wasting away;
為君重賦碩人詩。	Again, I write a poem for you, matching "A Splendid Woman."³⁵

As the title indicates, Wu wrote this poem for her second-eldest sister. The gathering of the sisters recorded in this poem seems to have taken place during this married sister's visit to her natal family. As the poet suggests, it was an unusual and moving reunion. They must have suffered tremendously from the war and probably had not expected to be reunited. On this precious occasion, they are exchanging poetry again beside their "small window." The moon and the lamp might have witnessed this activity many times before, but this meeting takes place under extraordinary circumstances. Outside their window, the world is teeming with soldiers and weapons. They are not sure when they will see one another again. The author dedicated this poem to her second-eldest sister, encouraging her to be strong and positive. Attempting to cheer her up, Wu also recalls a poem that she presumably wrote on the occasion of her sister's wedding, praising her beauty and virtue. This poem was modeled on the poem "A Splendid Woman" (Shuo ren), in the *Book of Songs*.³⁶ At this moment, the boudoir provides the sisters with a space in which to recollect their pleasant memories and seek emotional support from one another.

After writing the above poem recording their reunion, Wu Chai composed another poem, "Playfully I Reply to My Own Poem on Behalf of My Sister":

歲寒仗有故人知,	At year's end, thankfully, family and friends care for one;
一角湖山招隱時。	It's when we can retreat to a corner of the lakes and mountains.
持鐵曉吟梁苑雪,	Holding iron castanets in the morning, we sing about the snow in Liang Garden;
然脂暝寫漢宮詞。	Burning oil in the night, we write the lyrics of the Han Palace.
好懷續史他年志,	We should hold the ambition to write a supplementary history in the future;

莫作寄公流寓悲。	Do not compose poems on the sorrows of the fugitive's wandering.
長憶當年風雨夕,	Always remember in this stormy evening,
綠窗分韻共裁詩。	We allot rhymes and compose poetry together by the green window.[37]

In speaking for her sister, Wu Chai is in effect speaking to both herself and her sisters. She encourages herself and her sisters to maintain optimism and faith that they can manage to survive and live a meaningful life. Although they cannot control historical changes, they can count on one another and have their aspirations to keep their spirits high. They can also withdraw from the worldly realm to the mountains, where they can continue to engage in meaningful pursuits. As Wu Chai suggests in the second couplet, composing poetry, particularly poems that meditate on history, is a worthwhile ambition. Liang Garden (Liang Yuan) was an imperial garden in Kaifeng established by the Han prince Liu Wu. It later fell into ruin and was frequently invoked by literati poets to suggest the vicissitudes of history. The Tang poet Li Duan (fl. 770), for example, wrote lines such as "The Sui Palace is far away on the river; / The Liang Garden is buried in deep snow."[38] Wu Chai also desires that she and her sisters write poetry expressing their reflections on the historical situation. The phrase "burning oil and writing at night" (*ran zhi ming xie*), in the line "Burning oil in the night, we write the lyrics of the Han Palace," is borrowed from Xu Ling's preface to *New Songs from a Jade Terrace*. The poet uses it, on one level, to depict the sisters' diligence in writing and, on another level, to draw an association with feminine-style writings such as the subgenre of "palace lyrics" (*gongci*) established in the Tang, a genre similar to the boudoir plaint but focused on palace women. By paralleling two poetic styles—historical and feminine—in the couplet, the author suggests the range of their poetic writings. In the third couplet, with the line "We should hold the ambition to write a supplementary history [*xu shi*] in the future," alluding to Ban Zhao, who completed the *Book of the Former Han* (*Han shu*) after her brother Ban Gu's death, the author goes on to make more explicit her intention of being a subject witnessing and writing history, like Ban Zhao, rather than a refugee merely lamenting her sufferings.[39] Finally, the poem returns to the moment in which the sisters were composing poetry and supporting one another at their "green window," a moment to be remembered.

Referred to by the synecdoche "small window" or "green window," the boudoir is a central image in the above poems by Wu Chai. As in *The Anthology of Correct Beginnings*, the boudoir also functions in these poems as a space for the *guixiu*'s cultural activities, such as poetry composition. However, the vignette of the sisters' reunion in the *gui* is a smaller picture placed within the larger context of social disorder. As the small window reflects "soldiers and weapons" (*bing ge*) and the green window is shaken by the storms of war, these women are no longer circumscribed by the former peace and seclusion of the *gui*. Wu Chai pushes the women's sphere to the sociohistorical front.

The belief that she could retreat to her boudoir to pursue her goals indeed empowered Wu Chai when she faced difficult situations. In 1860, when the Taipings occupied Jiangsu, Wu Chai and her husband's family fled from their home city and were fugitives for months, during which time her one-year-old son fell ill and died. In the years that followed, she seemed to be always on the run. Most of the poems in the second half of her collection record moments of fleeing from place to place. Their titles indicate that in 1863 she traveled through at least five cities and towns in Jiangsu and Zhejiang, including Haimen, Meili, Shanghai, Loujiang, and Yinxi.[40] In a long poem titled "After Being Stopped by Wind at Huangpu, I Was Stopped by Snow Again When Arriving in Pudong," she recorded her experience of being caught by a snowstorm while traveling by boat near Shanghai. Having described the terrible conditions of the snowstorm, she continues with the following lines:

. . .

湖山無恙儻招隱，	If lakes and mountains are well, I could retreat there;
終期炙硯佩秋閣。	In the end I hope to heat up my inkstone at the Pavilion of Autumn Sash.
明發衝寒歸去來，	Tomorrow I set out in the chill air to return home;
故園梅樹定含萼。	Plum trees in my old garden must be in bud.[41]

Once the poet survives this storm or the country survives this period of disorder, she hopes to return to her boudoir/study and devote herself to the writing of poetry. The Pavilion of Autumn Sash may not have survived physically, but it has become a spiritual site to which she turns for hope and strength. A close friend, Yu Menghua (fl. 1864), painted a picture of the Pavilion of Autumn Sash and sent it to Wu Chai as a gift. She also inscribed four poems on the picture, which Wu Chai included in her poetry collection.⁴² The following are the second and the fourth:

POEM TWO

舊閣猶聞說佩秋，	I still hear people talking about your old boudoir, Autumn Sash;
紉蘭應許抵忘憂。	Wearing orchids may help us to forget sorrow.
而今為年家山遠，	Now you have been away from your homeland for a year;
尺幅批來當臥游。	I paint this picture for you to visit in spirit.⁴³

POEM FOUR

同是飛鴻踏雪泥，	Both are flying geese landing on snowy mud;
桃源暫借一枝棲。	Let's borrow a branch at the Peach Blossom Spring on which to perch.
故鄉尚有烽煙警，	Our hometown is still on alert with beacon smoke;
愁枕孤城聽鼓鼙。	On my sad pillow in the isolated city I listen to battle drums.⁴⁴

It seems that Wu Chai's Pavilion of Autumn Sash was famous among her friends. Yu Menghua may have been one of the frequent visitors. According to Wu Chai, Yu was also living an unsettled life as a refugee at the time.⁴⁵ The image of "flying geese landing on snowy mud," meaning the traces of a wanderer or fugitive's life, characterizes Yu's similar situation. Painting this picture also gave her a moment of escape from the depressing reality. Yu Menghua suggests to the absent Wu Chai that she can make a "visit in spirit" (*wo you*) to her former abode. The spiritual site of the boudoir plays the role of the Peach Blossom Spring for these women in a world full of beacon smoke.

Nostalgia for the peaceful life in the *gui* reveals these women's deeper sense of displacement as a specific social group, the *guixiu*. Despite its physical destruction, the boudoir still played a significant role in their writings. These displaced subjects invoke their normative location not only to reveal the degree to which social turmoil affected their lives but also to maintain their subjectivity in the context of social disintegration. However, while the turmoil of the larger world broke up these women's studies or pavilions, it also broadened their perspectives on life and history. Significantly, in their poetic depiction, the *gui* no longer is an isolated world of women but is connected to the larger social and historical background.

EMBRACING POLITICAL CONCERNS

War and social chaos brought tremendous trauma and loss to women. Women were not only distressed by their personal losses, however, but also began to reflect on broader social and political concerns, a significant change in Qing women's poetry at this critical juncture, rife with social disorder.[46] Women's concern with the sociopolitical realm as expressed in their writings is a prominent sign that they were beginning to address the world beyond the inner chambers. In expressing their political sentiments, writing women employed both *shi* and *ci* genres.

As the *ci* form is generally divided into two stylistic categories, masculine and feminine, these two categories also point to two distinct thematic foci: while the former expresses sentiments associated with social and political concerns (a distinctively male arena), the latter deals with private feelings and emotions that are often associated with the inner, domestic sphere. Women writers were presumed to belong "naturally" to the latter realm. Affected by their historical and personal contexts, however, many Ming-Qing women authors wrote lyrics that present a much more complicated reality. Their perspectives may still have been framed by the "small window" of the boudoir, but from this small window, they began to pay attention to national crises and offer their opinions on historical changes.

Their views were, of course, often different from those of men. Without access to office or political power, they did not express frustration over the difficulties of pursuing an official career. Loyalism, however, seemed to be a legitimate political stance for a woman to adopt under the extraordinary historical circumstances of dynastic transition. Regarded by her contemporary critics as "the greatest gentry woman poet since the Southern Song," Xu Can (ca. 1610—after 1677) is perhaps the best-known representative of an early expression of "loyalist lyrics" by women.[47] Writings by Xu Can and other women provide the first indication that women authors were beginning to represent their political sentiments in the *ci* genre.[48] Their interaction with the conventional poetics of the *ci* produced another vibrant arena in which women poets were able to transform the boudoir topos.

Xu Can was not alone as a witness to historic upheavals but was joined by many other women writers of her time. Given the substantial scholarship already dedicated to Xu Can, it will be useful to focus here on one of her lesser-known contemporaries, Zhu Zhongmei

(1622–1672). In her song lyric "In the Summer of Dingyou (1657), I Read Mme. Chen Su'an's *Ci*. Moved, I Harmonized with Her Rhyme," to the tune "Full River Red," Zhu Zhongmei writes, "Casting eyes toward the passes and rivers, I wipe my tears in vain; / Heartbroken, with a cup of wine I invite the moon to drink."[49] Written after reading a poem by Mme. Chen Su'an (Xu Can), Zhu's lyric is similarly replete with melancholy over the misfortunes of her country. Zhu Zhongmei was the wife of Li Yuanding (1595–1670), also a chief minister who served two dynasties. Zhu and Xu became acquainted with each other when they accompanied their husbands to posts in Beijing and exchanged several poems. She shared with Xu Can an interest in poetry and loyalist sentiments for the Ming.[50] Although she was less upset than Xu about her husband's decision to serve in the Qing and tried to understand his taking the office as service to the people, she herself was deeply distraught over the fall of the Ming. The following lines from one of her *shi* poems illustrate her feelings:

荒城處處傷離黍，	Every corner of the deserted city makes me mourn the millet crops;
舊燕飛飛覓畫梁。	Swallows of the past fly around, looking for painted beams.
家國可堪寥落甚，	How can I bear the misery of my home country?
怡情何地足滄浪。	To ease my feeling, where can I step in the Canglang River?[51]

Upon seeing the city scarred by war, the poet feels sorrow over the "millet" (*lishu*) crops. Though its syllable order is reversed, the term is derived from the poem "Millet" (Shuli) in the *Book of Songs*, in which the minister of Zhou mourns the loss of his kingdom. It later became a conventional term expressing sorrow over one's lost country.[52] The image of "swallows of the past"—derived from the well-known lines "the swallows from the halls of the Wangs and Xies of the past / Fly into the house of ordinary people" by the Tang poet Liu Yuxi—is also a nostalgic symbol of a vanished dynasty.[53] In adopting these poetic conventions, Zhu Zhongmei demonstrates her emotional reaction to the dynastic cataclysm. However, she does not end her poem here but offers her reflection on this historical tragedy in the final line "To ease my feeling, where can I step in the Canglang River?" The allusion to the Canglang River embraces several levels of meaning. The term originally comes from a folk song of Chu, "When the water of the Canglang is clear, it can be used to wash the strings of my cap. / When the water of the Canglang is muddy, it can be used to wash my

Inside Out

feet," which is cited in classics such as "Fisherman" (Yufu) in *Songs of the South* and *Mencius*.[54] While the former work discusses how one should adapt to one's broader historical milieu, the latter reaches the conclusion that, just as different conditions of the river cause people to react differently, a country's fall is due not to its enemy's attack but to the faults of its own people. Judging from the overall meaning of her poem, Zhu Zhongmei uses the allusion to express her profound sense of alienation as she confronts the new age.

Zhu Zhongmei also incorporates her historical reflections into the depiction of the boudoir space, as her *ci* to the tune "Waves Scour the Sands," subtitled "Stirred by Feelings in the Rain," shows:

香度小窗中，	Fragrance wafts through my small window;
燕啄花叢。	I see swallows pecking at the masses of flowers.
雨聲滴碎遠來鐘。	Rain spatters, interrupting the sounds of a far-off bell.
家信杳然何處覓，	Hearing nothing from my family, where can I seek news of them?
且待新鴻。	I wait for the new wild geese.
睽越此情同，	Gazing across, our feelings should be the same;
歸念匆匆。	My thoughts of returning home are hurried.
濕雲迢遞鎖明宮。	Moist clouds extending far off lock up the Ming palaces.
為問滄桑無限事，	If one asks about the profound matter of historical change,
今已三逢。	It's been three years.[55]

Zhu Zhongmei's husband, Li Yuanding, began to serve in the Qing court in 1645 and retired in 1659. As the final lines indicate, this song lyric must have been written around 1647, three years after the fall of the Ming. At the time, the author would have been living in Beijing, far from her home in Jishui, Jiangxi. Zhu Zhongmei begins by locating her perspective as from the "small window" and gradually reveals a gaze that looks far afield. The boudoir filled with fragrance and the swallows and flowers in the spring garden constitute a typical feminine setting, within which, according to boudoir poetic conventions, one expects to find tender sentiments such as lamentations over unrequited love. However, the rain that arrives disrupts the poet's contemplation of the serene garden scene, and the sounds of a bell perhaps signal the arrival of news from her distant home. The song lyric then turns to the motif of homesickness. Although Zhu Zhongmei shows in one poem an understanding of her husband's service for the new dynasty, she repeatedly expresses in other poems her desire that her husband withdraw from officialdom. The "return home" is a political gesture meant to preserve one's integrity. The author casts her gaze upon the palaces, which she still refers to as belonging to the past Ming, demonstrating that the sentiment of missing her home is intimately connected to that of mourning for her lost country. She seems to use the rain and clouds as metaphors of the Qing, a violent storm that locks up her native land. From the perspective of her small window, this song lyric by Zhu Zhongmei provides a broad view of her distant home and former country.

Women's *ci* writings, represented by Xu Can's and Zhu Zhongmei's loyalist lyrics, demonstrate that women's vision of the world went beyond the feminine space of the boudoir, and their political sentiments further expanded the thematic scope of boudoir poetry. Associating the boudoir with political sentiments was not these women's original contribution. The Southern Tang poet Li Yu had appropriated the boudoir plaint as tropes and conceits for expressing his nostalgic sentiments over the loss of his kingdom.[56] Lyrics by the late Ming poet Chen Zilong written in the context of his love affair with Liu Rushi and his loyalist activity also created a feminine space evoking mixed feelings of loyalism and personal love.[57] However, Xu Can's and Zhu Zhongmei's writings brought into the boudoir space women's own expression of political sentiments. By doing so, they crossed gender boundaries on both political and literary levels. The "small window" of the boudoir was opened even more.

CONSIDERING GENDER BOUNDARIES

When women began to confront the larger world and consider what kind of role they could play in reacting to historical change, some of them became aware of the gender restrictions imposed on females. In particular, they recognized the *gui* as a place defining and limiting women's role in society and began to use their poetry to protest the gender inequality it embodied.

This use of poetry is well illustrated by one of Gu Zhenli's song lyrics to the tune "Full River Red," subtitled "Hearing an Alarm in the Government Office at Chuhuang," another example of the subversive mode of articulation with which Gu addressed her life and position in relation to the *gui*. Considered "heterodox" by many because of her unconventional poetry, Gu was among the most outspoken critics of the subjection of women. This lyric also asserts her critical stance against gender inequality. More importantly for this chapter, it shows how her reflection on women's place in society was directly triggered by political concerns related to the Ming-Qing transition:

僕本恨人，	I am at root an aggrieved person,
那禁得，	How could I stand
悲哉秋氣。	The sad air of autumn?
恰又是，	Just then,
將歸送別，	It is again the moment to return home and say farewell,
登山臨水。	To climb the mountain overlooking the river.
一片角聲煙靄外，	The sounds of a horn rise beyond the mist,
數行雁字波光裡。	A few lines of wild geese reflected in the shimmering waves.
試憑高，	Trying to stand higher,
覓取舊妝樓，	I search for my former dressing tower,
誰同倚。	Yet who will be my companion?
鄉夢遠，	My native place distant as a dream,
書迢遞。	And letters far off.
人半載，	For half a year now,
辭家矣。	I have been away from home.
嘆吳頭楚尾，	I sigh that between the far ends of Wu and Chu,
倏然孤寄。	Suddenly I am a lone sojourner.
江上空憐商女曲，	On the river, in vain I'm moved by the melody of singing girls,
閨中漫灑神州淚。	In the boudoir, to no purpose I shed tears for my country.
算縞綦，	I must ask why women
何必讓男兒，	Must yield to men?
天應忌!	Heaven should forbid this![58]

The tune pattern of "Full River Red" was a well-recognized form in masculine-style lyrics. Ming-Qing women appropriated the form in different ways in order to express their political concerns.[59] Gu Zhenli's *ci* cited above bears many masculine qualities of self-representation. She begins by introducing herself in a strong first-person voice, which is rarely heard in women's writing: "I am at root an aggrieved person" (Pu ben henren). *Pu* is usually used by men as a first-person pronoun. This is a line quoted from "Rhyme Prose on Grief" (Hen fu), by the Southern Dynasties poet Jiang Yan. Identifying herself using literati rhetoric, Gu seems to consciously portray herself as a person with a masculine rather than a female nature. However, with the terms "dressing tower" (*zhuanglou*) and *gui* in the following lines, she also shows an awareness of her supposed place in society. This contradiction, as the lyric progresses, gradually reveals the problematic situation of her gender status.

The line "The sounds of a horn rise beyond the mist" echoes the subtitle "Hearing an Alarm in the Government Office at Chuhuang" and indicates the disorder of the times, as an alarm usually warns of a bandit attack or some other emergency. In these chaotic times, the poet was not only separated from her natal family but was also losing her country. The lines "Trying to stand higher, I search for my former dressing tower, / Yet who will be my companion?" suggest that, in searching for her former boudoir, she wishes to go back to her happy life as an unmarried daughter who had not yet experienced the miseries arising from her personal life or from political upheavals. However, even if she could physically return to her home, the larger world has changed.

Standing in the middle of nowhere, the author expresses a sense of displacement. The two lines "On the river, in vain I'm moved by the melody of singing girls" and "In the boudoir, to no purpose I shed tears for my country" further reveal that this displacement implicates gender and politics. The phrase "the melody of singing girls" (*shangnü qu*) alludes to "the music of people who have lost their country."[60] By this phrase and the term "my country" (*shenzhou*, literally "my sacrosanct land"), Gu unambiguously asserts her loyalty to the fallen Ming. Meanwhile, as the singing girl is associated with the entertainment quarters frequented by men, Gu may, from her gendered perspective, be suggesting a contrast between two different reactions to the historical change: while some spineless men are still entertaining themselves in the pleasure quarters after the loss of the state, she, a woman dwelling "in the boudoir" to whom politics is off limits, is concerned about the country. By noting her supposed social place and her apparently futile political concern, Gu Zhenli's lyric expresses not only bitter irony but also deep frustration. Thus, filled with sorrow and anger, she ends the lyric with a rejection of women's subordinate role: "I must ask why women must yield to men? / Heaven should forbid this!"

There were indeed a few exceptional women such as Liu Shu (b. 1620) and Qin Liangyu (d. 1668) who stepped out of the *gui* to participate in loyalist resistance.[61] But as women were socially and symbolically associated with the *gui*, they were in general denied access to the political world. This explains why other women poets continued to voice similar frustration. For example, women of later generations, such as Chen Yunlian (fl. 1840), also acknowledged that their consignment to the *gui* left women without an institutional place in the outer realm. In the beginning of her poem "Inscribed on the Painting of Mme. Cheng Joining the Army," Chen offers her observations and analysis of the frustrating reality women faced:

男兒生世間，	Men born into this world,
功業封王侯。	Their meritorious business is to pursue noble rank.
女兒處閨閣，	Women located in the inner chambers,
有志不得酬。	Their ambitions cannot be fulfilled.
讀書空是破萬卷，	Reading thousands of books in vain,
焉能簪筆登瀛洲？	How can a woman ascend up to Yingzhou by her brush?
胸懷韜略復何用，	Full of knowledge and tactics, what is the use?
焉能帷幄參軍謀？	How can she enter the general's camp to give military advice?[62]

. . .

The identity of this Mme. Cheng is not known. According to the clues provided by the title and content of the poem, she painted a portrait of herself carrying a sword. In inscribing this painting of Mme. Cheng (perhaps at the request of Cheng), Chen Yunlian composed a sixteen-line *yuefu* poem. She begins with a bold observation on the unequal allotment of gender roles. Confined to the inner chambers, there is no way for a woman to pursue the sort of career depicted in Cheng's picture. She then bursts with emotion as she poses two rhetorical questions on the purposelessness of women's learning and talents. "Yingzhou" refers to both an isle of immortals and the Hall of Literature established by the Tang emperor Taizong, who recruited scholars for their outstanding literary talent. Being admitted to this hall was a great honor, called "entering Yingzhou" (*deng Yingzhou*).[63] This honor and "to give military advice" (*can junmou*) are the highest forms of recognition for literary and political talent, but women have no access to them, even though they have mastered equivalent knowledge and skills. She goes on to acknowledge in the poem that there are indeed exceptional cases such as the legendary heroine Mulan:

千載僅聞木蘭事，	In a thousand years, I only heard the story of Mulan,
代父從征棄簪珥。	Who threw away hairpins and earrings to join the army on behalf of her father. . . .

夫人有志亦相同，	Madam also has the same aspiration,
畫作從軍佩劍容。	Painting a portrait carrying a sword to join the army.
但求聖代無征戰，	Let's wish that our august dynasty has no war;
莫嘆蛾眉老此中。[64]	Don't lament the woman in this picture growing old.

Although Chen Yunlian admires Cheng's aspiration to be a Mulan, she hopes that there will be no opportunity for Cheng to fulfill her ambition. With this ending, the poet both expresses her wish for peace and finds a solution that relieves the sorrow of women such as Cheng who are frustrated by gender restrictions. While Chen Yunlian was cognizant of the unfair treatment women received in her society, she could not do anything about it. Her later poems suggest that she reacted to disorder only from her prescribed social position.

Despite Chen Yunlian's wish for peace, war soon came to plague both her "august dynasty" and her home in Tianjin. Chen Yunlian was married to Zuo Chen, a native of present-day Changzhou. As one of Chen's poems suggests, in 1837, Zuo Chen went to take his official post in Tianjin,[65] and she later followed him.[66] A port city close to Beijing, Tianjin is a place of crucial military significance. In 1840, after the first Opium War broke out, the British navy sailed north from Guangdong and captured the Dagu forts of Tianjin.[67] Seeking to avoid the war, Chen Yunlian was forced to leave home and take refuge in Baoyang. She records this experience in a group of four poems titled "Writing My Feelings While Traveling at Night." Next to the title, she provides a brief preface: "There is a warning of foreign invaders at the gate of Tianjin, so I take shelter in Baoyang." The first poem is subtitled "Examining My Sword":

飄泊誰憐淚暗彈，	Blown about, who cares about me? I shed tears secretly.
出門草草返何難。	We left home hurriedly, how difficult it will be to return!
夜深膽怯挑燈坐，	Deep in the night, with heart beating I sit up and trim the lamp,
但把吳鉤仔細看。[68]	Only to examine carefully the sword of Wu.

Although she had hoped that Mme. Cheng would not have to use a sword in battle, she now prepares to use one herself. However, her sword would be put to a different use. Her action of examining a sword under a lamp may remind us of a similar gesture in a lyric by

Inside Out

Xin Qiji, but the desolate situation and disturbed feelings expressed in her poem are in sharp contrast with Xin's:

醉里挑燈看劍，	Drunk, I trimmed the lamp and examined my sword;
夢回吹角連營。	Waking up from a dream, I heard bugle calls sounding from camp to camp.
八百里分麾下炙，	Roasted meat of the "eight-hundred-*li*" oxen were portioned out to my soldiers.
五十弦翻塞外聲。	Frontier music rolled out from fifty zither strings.
沙場秋點兵。	On the battlefield I do the autumn inspection of my men.[69]

Whether reality or fantasy, Xin's lines depict the image of a proud and powerful general commanding his troops. He might be frustrated by difficulties, but he is not afraid. And he can be confident that his sword will be used in battle to kill his enemy. But the woman is in a very different situation. Homeless and helpless, the sword for her is a weapon of last resort more likely to be used for taking her own life rather than that of an enemy.[70]

The British navy's threat to Tianjin was temporarily resolved by negotiation, with the Qing government paying a hefty ransom.[71] However, Chen Yunlian did not live a peaceful life thereafter. A decade later, her life was threatened again by the Taiping rebels. In 1853, Taiping troops began their northern campaign, and in October, they pressed on the suburb of Tianjin.[72] Magistrate Xie Zicheng (d. 1853) organized local militias to defend the city.[73] Chen Yunlian witnessed this historical event. She composed a group of twelve quatrains, "Recording the Events of Destroying the Bandits at the Gates of Tianjin," which includes a preface noting the dates: "Beginning from the ninth month [October] of the Guichou year [1853] and ending in the second month [March] of the Jiayin year [1854]."[74] The first poem reads:

賊勢鴟張逼郡城，	Pressing on the city, the bandits are rampant;
自憐閨閣枉談兵。	In the inner chambers, I pity myself discussing military affairs in vain.
蚩尤妖霧如延及，	If the evil fog of Chi You extends to me,
便擬懷沙效屈平。	Composing "Huai sha," I plan to follow Qu Ping.[75]

Once again, the poet shows the powerlessness of a woman in the inner chambers when confronting social upheaval. She may want to react to the conflict as active male heroes do, but she knows that, as a woman, she has no institutional outlet for her actions. As always, she can only resort to the extreme form of self-defense, suicide, to protect her integrity and chastity. While Chen only suggests her suicidal thoughts in her previous poem, in this poem she unambiguously expresses her intention to commit suicide in case of emergency. The way in which the poet refers to the Taipings as Chi You, the evil rebel who defied the Yellow Emperor in legend, reveals her dread of the destructive force of the rebellion and her loyalty to the regime to which she belonged. If her integrity and chastity are threatened, she is determined to commit suicide as did Qu Yuan (courtesy name Yuan, name Ping). "Embracing Sands" (Huai sha) is believed to be the last piece Qu Yuan wrote before he drowned himself in the Miluo River upon learning that his country had fallen to the Qin.[76] By invoking Qu Yuan as her role model, Chen Yunlian demonstrates her intent to choose loyalty, purity, and integrity, values celebrated in her culture, over her own life. This seems to be the only way for her to empower herself from her gendered position under these extreme circumstances. The Taipings were defeated by the Qing troops and local military forces, and Chen Yunlian survived along with the city. However, countless women known and unknown did choose to end their lives during periods of turmoil in the Ming and Qing.[77] The issue of women's suicide in the context of disorder is beyond the purpose of this chapter, but it is necessary to point out that their suicidal tendency in extremely difficult situations had much to do with the social restrictions placed upon them that foreclosed other responses to disorder.

Chen Yunlian's contemporary He Huisheng (d. 1858) provides another example of a woman considering gender boundaries in a time of chaos. He Huisheng was a native of Shanhua, Hunan. In 1853, she became the second wife of Long Qirui (1814–58), a prominent scholar and official.[78] Long obtained his *jinshi* degree in 1841 and was appointed a compiler (*xiuzhuan*) in the Hanlin Academy.[79] He later worked as the provincial literary chancellor (*xuezheng*) in Hubei before returning to his hometown of Guilin, Guangxi, in 1850. When the Taipings attacked Guilin in 1852, he organized military forces and defeated the Taiping troops. In 1856, he was appointed to a post in Jiangxi, where he worked until his death in 1858.[80] Because of his career, He Huisheng and Long Qirui spent much of their five years of marriage living separately.

It is not clear when the following poem was written, but the poet clearly speaks as a longing wife:

思婦歎	THE LAMENT OF A LONGING WIFE
涼月皎皎涼風鳴，	Bright, bright the cool moon; a cool wind soughs,
打窗落葉無停聲。	Tapping the window, ceaseless the sound of falling leaves.
階前蟋蟀喞還駐，	On the front steps crickets chirr and pause,
金翦生寒露氣橫。	Gilded scissors generating chill, dewy air spreads.
縫君衣，淚空揮。	Sewing a robe for you, my tears shed in vain.
焉能化作長天雁，	How can I become a wild goose in the vast sky
從君萬里西南飛。	Flying southwest to follow you ten thousand *li* away?[81]

Here, the author adopts an ancient-style *yuefu*. Whether in terms of the speaking voice or the language, the poem is a typical version of the boudoir plaint. Given that the poet was indeed often separated from her husband, the performance of the abandoned-woman persona in this poem is not merely an exercise. In ending the poem, the persona expresses a strong desire to go beyond the *gui* to follow her beloved. Overdetermined by the longing-wife convention, the sense of being confined in the *gui* in these ending lines may appear to fall into the category of traditional boudoir sentiments. However, they may convey deeper meanings if read together with a poem that appears earlier in the same collection, "Wandering in the Fields after the Clear-Bright Day":

春老清明後，	After the Clear-Bright Day, spring grows old;
閒行負郭田。	Idly, I roam in the outskirts of the city.
草長盤馬地，	Grasses growing in the race course,
花落打魚船。	Flowers falling, beating on fishing boats.
新漲平隄闊，	The newly risen river broadens out, reaching the level of the dike;
長橋野寺連。	A long bridge links a temple in wilderness.
嗟余困巾幗，	Sighing over myself trapped in the camp of women,
空自度年年。	Living year after year in vain.[82]

In this poem, the poet describes what she views as she strolls in the suburbs in spring. But the natural scene outside the inner chambers does not make her forget where she belongs. The seasonal changes remind her that time passes, yet her years spent in the boudoir are meaningless. The feeling of ennui typifies poems with the theme of a woman contemplating spring scenes, but the motif of emptiness the poet brings up here does not fall into the conventional category of "mourning spring" (*shang chun*). The phrase "trapped in the camp of women" unambiguously points to the poet's reflection on her gender.

For her, it is because she is a woman that she cannot live a more meaningful life. The diction she chooses, "trap" (*kun*), reveals the degree to which she is plagued by the problem. Read in this context, her lines "How can I become a wild goose in the long sky / Flying southwest to follow you ten thousand *li* away?" in "The Lament of a Longing Wife" may also convey her desire to go to the outer realm as her husband freely did, although ironically by "following" (*cong*).

Having encountered the Taiping Rebellion firsthand, He Huisheng also played an active role in poetic witnessing. Her "Four Poems: Stirred by Events," written after 1853, records the worsening situation: "Imperial troops have been exhausted, / yet rebels and bandits are still rampant."[83] As she began to be concerned with the national cataclysm, He Huisheng felt more compelled to reflect on her place in society. Following the four poems mentioned above, she composed another group, "Four Poems: Boldly Expressing My Opinion," two of which further discuss the gender issue that she initiated in previous poems. The first poem reads:[84]

天涯擾擾盡風塵，	The world is disturbed, completely filled with wind and dust;
欲報君恩愧此身。	Wanting to requite the emperor's favor, I'm ashamed of this body.
若使朝廷用巾幗，	If the court could have used womankind,
高涼應有洗夫人。	There would definitely have been a Mme. Xian in Gaoliang.[85]

Having described the country in crisis, He Huisheng expresses her desire to dedicate herself to it. Like Chen Yunlian, however, she also realizes that because she is a woman, she is not qualified to enter the political sphere. She then suggests that if the court, by which she means the political system of her time, allowed a place for women, there would be heroines like Mme. Xian who could save the country (including, no doubt, herself). Mme. Xian (ca. 512–602), also known as Mme. Qiaoguo, was the wife of Feng Bao, the prefect of Gaoliang Prefecture in the Liang and Sui dynasties.[86] She played an instrumental role in helping her husband with administrative and political affairs and was especially recognized for her suppression of rebels in the region.[87] Gaoliang was located in the west of Guangdong, which was close to Guangxi, where the Taiping Rebellion started. The woman poet is confident that women could make significant contributions to curbing the chaos if they were allowed to do so. As she goes on to claim in the second poem, she is eager to play the part of a hero:

恨不沙場萬里行,	How I wish I could go to the battlefield ten thousand *li* away!
豈辭馬上請長纓?	Would I have refused to join the army on horseback?
笑他碌碌稱男子,	Laughing at those mediocre ones calling themselves men,
投筆何嘗為聖明。	Did they throw aside brushes for our sacred emperor?[88]

In direct and forceful tones, He Huisheng voices her eagerness to participate in military campaigns. The beginning two lines read as though she is talking back to someone questioning her intentions. After providing an affirmative answer, He Huisheng goes on to criticize men, the first-class citizens in her society who, in her opinion, lack first-class qualities. "Throw aside brushes" (*toubi*), an allusion to the story of Ban Chao (32–102), refers to those who abandoned their scholarly careers to join the army when the country was in a state of emergency.[89] Yet He Huisheng is not convinced that those so-called men indeed care about the country. As the title "Bold Words" (Fang yan) suggests, these poems were intended to boldly voice her opinion. Although the woman's voice had been used to express criticism of incapable men in earlier poetry, He Huisheng's proclamation of herself as a heroine who could save the country and her condemnation of incapable and disloyal men would still have been striking statements in her time.[90] Frustrated by the unfair treatment they received, women such as Gu Zhenli and He Huisheng turned their frustration into cynicism about male incompetence.

Although He Huisheng could openly express her critique of gender inequality, she could not actually fulfill her ambition. She could only entrust to her husband the fulfillment of her ambitious goals:

贈外	POEM PRESENTED TO MY HUSBAND
回思繡閣昔塗鴉,	Recalling the old days scribbling in the embroidered boudoir,
楊柳依依謝女家。	Among fresh green willows, it is the home of the Xie daughter.
不是流鶯傳消息,	If it is not migrating orioles who pass on news,
誰傳春信與秦嘉?	Who will convey the spring message to Qin Jia?
橫流四海盡煙塵,	All over the world is smoke and dust,
哪有心言兒女情。	Who has the mood to talk about love?
我已無才困巾幗,	Trapped in the camp of women, I'm without talent,
願君勳業繼文成。	But I hope that your meritorious efforts continue to build on Wencheng's.[91]

This poem appears almost at the end of He Huisheng's collection. It was most likely written between 1856 and 1858 while Long Qirui was serving in his post in Jiangxi. In it, the poet begins by nostalgically recalling her earlier years as an unmarried daughter in her *gui*. Despite the humble way of referring to her writing (or painting) as "scribbling," her self-identification as "the Xie daughter," the recognized talented woman Xie Daoyun, demonstrates the pride she takes in her learning and poetic talent. On the basis of this talent, she fashions herself as a wife who is intellectually compatible with her husband. Qin Jia and his wife Xu Shu in the Han period were the earliest example of a couple who exchanged poetry.[92] By calling her husband "Qin Jia," the woman poet is in fact emphasizing their matched talent. However, in the world of beacon smoke and battlefield dust, she is in no mood to express love. Instead, she encourages him to establish himself in his political career, because there is no way for her, a woman, to achieve similar status. In the last couplet, the poet repeats herself by mentioning "being trapped in the camp of women"; she contrasts this with her husband's career through which he could match the accomplishments of Wencheng, the Ming scholar and minister Liu Ji (1311–75), who helped found the Ming.[93] This contrast again conveys her discontent with her gender status.

In 1858, Long Qirui died in office in Jiangxi, and He Huisheng committed suicide soon after.[94] Four sons survived her, including her stepson Long Jidong. According to Long Jidong's recollection, she was extremely saddened by her husband's death. Her suicide appeared to be well planned and determined: she dressed up and then hanged herself on the lintel of her bed after the completion of her husband's funeral.[95] He Huisheng wrote a letter before committing suicide, but Long Jidong does not mention its contents nor is it included in her collection. It is curious that as an outspoken poet, she did not write a poem before ending her life. Perhaps she thought that the reasons for her suicide were personal and felt no need to justify her act. As Long Jidong suggested, the direct cause of He Huisheng's suicide was most likely her overwhelming sadness over her husband's death.[96] Regardless of the reasons for her suicide, one thing is certain: she had no good reason to convince herself to live. Her death physically perpetuated the predicament repeatedly expressed in her poems, "trapped in the camp of women."

However, the poems she left behind symbolically transcended the physical frame in which she was trapped. He Huisheng's collection,

The Poetic Drafts from the Plum-Blossom Immortal's Studio (Meishenyinguan shicao), was published posthumously in 1874 by her stepson, Long Jidong. It contains one *juan* of sixty *shi* and four *ci* poems. In addition to Long Jidong's postscript, there are prefaces and inscription poems to the collection written by more than ten contributors (all of whom appear to be men). Almost everyone remarks on the poet's distinctive voice and gives a high evaluation of her transformation of the feminine poetics generally associated with women poets. Most of these comments focus on He Huisheng's unusual gesture—her intention to "throw aside the brush"—and offer their admiration for the unusual qualities of both her poems and her personality. Jiang Da, for example, expresses his amazement in his endorsement poem: "Surprisingly nowadays the inner chambers can generate such writing!"[97] In lavishing their admiration on her, some also point out that it was the chaotic times that helped produce such an unusual woman poet. In his preface, Zhang Jinyong especially elaborates on this point:

> Several times, she expresses her wish to follow the example of Ban Chao to discard the brush (for action). How profound and forceful she sounds! As we see in this world, others make their words as if they inhaled clouds, cut jade to be elegant, rouge themselves to become beautiful, and wear jewels to enhance their brilliance; these really cannot be spoken of in the same breath as her! However, willow catkins rise because of wind. What [ordinary women] compose are all lines like those characterizing snowflakes in the Xie family. In their poetry, spring is better than autumn; lines like Su's [Su Shi's] comments on the moon are rare. Hanchen's [Long Qirui's courtesy name] words are indeed true. Isn't her style created by the times?[98]

In this passage, Zhang attempts to analyze why He Huisheng's poetry stands out with its weighty thematic matter and vigorous style. Having criticized poems of superficial, artistic beauty (ironically, Zhang's own parallel prose falls into the same category), Zhang claims that this style, presumably feminine for him, has shaped a tradition that can be traced back to Xie Daoyun. Xie Daoyun was often invoked by Qing writers as an emblem of talented literary women; the catkin motif also becomes a cliché referring to women's "poetic talent" (*yongxu cai*). The phrase "willow catkins rise because of wind" carries double meanings. On the one hand, it is an adaptation of Xie's original line "More like willow catkins tossed up by the wind," a line with which Xie won a poetic contest on writing about falling snow.[99] On the other hand, Zhang means that women imitate Xie's style like catkins driven by wind. He is suggesting that women writers, modeled on Xie Daoyun, generally engage with poetry of tender sentiments and superficial beauty rather than with Su Shi's style of poetry on heroic and political matters. For Zhang, He Huisheng's poetry could fall into the former category, but at an historical juncture of social disorder, the woman poet developed a style similar to masculine poetics. In agreement with Long Qirui, Zhang concludes that He Huisheng's poetry was the product of her time. Zhang's mention of Long Qirui here echoes Long's words quoted earlier in this preface:

> [Long] told me: "Since she was married to me, she has encountered chaotic times and our life has encountered many incidents. Her talent is buried in the domestic chores . . . feeding the family has become her responsibility. Therefore, she has rarely composed poetic pieces recently."[100]

This passage illuminates the circumstances of He Huisheng's poetic practice after she was married; two factors influenced her poetry, the larger historical background and her personal situation as a housewife. Although Long focuses more on how the latter affected the quantity of his wife's poetic production, Zhang, drawing on Long's information, reaches a conclusion that focuses on the former. Perhaps Zhang was more inspired by He Huisheng's own poetic voice. As mentioned earlier, He Huisheng once referred to herself as "the Xie daughter'" when recalling her unmarried life. But in asking "All over the world is smoke and dust, / Who is in the mood to talk about love?" she seems to suggest that she has already given up the tender, delicate poetics associated with Xie Daoyun.

An endorsement poem for He Huisheng's collection signed by He Guochen reads:

烽火關山苦未休,	Beacon fires leap across passes and mountains— suffering is not yet over;
深閨覓句動悲秋。	Deep in the boudoir, she searches for poetic lines— stirred by autumn's lament.
掃除粉黛思投筆,	Sweeping away powder and rouge, she intends to set aside the brush;
吟眺風雲愛倚樓。	Reciting, she gazes upon winds and clouds, leaning against the tower.[101]

From the secluded boudoir to the world burning with beacon fires, from a concern with powder and rouge to a focus on the "winds and clouds" (historical changes), this poem aptly summarizes He Huisheng's life and works. It captures the poetic transformation that not only He Huisheng but also other women discussed in this chapter achieved in their poetry. Inspired by He Huisheng's self-representation, He Guoshen could reproduce the new textual position and voice constructed in the former's writing. This case demonstrates that the new mode of representing women in the boudoir brought forth by women poets did influence their contemporaries' literary representations of women.

While social upheaval destroyed the placid lives of countless women, it also prompted them to reflect on their place in society. Unlike the poems examined in previous chapters that depict the *gui* as a central setting, in the poems discussed here, it more often functions as a critical notion that the authors discuss as they are displaced from this space or examine from a critical distance. Whether it is a visible poetic setting or a discursive concept, the *gui* merges into a larger background of the author's social and historical experiences of war and chaos or becomes a framework within which to reflect on her social, political and personal circumstances. In other words, it is not treated as an enclosed feminine space paralleling the author's interiority but examined externally by the author. If women authors as represented by those in *The Anthology of Correct Beginnings* negotiate the conventional boudoir poetics in order to craft a new feminine space, the authors examined in this chapter are not concerned with the textual representations of the *gui* but connect it to their broader social and historical concerns and begin to consider its social meaning.

Compared with those in *The Anthology of Correct Beginnings*, the poetic voices examined in this chapter—with the exception of Wu Chai—tend to be aggrieved and plaintive: some complain that war destroyed their peaceful and comfortable life in the *gui*, some express their deep sorrow over the loss of their beloveds, some mourn the fall of their native dynasty, and some protest the restrictive boundaries of women defined by the inner chambers. As the voices in *The Anthology of Correct Beginnings* represent "the tones of a well-managed age" that are "at rest and happy," the voices examined in this chapter can be characterized primarily as "the tones of an age of turmoil" that are "bitter and full of anger."[102] Living through times of chaos, these women's writings indeed reflect their social and historical contexts. Although their bitter and angry voices are far from the ideals of orthodox poetics, their contemporary critics understood the extraordinary circumstances under which these voices were produced. For example, in his preface to the poetic collection of Wang Caipin (1827–after 1893), a widow living through the Taiping Rebellion, Xu Zhenyi begins by claiming, "Since ancient times, works by outstanding women of the inner chambers can express plaint!"[103] Not to be mistaken, here, he does not mean the boudoir plaint in the conventional sense, as he goes on to link her poetry with Qu Yuan's writing and the lamentation songs of complaint in the *Book of Songs*. For him, one can create immortal works from the experiences of adversity as long as one upholds one's integrity. Male critics affirmed women's embrace of high cultural values such as loyalism in their poetry, seeing it as an admirable transcendence by women of gender boundaries.

Curiously, none of these male critics touches upon the issue of systemic gender inequality raised by women such as Gu Zhenli and He Huisheng. Perhaps this issue was too sensitive to discuss or posed a social impasse for which they had no solution. Or they simply were completely unconscious of gender inequality as a problem.

CHAPTER 5

The Old Boudoir and the "New Woman"

The Late Qing and Early Republican Era

Right in front of me the vast sea has actually become dust.
Wretchedness locks the deserted corner; all kinds of feelings are frequently stirred.
Folks are waiting to see the old evil practices eradicated;
The one in the secluded boudoir wishes to be a new citizen.

眼看滄海竟成塵, 寂鎖荒陬百感頻。流俗待看除舊弊, 深閨有願作新民。

—LÜ BICHENG

Social and political turmoil in the late imperial period affected women's lives, engendering changes in their conceptions and poetic depictions of the *gui*. Whether nostalgic about their formerly peaceful lives in the inner chambers or protesting its constraints, which hindered them from participating in the political sphere alongside men, women were already thinking outside the frame of the *gui*. However, the late Qing and early Republican era saw profound changes that more radically altered women's lifestyles, social roles, and their self-representations in literature. Women like He Huisheng, whose sense of confinement in the inner chambers led her to hang herself in 1858, would have found it inconceivable that in the near future women could actually leave their houses to go to school, have professional careers, or even study abroad.

What was happening in women's lives and writing in the very late Qing and very early Republican period, an era in which institutional and ideological changes produced an unprecedented mixing of old and new? During this time, the story of the boudoir continued in both familiar and unfamiliar ways. These developments are exemplified in the writing of Qiu Jin (1875–1907) and Lü Bicheng (1884–1943), two revolutionary women who continued to employ the time-honored cultural signifier *gui* but adapted it to their new expressive needs.¹ The ways in which these two women engaged with the *gui* both in classical forms and in the context of their complex relationship to Chinese literary tradition and modernity show that the *gui* was not only a determinant of late imperial Chinese women's approach to the writing of poetry but also a factor subject to constant rewriting.

GOING TO SCHOOL AND GOING PUBLIC

For late Qing reformers such as Liang Qichao (1873–1929), women's liberation was at the forefront of their attempts to form a modern state out of an empire battered by both internal and foreign attacks. They believed that women's nonparticipation in production was a waste of potential and a drain on the strength of the nation. The solution to this problem, they believed, was to emancipate women from the confinement of the inner chambers and the constraints of bound feet and teach them modern knowledge and skills. Their goal was to transform women into capable "mothers of citizens" or "female citizens" equal to men. Although there were debates regarding the purpose of women's education, all of the reformers and activists shared the view that education was where change had to begin.

Not counting the schools founded by Western Christian missionaries,² the first girls' school in China was founded by Kang Guangren (1867–1898) and Liang Qichao in 1897 in Shanghai.³ Although the emergence of girls' schools caused a great deal of controversy, the modernization of female education quickly became an irreversible trend. Indeed, even the Qing government participated in the promotion of modern education for women. Empress Dowager Cixi and Manchu noblewomen played a leading role in mobilizing resources to establish girls' schools.⁴ In 1907, the board of education issued regulations for the standard system of female education, indicating the legitimization and institutionalization of female education.⁵ On April 23, 1919, right before the May Fourth Movement began, the Republican government founded the first postsecondary educational institution for women, Beijing Women's Normal College. Coeducation was also gradually institutionalized, beginning with elementary schools in 1912.

However, the purpose of female education was a matter of some debate in the late Qing and early Republican period, whether women's education should benefit society or women themselves and whether women's education should be different from men's. The cultivation of "capable wives and good mothers" (*xianqi liangmu*) had been taken up as a slogan by late Qing reformers in their campaign for female education, but feminist activists who were concerned primarily with women's own rights questioned such a purpose. Given the controversy, many Republican schools began to adopt an ambivalent attitude toward this goal,[6] which was further marginalized with the rise of the May Fourth Movement and the practice of coeducation. However, the idea of cultivating good mothers was never entirely discarded when gender-specific education was addressed. For the purpose of cultivating female moral character, the old "four books" for women remained the core textbooks in late Qing girls' schools. Lü Kun's *Regulations for the Inner Chambers* and Chen Hongmou's *Inherited Guide for My Daughters* were also commonly used.

Most schools, except those that were Christian-run, targeted the daughters of wealthy families who not only could afford schooling (they had leisure and money) but also were in an advantageous position because of their readier access to networks, information, and new ideas. For example, the founders of the first girls' school in Shanghai announced that they would enroll "cultivated daughters of the inner chambers from good families" (*liangjia guixiu*) to be their students.[7] Although the earlier schools, especially the ones founded in the late Qing, set strict rules for maintaining sex segregation and minimizing exposure of schoolgirls to the public, most of these students, who would otherwise still have been cloistered *guixiu*, could for the first time study outside their homes and meet female peers from different families and areas. When coeducation was implemented, they were also able to mingle with the opposite sex on public occasions.[8]

Schooling not only provided channels for women to enter the public realm but often opened the way for professional careers. Women who graduated from a normal school, for instance, could become teachers in girls' schools. The knowledge and skills obtained in schools also enabled female graduates to pursue other professions, such as medical workers and newspaper and magazine editors. Some schools, established during the 1911 revolutionary period and given secret revolutionary missions, even trained their girl students to be spies and assassins.[9] Education and professional careers finally broke down the walls of the inner chambers and enabled women to participate in public, political and military events, entering a world that used to be beyond their reach. They were plunged into sociohistorical changes and political turmoil and could take up the many unconventional roles thus opened up.

Modernized female education was one of the most important processes through which women were reformed into modern subjects. The Jingzheng Girls' School, for example, one of the earliest girls' schools, may have enrolled "cultivated daughters of the inner chambers from good families," but what it aimed to achieve was the transformation of its schoolgirls into women of modern learning.[10] In the words of Pan Xuan, one of the chief editors of *Women's Education*, in 1898, "With the establishment of women's schools, those young ladies of the inner chambers [*guixiu xiaojie*], whether they used to read or not, can study together day in and day out so that they can easily make progress. In the future, when they are accomplished in their studies, it won't be hard for them to be above average and to be good at both Chinese and Western learning."[11]

Modern newspapers and periodicals that proliferated from the late years of the Qing through the May Fourth era provided another unprecedented public forum for women. Both men and women activists who were interested in the Woman Question published their opinions or founded their own presses so that they could take better advantage of modern mass media and disseminate their political beliefs and ideas. As many scholars have observed, these women's periodicals became one of the major sources producing and spreading new gender ideology and discourses. They introduced, coined, and circulated a terminology for discussing nationalist and/or feminist issues in a public forum opened for and by women. Keywords such as "women's world" (*nüjie*), "women's rights" (*nüquan*), and "gender equality" (*nannü pingdeng*) thus entered circulation.[12] With their specific gender orientation, women's periodicals also gendered the conceptions of "civil rights" (*minquan*) and "human rights" (*renquan*) promoted by nationalists. The reform journals and newspapers had a direct impact on women's lives and self-perceptions by providing specific role models and calling on them to perform these roles. Texts published in the mass media are an important resource in investigating the discursive formation of new female subjectivities and identities.

FROM *GUIXIU* TO NEW WOMAN

The central agenda of late Qing reformers as well as New Culturalists in the May Fourth era was to transform the "senile" Chinese empire into a modern state and the Chinese people into modern subjects in order to survive the clash with Western and Japanese imperialist powers. That is to say, the formation of new subjects was central to the process of modernization. From the very beginning, alongside the transformation from "subjects of the emperor" (*chenmin*) or "slave" (*nuli*) to "citizen" (*guomin*) or "new youth" (*xin qingnian*), there were also calls for gender-specific changes from "the slave of the slave" (*nu zhi nu*) or cloistered *guixiu* to "mother of a citizen" (*guomin zhi mu*), "female citizen" (*nü guomin*), or "the woman of new China" (*xin zhongguo zhi nüzi*). These new roles generated in the context of nation and race building transcended the inner/outer spatial boundaries and associated women with the polity. In discourses that placed women in the context of nation building, the *Book of Rites*' prescription of a spatial division between the male or outer spheres and the female or inner spheres began to be viewed as a way of victimizing and demonizing women. The inner-chambers regime was described as a trap for women: "The ancient sage. . . views women as demons and monsters, dangerous venomous snakes, who can only be shut in cowpens and pig-folds and are forbidden to go out even for one step."[13]

Even as the women's liberation agenda targeted the *gui* as the symbol of women's separation from society, the term *guixiu* remained in frequent use during the late Qing and Republican periods. It was used not only as a dated term to refer to women who kept their traditional lifestyle but also as a respectful title for women in general. For example, a female teacher from the United States was called "American *guixiu* [*meiguo guixiu*]."[14] This combination of continuity and change is apparent in three prevalent categories of female identities and subjectivities constructed in late Qing discourses: good wife and wise mother or mother of a citizen; woman citizen; and woman of New China.

When late Qing reformers such as Liang Qichao first institutionalized female education, they announced that their goal was to train the students to become wives and mothers who could benefit their husbands, children, and, by extension, their country. In this sense, the first modern schools carried on traditional women's learning in many ways, only with a revised content and purpose. According to Liang Qichao, "The foundation of a nation is rooted in the family; the importance of family education lies in the virtue of the mother; the reason for establishing girls' schools is to produce virtuous and capable mothers."[15] Following this logic, the most important task of good mothers is rearing sons who can restore and strengthen the nation. Liang's educational philosophy, as many have pointed out, was a reflection of the Japanese notion of "good wife and wise mother" (*liangqi xianmu*), which integrated traditional Confucian feminine virtues and nationalist utilitarianism.[16] Another phrase, "mother of a citizen," perhaps coined by Jin Tianhe (pen name Jin Yi, 1874–1947) when he published his influential text *Women's Bell* (Nüjie zhong) in 1903, directly indicates women's role as reproducers of modern political subjects, although Jin had a more advanced and complicated scheme for transforming traditional womanhood.

While nationalist reformers such as Liang Qichao called on women to be virtuous and good mothers, their insistence on the traditionally defined domestic roles of women also caused strong counterreactions. Some who were more concerned with women's own rights countered with the notion of a woman citizen or, simply, a citizen without gender connotations in order to claim for women a political subjecthood equal to that of men. They argued that an educated woman should play more important public roles than simply "supporting her husband and educating her children." For example, in a petition letter written to Empress Dowager Cixi requesting more support for women's education, Lu Cui (fl. 1898) seeks the participation of other women: "Speaking of the notion of citizen, as men are considered to be citizens, women should be also considered citizens. All of us women can also submit political petitions with our joined signatures."[17] In emphasizing that women can *also* "submit a petition" (*shangshu*), Lu Cui was suggesting that women could participate in the political sphere with the same techniques used by male reformers such as Kang Youwei and Liang Qichao.[18]

Another important woman author active in this period, Gao Susu, elaborated further on why the idea of good wives and wise mothers was not good for Chinese women: "A woman, also a citizen, is neither privately owned by her family or by men but belongs to the country. She has full personhood. Therefore, the educational philosophy of women should be planned for women's own good and for the future of the country rather than for the private service of men."[19] Gao goes on to identify Japan as the source of the ideology of good wives and wise mothers and points out that Japan, a society in which women are subordinate, should not be taken as a model for China. Finally, she portrays the ideology as an outdated value, at odds with the ideal of women as independent national subjects.

The term "new woman" (*xin nüxing*), often used to refer to the image of women popular in the May Fourth cultural context, entered circulation during the 1920s.[20] Even without the modifying morpheme *xin* (new), the term *nüxing* (female) itself, a sex identity independent from kin roles, was new. If these terms dated to the 1920s, the concept of new woman versus traditional womanhood had already emerged in the late Qing context when a similar term, "woman" (*nüzi*), vis-à-vis "man" (*nanzi*), was in frequent use. Increasing calls for the two hundred million women of the Chinese nation to participate in the process of state building and the liberation of women were accompanied with the construction of a new subject position of *nüzi*. Jin Tianhe, in his *Women's Bell*, also coined the term "the woman of new China." He even draws a vivid portrait of this new woman: "Between her handsome eyebrows her brisk spirit is revealed, and her speech is confident and sharp. A beauty carrying a precious sword, she is the divine dragon that has come alive. Who is this person? The woman of new China."[21]

Although Jin Tianhe was not the first person to discuss feminism in explicit terms, his work, hailed as one of the classical texts promoting women's liberation, was among the most influential. It provided not only a lexicon and rhetoric that was repeatedly used in later feminist speeches but also specific role models for women to emulate. Some scholars have argued that Jin Tianhe's construction of the new roles of women is in fact a construction of male subjectivity in reaction to his own identity crisis.[22] For the purpose of this chapter, it is more important that the multiple roles Jin Tianhe intends women to perform, however contradictory, had a profound impact on women's movements and their self-perception.

LITERARY REFORM

In calling on women to reject traditional womanhood, reform-minded men and women also urged them to break with women's literary past.[23] In his 1897 essay "On Women's Learning" (Lun nüxue), Liang Qichao first frowns upon the illiteracy of the majority of women and then criticizes the traditional "woman of talent" (*cainü*): "As for what were called 'women of talent' in ancient times, they depicted the romance of the wind and the moon and toyed with the images of flowers and grass. They were capable of nothing more than accumulating volumes of *shi* and *ci* collections lamenting spring and separation.

However, such things cannot be viewed as learning."[24] It is unlikely that a knowledgeable man like Liang was unaware of the existence of literary women among his contemporaries. However, his use of the term "ancient" (*gu*) in describing them suggests his eagerness to leave them behind. Ironically, he recognized the woman of talent only in order to dismiss her. While this may have been part of his strategy for radically rejecting the immediate literary past, the effect was to reduce the woman of talent's poetic tradition to trivial and trite verses on romances and tender pathos and consequently to disqualify it as serious learning.

Liang was an influential reformist figure, so his deprecation of the traditional woman of talent continued to circulate in later reform-oriented discourses on women.[25] For instance, the woman author Liu Renlan picked up his message and elaborated on it in her essay published only one year later in the *Women's Education Journal* (Nü xuebao). She even borrows some phrases from Liang's essay:

> Those who are above average depict the romances of the wind and the moon, sing about the grass and the flowers. They write erotic and bewildering lyrics and articulate amorous lines. They pick up the leftovers of Li Qingzhao's "saliva" and collect the remnants of Zhu Shuzhen but think they are as talented as the pepper flowers and the willow catkin without the knowledge that they actually fall into the category of lasciviousness and loose morality.[26] How are they different from prostitutes amid the places of profligacy? Suppose that women all over the country were all like Xie Daoyun and Cai Wenji [Cai Yan], what can the world benefit from them? What can the household benefit from them?[27]

Like Liang, Liu first exposes all the "evil" aspects of traditional womanhood and then moves on to criticize literary women. The only difference is that the woman author adopts a much harsher tone and more radical stance as she attacks the woman of talent indiscriminately. She collapses all women's writings into a single category of the erotic and amorous and confuses *guixiu*, the talented of the inner chambers, and prostitutes, the two groups of women authors that had been painstakingly distinguished by Yun Zhu and other anthologists. Furthermore, the image of the talented woman Xie Daoyun, popular in the late imperial period, is portrayed as useless for either nation or family. Commentators on He Huisheng's poetry indirectly suggest the insignificant, feminine poetics represented by the trope of Xie Daoyun, but Liu seems to have been the first to openly attack this generally worshiped female icon. In this way, Liu attempts to deconstruct the poetic tradition established by writing women in the late imperial era.

Echoing both Liang Qichao and the woman author Liu Renlan, Jin Tianhe, in his famous *Women's Bell*, also explicitly identifies the women writers he targets as "young wives in the inner cham-bers" and criticizes their poetry as not only useless but harmful to the revolution:

> In the past, men carried their swords, traveled outside their homes, and never had concerns about the inner sphere. However, [women] cause them to be bound up with the bedchambers, with singing and crying in the boudoir, and consume their hearts that should have been concerned about the country, and destroy their heroic morality. Whenever I read the poetry of young wives in the inner chambers, I have never been able to close the volume without many sighs, even though they are the excellent ones.[28]

Using similar logic and rhetoric, these influential authors of both genders express the same negative attitude toward the feminine poetic tradition established by the "woman of talent" or "young wives in the inner chambers." Their determined misreading of this tradition derived from their agenda to liberate women from traditional womanhood and learning and usher in literary reforms. The reforms that they intended to carry out had two main features. First, they attempted to elevate the fiction (*xiaoshuo*) genre as the most efficient vehicle for cultural and moral renovation.[29] Second, they promoted a revolution within the poetic genre, that is, to express new ideas and concepts in classical forms. The complete negation of the preexisting feminine poetic tradition was necessary so that they could pave the way for the literary reform they envisioned. Although both men and women disagreed with these critics' "wholesale condemnation of past traditions of women's learning," this criticism of the traditional poetics of women, though reductive and distorted, had begun to influence the representation of women in literature before the May Fourth vernacular movement.[30]

As a crucial topos for representing women and femininity, the *gui*, once again, was subject to rewriting by reform-minded poets. This time, however, men as well as women introduced new meanings into this age-old poetic space. The "new mode of boudoir sentiments" (*xinshi guiqing*) involved a small number of male poets who echoed women's poetic innovations.[31] Like literati poets in earlier times, these male poets also performed ventriloquism, exercising their imaginations and expressing their concerns in the voices of women. However, in the new historical context, they had an explicit agenda, that is, to reform the conventions of the boudoir plaint and make it serve new politics such as state and nation building and women's liberation. As Zhou Shi writes in the preface to his poems "Guiqing" (Boudoir feeling): "In our country's poetry, verses expressing the boudoir plaint and other sentiments are nothing but words comprising gauzes, satins, rouge, and powder. In my spare time I composed these poems so as to usher in a boom in new Chinese women's learning."[32] These poems consist of six quatrains:

POEM NO. 2

幾年夫婿覓封侯，	In these few years, my husband has been seeking noble rank;
十幅鸞箋昨付郵。	Yesterday I sent him a letter of ten colorful pages.
大好河山須努力，	To protect our wonderful country, you should work hard;
男兒誤國女兒羞。	If a man fails to fight for his country, his woman will be ashamed.

POEM NO. 3

欲憑纖手拯沉淪，	I desire to brace up the fallen state with my slender hands,
自怨釵裙累此身。	But blame my body trapped in hairpins and skirts.
寄語征人倘殉國，	Thus I send a message to my husband on the battlefield: "If you die a martyr,
阿儂便作墜樓人。	I will be the person committing suicide by throwing myself off the tower!"[33]

POEM NO. 6

拈花鬥草自年年，	Plucking flowers and toying with grass, we've spent year after year.
誰向神州倡女權？	Who will promote women's rights in the wondrous land of our country?
夜氣沉沉人語寂，	On this dark night, the human voice is silent.
江山破碎月孤圓。	Above the broken rivers and mountains, only the lonely moon is full.[34]

In these poems, the male poet adopts plain language and an explicit feminine voice. In doing so, he may have intended the "new" voice he created to reach out to and elicit the response of more women. In fact, the voice of an understanding and supportive wife in "Poem No. 2" and "Poem No. 3" is familiar to readers who recall the poems women like Qin Puzhen wrote to their husbands. Moreover, women's poetry makes use of the motif of blaming gender restriction for women's inability to participate in the political sphere. It is not known whether or not Zhou Shi had actually read or been influenced by those poems, but as an active male poet, his imitation of the woman's voice would have been more widely circulated than women's texts. The voice in "Poem No. 6," the last of the group, was unheard of in earlier times, but he was preceded by contemporary women poets.

As both product and part of the discursive process of redefining womanhood and femininity, women's literature at the turn of the century was also taking a critical turn. Pioneering women writers in the late Qing had launched linguistic and literary reforms well before the rise of the May Fourth women writers. They started to express themselves in language and forms that women had rarely used, such as essays in vernacular style, popular songs, and prose fiction. In the meantime, they conducted significant literary reforms or textual revolutions without necessarily discarding the traditional.[35] The transitional stages in the literary lives of Qiu Jin and Lü Bicheng were deeply informed by the context outlined above. They engaged with the cultural signifier *gui* in classical forms and in the context of their changing lives and evolving subjectivities.

A REVOLUTIONARY'S TEXTUAL REVOLUTION

Qiu Jin, a significant transitional figure in Chinese history, has been well studied. Her life was as dramatic as the era in which she lived. Mirroring the historical changes of her time, her life and writing can be divided into two stages: traditional and revolutionary. Although many of her biographers tend to highlight her unusual upbringing by doting parents, which contributed to her extraordinary personality, the first half of her life was not completely unconventional: besides martial arts, horseback riding, and swordsmanship, she received the typical *guixiu* training in embroidering, sewing, calligraphy, and poetry writing. In this regard, Qiu Jin's life and writing should be examined "first of all within the female literary tradition of late imperial China."[36]

Qiu Jin was well versed in classical poetry, including the *shi* and *ci* forms. During the period from 1890 to 1902, when she lived in Hunan with her parents and, later, her husband before they moved to Beijing, Qiu Jin was a prolific *guixiu* poet. In one of her earlier verses, she, like many women poets in the Qing period, explicitly identifies with the popular icon Xie Daoyun, admiring not only her poetic talent but also her flamboyant personality. The verses Qiu Jin produced during her years in Hunan were well situated within the existing *guixiu* tradition and include many familiar boudoir scenarios. For example, in the following verse, set in springtime, the woman persona, annoyed by the contrast of the beautiful, amorous season and her loneliness, is in no mood to raise the curtain of her boudoir:

花朝過了逢寒食，	The Day of Flowers has now passed, and again it's Cold Food:
惱人最是春時節。	Nothing is more wearisome than the season of spring!
窗外草如煙，	Outside the window, the grass is like mist;
幽閨懶捲簾。	Inside my room, I'm too lazy to roll up the screens.
絳桃臨水照，	Crimson peach blossoms blaze along the river;
翠竹迎風笑。	Verdant bamboos smile against the wind.
鶯燕不知愁，	Oriole and swallow who know not sorrow
雙飛傍小樓。	Together swoop and fly around the little tower.[37]

On a summer evening, the woman persona has taken an aromatic bath and enjoys the flowers and jewelry that flatter her beauty:

…	
夏晝初長，	The summer days are just becoming long;
紈扇輕攜納晚涼。	Carrying my light silk fan, I enjoy the cool evening.
含桃落盡，	Cherry flowers fall off;
鶯語心驚蝶褪粉。	Startled orioles twitter, and butterflies shed powder.
浴罷蘭泉，	After the bath in the orchid spring,
斜插茉花映翠鈿。	I set jasmine flowers aslant in my hair to match the kingfisher hairpin.[38]

In autumn, there are sleepless nights when she is alone and stirred by the sorrows of the season:

窗外落梧聲，	The sounds of falling wutong leaves
無限淒清，	Are endlessly saddening;
蛩鳴啾唧夜黃昏。	The night falls in the chirps of insects.
秋氣感人眠不得，	The autumn atmosphere so stirring that one cannot sleep,
細數鼉更。	I make a careful count of the sounds of the watches.
斜月上簾紋，	The slanted moon shows up through the patterned blinds;
竹影縱橫，	The shadows of bamboo are crisscrossing.

The Old Boudoir and the "New Woman" 157

一分愁作十分痕！	Each fraction of my sorrow is amplified ten times by their traces!
幾陣吹來風乍冷，	Several gusts of wind are suddenly cold;
寒透羅衾。	Chill penetrates my silk quilt.

However, there are also nights of sharing secrets and pleasures while partying with female companions and celebrating a holiday of their own, the Double-Seven Festival:

金針度，	To pass a thread through a golden needle,
晚妝初罷陳瓜果；	We arrange melons and fruits as soon as we finish our evening dressing;
陳瓜果，	Arranging melons and fruits,
無限心事，	We have endless secrets
背人偷訴。	To share behind others.
夜深小憑欄杆語，	Late in the night we chat while leaning against railings;
階前促織聲悽楚；	The crickets on the steps chirp sadly.
聲悽楚，	As they chirp sadly,
笑倩同儔，	I ask my party with a smile,
不如歸去。	Why don't we return?[39]

Finally, when the year comes to an end, she is in the mood to appreciate winter snow and plum blossoms, just like many of her poetic predecessors:

雲漠漠，	An expanse of clouds,
風瑟瑟，	A soughing wind
飄盡玉階瓊屑。	Blows off jasper crumbs on jade steps.
疏蕊放，	Scattered buds are opening,
暗香來，	Hidden fragrance comes over,
窗前開早梅。	Early plum blossoms are blooming in front of my window.[40]

Qiu Jin's poems in the boudoir setting demonstrate a broad spectrum of themes, motifs, and images developed in the *guixiu* tradition. These not only incorporate the older literati convention but also create newer poetic modes. Whether these poems should be read as merely exercises imitative of popular poetic modes or related to her real experience, they at least show that Qiu Jin was once well connected to the preexisting poetic tradition in which she found useful voices and expressions for her own writing.

Her ways of engaging with the signifier *gui* in her poetry, especially those instances related to her life experiences, also reveal a deep sense of her identification of the *gui* as a proper subject position for women. In a poem requesting a handwritten couplet for her study from the famous calligrapher Chen Meisheng, she writes:

如雷久耳右軍名,	Having long heard of the master's name as thundering as Wang Xizhi,
問字愁難列講庭。	I wish to learn calligraphy, but I'm grieved it's hard to present myself in your teaching hall.
欲乞一聯奇麗筆,	Writing to beg for a scroll of your marvelous handwriting,
閨中曾讀養鵝經。	In the boudoir I used to read the Classic of Raising Geese.[41]

In this poem, Qiu praises Chen's fame and art as a master in calligraphy by referring to him as Wang Xizhi (ca. 303–ca. 379), one of the greatest calligraphers in Chinese history, and expresses her wish to obtain a piece of his work. In expressing this wish, she emphasizes that although her gender status in the inner chambers does not allow her to study with him in person, it does not hinder her learning from works such as the Classic of Raising Geese, instructional material for calligraphy learners. In this way, she acknowledges her own gendered position in the inner chambers when communicating with a respectable male literatus.

Qiu Jin's identification of the *gui* as the women's place is also confirmed in her reference to the place as not only hers but also belonging to other women. In lines written to her mother, sisters, and friends, such as "In the secluded boudoir, our gathering and separation are in too much of a hurry" and "I'm delighted at our poetic exchange in the inner chambers. / Together we lean against railings under the moon,"[42] she provides a record of the *gui* as an important homosocial space. Even in her later poems, written after she had both physically and symbolically stepped out of the *gui*, she still reserves the term for the special women in her life. For example, in one poem, she uses the term "the legacy of the orchid boudoir" to refer to the words of her late mother.[43] The spatial term "orchid boudoir" (*langui*) had thus come to stand for the person, suggesting its symbolic significance.

In 1895, she was married to the son of a merchant family, a match that had been arranged by her parents. She bore her husband two children and followed him to his post in Beijing. However, this arranged marriage turned out to be a mismatch. Qiu Jin was extremely unhappy, and her husband's dissolute behavior, which included frequenting brothels and taking concubines, troubled her even more. Under such circumstances, it seems that Qiu Jin found that the abandoned-woman persona could speak for her:

江煙漠漠雨霏霏，	Boundless river mist and fine rain,
料峭輕寒襲繡幃。	Light chill hits on the embroidered curtains.
曉鏡頻彈鉛水淚，	In the morning mirror, I frequently shed tears mixed with powder and rouge;
晚妝應換袷羅衣。	When doing my evening makeup, I should change into a lined silk dress.
折余楊柳情難繫，	I broke a willow branch but cannot retain love;
采罷蘼蕪郎不歸。	I picked parsley leaves but you haven't returned.
珍重九鸞釵一股，	Do treasure the nine-phoenix on this one single hairpin,
玉璫緘劄倍依依。	And this letter sealed by jade earrings—my feelings go on and on.[44]

This poem employs many allusions to the abandoned-woman persona. The motif of "picking parsley leaves" (*cai miwu*) is derived from an anonymous ancient poem included in *New Songs from a Jade Terrace*, in which an abandoned wife runs into her former husband and inquires about his new woman.[45] Another motif in Qiu's poem, of breaking a willow branch, refers to the ancient custom of giving a willow branch to the traveler setting off on a journey. It is also a poetic convention that poets have long used to express sorrow over parting.[46] Regardless of its specific source of inspiration, the conventions clearly resonated with the deep sense of betrayal engendered by her husband's behavior.

Qiu Jin might have ended up living the rest of her life in misery like many other unfortunate *guixiu* if she had not found a revolutionary career with which to reinvent herself. After her marriage fell apart in 1903, Qiu Jin wrote: "I have already learned I have no share of the ordinary happiness, / But I don't believe that there are others who are concerned with the nation's situation as much as I am."[47] These lines confirm that political participation was Qiu's chosen strategy "for self-redemption and integration into the new society."[48] After following her husband to Beijing, she began to embrace the new ideas of late Qing reformers, which opened up a brand-new world to her. She became an extreme case of a woman consciously and fervently taking up Jin Tianhe's imagined new-woman persona.

In her brief late years, she played out almost every aspect of ideal womanhood described by Jin Tianhe in his *Women's Bell*: first, she completely freed herself from all restrictions and attachments by leaving her husband, children, and home in order to become a free and independent person. Second, she fully devoted herself to revolutionary activities in order to save her nation: she studied abroad to learn from Japan's successful experience; through her writing, speeches, and educational endeavors, she called on women to stand up for themselves and for the nation; and she planned uprisings intended to overthrow what she viewed as the alien, suppressive Manchu regime, for which she was finally beheaded. Third, she not only expressed manly thoughts and took up manly roles but also literally dressed in male attire. She was indeed embodying "manly nature" in Jin Tianhe's terms.[49]

When Qiu Jin consciously echoed the call of Jin Tianhe to turn herself into a free, independent, compassionate, revolutionary woman, a "woman of new China," she also undertook a textual revolution in her literary practice. Her poem "Moved by the Event" (Gan shi) can be taken as one written at the turning point:

竟有危巢燕，	Surprisingly swallows are in a dangerous nest;[50]
應憐故國駝。	Pitiable camels' country will become the past.[51]
東侵憂未已，	An invasion from the east is still afflicting us.
西望計如何？	A peep from the west, what is our strategy against it?
儒士思投筆，	Confucian scholars want to toss their brushes;
閨人欲負戈。	The people of the inner chambers wish to carry weapons.
誰為濟時彥，	Who can be the heroes to help with the situation
相與挽頹波。	So that I can be with them to restore the declining waves?

In this regulated verse, Qiu Jin's use of its structure of parallelism manages to perfectly depict two parallel situations. The first is the crisis facing China: invasion by Japan from the east, and the threat of European imperialist powers from the west. The allusions to swallows and camels are tropes for innocent Chinese people unaware that the loss of their homes and country is imminent. Second is the eagerness of patriotic Chinese civilians, male scholars as well as women, to fight for their country: just as extraordinary as a scholar who discarded his brush, a woman who is supposed to be sequestered in the inner chambers now desires to carry a weapon. Here, Qiu Jin is speaking for herself. She identifies herself as a *guiren* but expresses a boundary-crossing wish for political participation. This poem marks a turning point in both her personal and literary lives. After her plunge into the revolutionary movement, not only did she literally remove the character *gui* from her name,[52] symbolically rejecting the old gender position, but she also gave up writing on conventional boudoir themes. She no longer spoke from her position in the *gui* but became an ardent spokesperson of nationalist and feminist topics and a harbinger of revolution. As Qiu Jin wrote in 1906:

英雄事業憑身造，	The heroic deed is dependent on my creation;
天職甯容袖手觀？	This is the career I was born to take: how can I merely be an onlooker?
廿紀風雲爭競烈，	In the twentieth century, political competition is heated;
喚回閨夢說平權。	I will awaken the ones dreaming in the inner chambers to talk about equal rights.[53]

In imagining the ideal "woman of new China," Jin Tianhe provides the following description in his *Women's Bell*: "She rides on the peach-flower horse and articulates her speech eloquently.[54] She must be the one who will waken those bewitched in the dreams of the inner chambers."[55] Here, her line "I will waken the ones dreaming in the inner chambers to talk about equal rights" is an explicit positive response to Jin Tianhe's call. She views the creation of a heroic deed as her "heavenly assigned career" (*tianzhi*), and she indeed realized it through her brief yet extraordinary life.

One of the means Qiu Jin adopted to "waken the ones dreaming in the inner chambers" was the writing of poems and songs that would spread the idea that consignment to the *gui* was a constraint that women should overcome in order to participate in the public sphere. Writing became part of her political career and mission. Her song lyrics on this theme have been well explored by scholars, but her *shi* poems merit analysis as well. In a poem written to Xu Xiaoshu (1887–1962), the sister of her friend, Xu Zihua (1875–1935), Qiu urges her to beware of the critical situation facing them, overcome the conventional gender barriers, and join her to fight for the nation:

何人慷慨說同仇？	Who can be as chivalrous as us to go against our common enemy?
誰識當年郭解流？	Who appreciates the knight-errantry of people like Guo Jie?[56]
時局如斯危已甚，	The situation is extremely critical;
閨裝願爾換吳鉤。	I urge you to replace your boudoir dress with a sword.[57]

Qiu Jin sacrificed her family for her political career, but she relied on her female peers, especially understanding and supportive women friends, for comradeship. The Xu sisters were among those on whom she could count. During the last few years of her life, Qiu Jin crossdressed in men's clothes, a dramatic gesture symbolizing her transformation of gender roles. It may also suggest, as Wang Lingzhen points out, a dramatization of "the lack of alternative new roles for women at the turn of the century."[58] In this poem, written during the years in which Qiu Jin discarded her traditional womanhood both symbolically and functionally, she is asking her close friend to do something similar: to take off her feminine clothes and undertake political and military exploits.

Calling on women to step out of the inner chambers was one of the major motifs of Qiu Jin's later poems. In 1984, Jiang Shumin (b. 1894), a ninety-year-old woman who claimed to be Qiu's former student, brought four poems, including the following, to public attention:[59]

女子平權當自強，	Women should have equal rights and be self-strengthening.
豈能受株在閨房。	How can they be passively waiting in the inner chambers?
精忠報國英雄事，	To requite the country with pure loyalty is a heroic deed;
一樣持槍上戰場。	Women too can carry arms to go to battlefields.[60]

Jiang claimed that these poems had been written for her by Qiu Jin so that she could show them to her father who was opposed to her attending school. Some scholars have questioned the credibility of the authorship of this poem as well as Jiang's story.[61] Whether or not her story is true, it shows that Qiu Jin had indeed established a recognizable voice in this regard, a style that was recognized and could be reproduced.

In many ways, Qiu Jin still relied on classical poetry and traditional references and imagery to which she brought new ideas and phrases. However, in order to spread ideas about women's emancipation more widely, she also experimented with new forms that would better serve her political agenda, as is evident in the first stanza of "Song of Women: Four Stanzas":

我女子等蜉蝣，	We women are equal to ants and ephemera;
困守閨中不自由。	Trapped in the inner chambers, we don't have freedom.
堂堂巾幗冑，	We are the dignified and noble female descendants of our ancestors
辱為男兒羞。	Yet have been insulted and shamed by men.
昏昏辜負好春秋，	Muddling away our prime years,

我女子等蜉蝣。	Women are equal to ants and ephemera.[62]

This piece was published in the journal *Women's World* in July 1907, the same month in which Qiu Jin was beheaded. As one of the major forums distributing women's-movement propaganda, this journal published similar songs in almost every volume. Some even included musical scores, allowing them to be sung or recited as slogans. Popular song forms, rather than the classical song-lyric genre, became an important instrument of propaganda in the 1911 revolution.[63] Using relatively easy vocabulary and a semi-colloquial style, feminist songs created by Qiu Jin and others were intended to communicate to a larger audience the idea that was repeatedly expressed in late Qing discourses: the inner chambers were a prison for women; women should reject them as well as the subject position women held within them, embracing instead the new ideal of modern citizenship. The third stanza of the same song continues:

我女子亦國民，	We women are also citizens;
億兆同胞苦沉淪。	Myriads of our compatriots are sinking into degradation.
嗚呼我同胞，	Alas, my compatriots,
焉可再因循。	How can we still follow the old pattern?
社會進化權力伸，	Society has evolved, and our rights should be asserted.
我女子亦國民。	We women are also citizens.

He Huisheng, the young wife of Long Qirui examined in chapter 4, repeatedly expressed her sorrow over "confinement in the camps of women" and exclusion from the public, political sphere. In contrast, Qiu Jin's song displays her belief in social evolution and faith in the possibility of bringing about a transformation of women's rights. Living in a time of rapid social change, she was able to break with gender restrictions and produce a poetic mode that rejected the *gui* as both a gender and a poetic convention.

At the same time, she sometimes retained the *gui* as a position for other women under particular circumstances. For example, in the following poem addressed to her female companion Xu Zihua, she writes:

珍重香閨莫太癡，	Take care in the fragrant boudoir; don't indulge too much in emotion.
留卿小影慰卿思。	I left my small picture to comfort your feelings.
不為無定河邊骨，	If I don't turn into bones on the Restless River's bank,

吹聚萍蹤總有時。   There must be a time when the floating duckweeds are blown together.⁶⁴

The important images in Qiu Jin's poem are borrowed from the Tang poet Chen Tao's (812–885) lines "I pity the bones on the Restless River's bank; / They are still the person in the dream of the spring boudoir." Chen's poem is in the subgenre of frontier poetry, which creates powerful aesthetic and emotional effects by linking two striking images: the long-dead soldiers and the undying feelings of their women in the boudoir. Qiu Jin's poem was written in May 14, 1907, when she was leaving her soul mate, Xu Zihua, to participate in the revolution. She must have been aware of the danger of her journey and wrote this poem as a farewell.

Because she was determined to take up the soldier's role, she assigned the feminine role, the one in the "fragrant boudoir," to her female companion (though in other poems she often urges Xu to join her in revolutionary activities). About two months after Qiu wrote the poem, she was executed and indeed became "bones on the Restless River's bank," leaving her companion alone in the boudoir.

ANOTHER NEW WOMAN'S SUBTLE REVOLUTION

A contemporary of Qiu Jin's, Lü Bicheng, was another well-known "new woman." Like Qiu Jin, she was also raised as a traditional *guixiu* and had acquired a mastery of classical poetry before achieving self-transformation. Her transformation was different from but no less dramatic than Qiu's. She has only recently been rescued from near oblivion by a number of Chinese and English scholars.⁶⁵ Focusing on her mature writings in the *ci* genre, scholars have paid particular attention to her alternative, individualistic position that resisted subordination to either traditional womanhood or universal modernity and to her persistence in retaining classical language and forms in expressing such a position. An examination of Lü's poetic transformation of the *gui* in the context of her shifting political concerns and subjectivity illuminates with more specificity and depth the ways in which she related her poetic voice to tradition and modernity. The examples that show her subject position in relation to the *gui* are mostly *shi* poems written not only in later years but also around the time she first entered the public sphere. These *shi* poems have not been translated into

English, and most have not been discussed in either Chinese- or English-language scholarship.

Although Lü Bicheng was nine years younger than Qiu Jin, they started their public lives and careers at almost the same time. While Qiu went to Beijing in 1903, studied abroad in Japan in 1904, and came back to China in 1905, Lü left her home in Shanxi in 1904 and went to Tianjin, where she established her fame as an author and editor at the newspaper *L'Impartial* (Dagong bao). Qiu and Lü knew each other by reputation and admired each other's extraordinary personality and talent before they met briefly in Tianjin in 1904 when Qiu Jin was on her way to Japan. Qiu failed to persuade Lü to accompany her to Japan and participate in more radical political activities, but both women shared an ambition to promote women's education and gender equality. Furthermore, both favored the classical poetic forms. Because they shared the same style name, Bicheng (Qiu Jin stopped using the name only after meeting Lü), and a similar writing style for a period of time, readers often thought that writings published under the name Bicheng were by the same author. Between 1904 and 1907, before Lü's literary practice underwent further transformation, she was also active in formulating nationalist and feminist ideas, though in ways subtly different from those of Qiu Jin.

Although she was younger than Qiu Jin, Lü Bicheng may have established her literary fame as a progressive woman writer even earlier. With her privileged access to *L'Impartial*, she had been published frequently in this influential national newspaper since 1904, when she was in her early twenties, and immediately became a celebrity in literary circles. As both Grace Fong and Shengqing Wu note, her first work to attract the attention of *L'Impartial* founder Ying Lianzhi and ultimately a nationwide readership, was the following song lyric, "To the Tune 'Full River Red': Stirred by My Thoughts." The first stanza reads:

晦黯神州，	Dark is our motherland—
欣曙光，	I rejoice that a ray of dawn is
一線遙射。	Shooting up in the distance.
問何人，	I ask who will
女權高唱，	Sing loudly of women's rights?
若安達克？	Joan of Arc?
雪浪千尋悲業海，	Thousands of snowcapped waves—I am saddened by a sea of sin;
風潮廿紀看東亞。	In the stormy twentieth century—I look at East Asia.

聽青閨，	If you hear me, from the green boudoir,
揮涕發狂言，	Weeping and voicing mad words,
君休訝。	Don't be surprised.⁶⁶

This work is significant on three interrelated levels: first, it is connected to late imperial Chinese women's expression of gender inequality through negotiation with the convention of masculine heroism expressed in the form of "Full River Red"; second, it introduces modern feminist ideas in classical form and language; third, it explicitly associates the conventional feminine subject position in the *gui* with the utterance of the new gender politics. Lü Bicheng was aware that the ideas to which she gave voice in the poem would not be readily accepted by her contemporaries. She therefore refers to her writing as "mad words" (*kuangyan*) and warns her readers not to be surprised. In situating the speaker in the "green boudoir" (*qing gui*), she suggests that the words are considered mad because they are voiced from a subject position that is supposed to follow gender conventions.

This song lyric was written before Lü came to Tianjin, demonstrating that she had been exposed to modern ideas and discourses and was able to incorporate them masterfully in the classical lyrical form even before she landed the job at *L'Impartial*. It is not surprising, then, that Ying Lianzhi offered her the position of assistant editor immediately after getting to know her, although she had been planning to continue as a student at the girls' school in Tianjin. After the extremely positive reception the song lyric subtitled "Stirred by My Thoughts" received, Lü also published several *shi* poems with similar titles, such as "Describing My Thoughts" (Xie huai) and "Expressing My Thoughts" (Shu huai), continuously asserting her "mad words":

大千苦惱歎紅顏，	In this world, I sigh over the affliction of women;
幽鎖終身等白鷳。	Cloistered for a lifetime, they are like white cranes.
安得手提三尺劍，	How could I carry a three-foot sword
親為同類斬重關。	To break through multiple passes for those of my kind?
任人嘲笑是清狂，	Let some laugh at me as purely mad;
痛惜群生憂患長。	Deeply pitying all the people, my concerns are constant.⁶⁷

. . .

Once again, the speaker in Lü's poem boldly affirms her concerns about not only women, "people of my kind" (*tonglei*), but "all people" (*qunsheng*). Being aware of her vanguard position in making these assertions, she also displays her gallant attitude toward the negative reactions they may provoke. Troubled by a situation in which women are confined like caged white cranes, she eagerly wishes she could wield a magic weapon to rescue them. The "three-foot sword" that used to be a metaphor for women's desire to enter men's political and military fields becomes a weapon for launching a feminist revolution. Lü's use of the sword image echoes the image adopted in Jin Tianhe's *Women's Bell*.[68] Unlike Qiu Jin, who answered Jin Tianhe's call with action, however, Lü only expresses a wish in writing to be a warrior. All she can do is carry out a revolution in the text, voicing her concerns and calling on others to take action.

In another similarly titled poem, "Expressing My Thoughts," Lü continues to articulate her bold wishes:

眼看滄海竟成塵，	Right in front of me the vast sea has actually become dust.
寂鎖荒陬百感頻。	Wretchedness locks the deserted corner; all kinds of feelings are frequently stirred.
流俗待看除舊弊，	Folks are waiting to see the old evil practices eradicated;
深閨有願作新民。	The one in the secluded boudoir wishes to be a new citizen.
江湖以外留餘興，	I place my surplus interest in the world beyond rivers and lakes;
脂粉叢中息此身。	Amidst rouge and powder I rest this body.
誰起平權倡獨立，	Who is going to initiate equal rights and advocate independence
普天尺蠖待同伸。	So that all the crouching looper caterpillars can stretch and rise?[69]

This poem was first published in 1905 and then repeatedly republished in newspapers and journals such as *Women's World*. It received increased attention because it translates nationalistic feminist ideas into a poetic form in exact and explicit terms: it outlines historical changes, urges women to give up their traditional positions and take up new public roles, and expresses the hope that leaders will emerge to lead women's emancipation.

The fourth line is most striking: "The one in the secluded boudoir wishes to be a new citizen." This is an unusual combination of old and new, a peculiar juxtaposition of two incongruous images—"the secluded boudoir" and "a new citizen." The secluded boudoir is a place in which a woman is cloistered, whether the older abandoned-woman persona longing for her absent lover or the newer *guixiu* image engaged in domestic and cultured activities. This image is so inscribed with convention that both Lü's contemporaries and readers today are struck when her new-woman persona desires to take on the modern political identity of citizen. Ding Chuwo, the founder of the journal *Women's World*, made this comment: "She is a young woman but wants to become a new citizen. How limitless is her aspiration!"[70]

This also appears to be a contradictory juxtaposition, the private inner chambers vis-à-vis the public, political subject citizen. However, it is precisely this gap between two incongruous worlds that engenders the desire to transcend, the wish to become that which was inconceivable before. The change needs to be effected through radical revolution. The poet therefore writes in the hope that there are extraordinary leaders for the movement of emancipation. Interestingly, she excuses herself from the leading role.

Despite the differences between Lü Bicheng's and Qiu Jin's poems in terms of the speakers' political stances, their reformed poetics can be taken as innovations in both gender and poetic conventions. Like earlier *guixiu* poets represented in *The Anthology of Correct Beginnings*, they infused new ideas into the age-old signifier *gui*. Only their ideas were stamped with the marks of their time. Having unconventionally combined the feminine boudoir woman and a sword, the secluded inner chambers and the desire to be a new citizen, they literally *revolutionized* the topos *gui*. Their reformed poetic theme and style were connected to both the political movements in which they were involved and the late Qing Poetic Revolution (Shijie Geming). Liang Qichao coined the term "Poetic Revolution," and Huang Zunxian has been considered the movement's most representative poet. However, women like Qiu Jin and Lü Bicheng also carried out a revolution in their poetry:

> In a transitional age there must be revolution. But when speaking of revolution, we mean revolutionizing the spirit of something, not the form. Recently our party has talked a lot about a Poetic Revolution. However, if one considers piling up new expressions on a page revolutionary, this is the same as the Manchu government's "reform" of laws or "restoration." If one can use old poetic forms to contain new ideas, this is really putting revolution into practice.[71]

Huang often turned to poetry in classical forms for recording his various personal experiences, such as his trips to Japan and the United States, which yielded unprecedented poetic expressions.[72] In illustrating his idea of a revolution in poetry, Liang Qichao took Huang

Zunxian's poetry as an outstanding example and claimed that Huang "stands alone in the world of twentieth-century poetry." Liang, however, had not taken women poets such as Qiu and Lü into account. Although they used their poetry to formulate nationalist and feminist ideas that were popular in their time, they also altered poetic conventions, whether the older literati or newer *guixiu* traditions, and created a new dimension of themes and imageries. The new ideas and phrases they brought into the classical forms and signifiers indeed "opened a new realm of poetry." In particular, their innovations with the *gui* topos belonged to what Liu Na termed "new boudoir feelings." It is important to note, however, that some of their poems that spread feminist words such as "women's rights" were published earlier than the "Guiqing" poems by Zhou Shi, the male poet whom Liu Na considers the predecessor of the new feminine voice from the boudoir.[73] It is difficult to tell who had influenced whom in a time when both men and women could actively participate in public writing.

This combination of new ideas and old forms was not generally appreciated in the late Qing and early Republican context. Zhou Zuoren (1885–1967), for example, spoke negatively about the practice of expressing new content in old forms in his preface to Huang Zunxian's poetry collection:

> I certainly admit that there are many excellent works of old poetry, which we can appreciate and should respect . . . , yet if one uses the analogy of putting new wine into old skins in the hope of using old forms to write about modern thought, I think the effort is futile. This is, of course, my personal prejudice, and I would hardly dare use it as an excuse to rank the moderns above the ancients, but I do not believe that old poetry can be made new, and thus I am not very interested in the old-style [classical Chinese] poetry of this new age.[74]

Zhou Zuoren was a representative of vernacular writers, so it is not surprising that he found the practice of pushing old-style poetry in order to incorporate modern ideas awkward. For him, one should simply give up the old form and instead try the brand-new free-style poetry. The rise of the vernacular movement, alongside other processes of modernization, dramatically changed the literary scene in China. The poetic reform carried out by Qiu Jin and Lü Bicheng, however unappreciated by some like Zhou Zuoren, was their way of responding to this rapidly changing world.

Although Lü was active in the Poetic Revolution in her earlier literary practice, in her later years, she tended to think differently about engaging in social criticism through poetry and openly defended the traditional feminine poetics that was under attack from both late Qing reformists and May Fourth New Culturalists. Parallel to this further self-transformation, her poetry shifted from the obvious insertion of newly coined vocabulary to a subtler blend of unprecedented elements along with classical language and form. Unlike Qiu Jin, who radically rejected the *gui* as a subject position for herself after she plunged into political movements, marking a discontinuity with the feminine poetic tradition established in the late imperial era, Lü Bicheng continuously reconfigured the signifier *gui* in both her *shi* and her *ci* poetry in order to fashion herself as an alternative new woman. Further examination of her more complex self-transformation and representation in the context of her literary practice in the Republican era can lead to a deeper understanding of the different relationships individual women had with literary tradition and the different approaches they took in transforming that tradition into a more personal technique of expression.

AN ALTERNATIVE ENDING?: LÜ BICHENG CONTINUED

In 1917, Chen Hengzhe (1890–1976), a young woman student, published the short story "One Day" (Yi ri).[75] The story has been acknowledged as "the first piece of literature in modern vernacular Chinese (*baihua*)," even earlier than Lu Xun's "The Madman's Diary" (Kuangren riji), published in 1918. It marks the rise of modern women writers who wrote in "a newly modernized, Westernized, semicolloquial language" and in newly emergent genres such as fiction, drama, and essays.[76] The Literary Association (Wenxue Yanjiu Hui) was founded in the beginning of the 1920s, indicating another crucial phase in the development of modern Chinese literature: the establishment of the newly imported notion of literature (*wenxue*). Scholars in modern Chinese literature have focused on these unprecedented literary trends and presented them as the mainstream.

However, one cannot simply announce the demise of classical literary culture. Outside the literary scene that has been the focus of scholars, there were writers who still insisted on classical language and forms in their literary practice. Lü Bicheng was one such a writer.[77] Unlike Qiu Jin, Lü never abandoned the *gui* as a speaking position. In the poems quoted earlier, her speech about women's rights, self-labeled "mad words," are voiced from her "green boudoir," and her wish to become a new citizen also originates in the secluded inner chambers. In her later poems, she continues to use the conventional term *gui* to signify her gender status and subject position. One example is the following poem published in 1917. The poem was written to the famous male Daoist Chen Yingning (1880–1969), whom she refers to as "Yingning daoren" in the poem:

妙諦初聆苦未詳，	Troubled, she was unable to grasp your wonderful ideas as soon as she heard them;
異同堅白費評量。	She tried hard to discuss issues of "difference, sameness, hard and white."[78]
辯才自悔聰明誤，	The arguing talent regrets being misled by her cleverness,
乞向紅閨恕狷狂。	Begging you to forgive the red boudoir for her wildness and ignorance.[79]

As the title indicates, this poem was written after Lü had argued with Yingning about Daoist ideas and sought his forgiveness. Read in this context, her self-identification with the red boudoir can be taken, on the one hand, as a way of adopting a humble position: as a member of the "weaker" sex, she may not be as wise as a man. In this way, she may be attempting to smooth out the hard feelings caused by her argument with the male master. On the other hand, this gesture of admitting ignorance and begging for forgiveness also demonstrates her grasp of the master's ideas or even her own self-enlightenment. Whether strategic or not, her choice of the conventional term "red boudoir" (*hong gui*), with its connotation of feminine sensuality, suggests her identification with the older, gender-signifying system.

Whether (in) the green boudoir voicing mad words, or (in) the "secluded boudoir" (*shen gui*) desiring entry into the new citizenry, or (in) the red boudoir begging for the master's forgiveness, Lü uses the *gui* signifier not only as a speaking position but also as a gendered self-identity. The metonymic way of using the gendered location as an identity for women was not Lü's invention but a convention in the context of late imperial China. This convention is present in Qiu Jin's poems written in her earlier years and to other women in her life; however, she discarded it after she redefined her gender role. It is ironic and intriguing that a new woman such as Lü Bicheng, who physically left the inner sphere of the *gui* and became a professional and public figure, still retains the *gui* for her self-representation, even in poems expressing ideas about women's liberation. How should we understand this *gui* position she claims in relation to gender ideology and poetic convention? In what sense does she identify with this subject position?

Between 1926 and 1929, Lü wrote an essay, "Random Things on Contemporary Women's Circles" (Nüjie jinkuang zatan), that included a section devoted to women's writings.[80] The discussion in this section provides important clues for understanding the classical, aesthetic, and gendered orientations of her poetics in the mature years of her literary practice. First of all, one should note that in this essay she addresses not women's literary practice of her time in general but the preexisting and existing feminine poetic tradition in classical forms in particular. She begins by pointing out that the imbalance between men's and women's writings in the long history of China was due not to women's inferior intelligence but rather to their lack of access to educational opportunities. Specifically, she observes that women's works are rarely seen in the Qing dynasty *Complete Library of the Four Treasuries* (Siku quanshu). Having analyzed the historical conditions, she goes on to observe the circumstances of her time: although women did in general enjoy the offerings of institutionalized education, they were often distracted by the study of modern subjects and consequently not able to concentrate on serious classical learning and writing.[81] After talking about the past and the present in one breath, she then turns to address the following critical issues:

> With regard to *ci* verses, many often criticize women's works as mostly tailoring the red silks and inscribing the green jades, writing about resentments and expressing romantic sentiments, all written in the same style, and unable to transcend the voice of those of the inner chambers. In my opinion, expressing nature and feelings should follow their own ways. One must produce the new out of the old, not fall into the old ruts. We should especially value works that are profound and elegant in meter and express genuine nature and feelings; these should be considered as fine pieces. Wen Tingyun and Li Shangyin in the *shi* genre and Zhou Bangyan and Liu Yong in the *ci* are all good at depicting tender love and beauty. If men can write like this, what's the harm for women in expressing their own nature? If words and expressions must be concerned with people and thoughts should never be separated from state politics, I would be privately sick of their artificiality if they were written by men and wonder: how can this be proper for the ones of the inner chambers? Women love beauty and are full of emotions and feelings and are feminine in nature. Why on earth do they have to admire the virtue of masculinity? If they deeply efface themselves, they must be self-abasing and feel ashamed to be women.[82]

Phrases such as "tailoring the red silks and inscribing the green jades" and "writing about resentments and expressing romantic sentiments" are clichés remarking on the ornateness and sentimentality of traditional feminine poetics. They were used not only in late Qing and May Fourth reform discourse but also by critics of earlier generations. In repeating these clichés, Lü is engaging in this critical colloquy on the same subject, women's writings in traditional poetic modes. She is reacting not only against the May Fourth new literature movement's emphasis on social commitment but also against the earlier attack on women's poetic tradition launched by late Qing reformists such as Liang Qichao and Jin Tianhe. Directly addressing their implications regarding the triviality of feminine sentiments in women's poetry, Lü argues that women should express what is "naturally" appropriate to their gender, that is, beautiful and emotional as opposed to artificial and political. In associating women with beauty and emotion, Lü holds an essentialist point of view on gender. As Shengqing Wu aptly points out, this is a strategy intended to rearticulate gender and textual differences.[83] Her essentialist stance should be understood as a reaction against a social commitment and nationalist agenda that, for her, would not only obliterate gender difference in the text but, more important, disrupt women's poetic tradition. Her exclusion of social issues and state politics from the feminine poetics she envisions is not so much directly against modern nation-state building as against a universal modernization that would destroy traditional Chinese culture in general and women's poetic tradition in particular. Moreover, by naming literati poets who were good at performing feminine voice and style, she suggests that, to her, femininity was a textual effect after all.

Indeed, Lü insists on a continuing feminine poetic tradition without distinguishing the past from the present or even the genders of the authors. Her transhistorical point of view is further revealed in her use of the term "the ones of the inner chambers" in discussing women's poetic voice. Moreover, she has no intention of distinguishing it from women or *nüzi* or female or *nüxing*, the more popular new terms of her time, but uses them interchangeably, arguing that the "voice of the inner chambers" (*guiren kouwen*) is proper to women and is integral to the tradition of "women's writing" (*nüzi zhuzuo*). This suggests that it is not necessary for her to change the subject, at least not on the surface.

In light of Lü's insistence on the continuity of traditional women's writing in an era that gradually came to be dominated by new forms of literature, maintaining the old signifier *gui* as a subject position was a way for her to stay connected to the preexisting poetic tradition. Of course, while insisting on the classical forms and tradition, she also emphasized that poets should be innovative and surpass conventional patterns. In her words, "One must produce the new out of the old, not fall into the old ruts." Lü Bicheng herself was one of the best examples of writing within but innovating upon the poetic tradition. Both Fong and Wu have shown in their seminal studies of Lü's song lyrics that she "significantly expanded natural, cultural, and imaginary spaces in poetry." Wu's argument that Lü's song lyrics arrived at "a more fluid sense of femininity that helped develop a distinctive identity in her poetry" is particularly inspirational for understanding Lü's transcendent subject position in the *gui*.[84] This position is intended to take up neither the woman persona constructed in the older literati tradition nor that of the virtuous woman guarding Confucian ideology as portrayed by some of the authors favored by Yun Zhu. Rather, it is an updated, hybridized or reconstituted subject position with which she bridges old and new worlds and represents her evolving subjectivity informed by her time and her changing sense of self.

At the same time, Lü's continuous use of the *gui* as an indicator of her speaking position is also her way of distancing herself from the new literary currents—that is to say, by using a gender signifier that was generally determined to be outdated, she was refusing to enter into the new signifying system. But by using the age-old feminine subject position to articulate her unconventional experiences and shifting self-perception, she was also riding the waves of historical change. In this way, she subtly carved out a poetic space for herself in which she could maintain a unique relationship to old and new discursive systems. What Lü strove to achieve was an expansion of the expressive parameters of classical poetry while carrying on the preexisting feminine poetic tradition.

In the critical narrative quoted above, she does not reflect on her own literary practice, but her critique of socially committed literature concerned with people (*cangsheng*) and state or country (*langmiao*) suggests a self-negation of her earlier writings, such as the poem "Describing My Thoughts," in which she formulates feminist ideas in classical poetic forms. In the poem, she explicitly expresses her concerns about people (*qunsheng*). The removal of some similar works in her later publications also suggests such a self-critical tendency.

When she first stepped out of the household and began working for *L'Impartial*, the young, ambitious Lü Bicheng was excited about entering the emerging urban intelligentsia and eager to impress this public world that had opened up to her by projecting her "progressive" way of thinking through her poetry. However, her self-perception in relation to literary tradition in general and the feminine position in the *gui* in particular was much more complicated than the progressive ideas formulated in those poems.

To give another example, in the same poem she takes no radical actions but merely articulates a wish to be able to rescue her fellow women. This is similar to the poem "Expressing My Thoughts," discussed earlier, in which she calls for women's emancipation but excuses herself from a leading role. This poem has two lines that bear repeating here: "I place my surplus interest in the world beyond rivers and lakes; / Amidst rouge and powder I rest this body." Read together with other lines, this couplet can be understood as suggesting that before women gained rights equal to those of men, they were excluded from the public, political sphere and could devote their time and energy only to marginal matters. Read in relation to the poet's life, they may also imply Lü's personal stance: she has an alternative interest, which does not lie in radical politics but elsewhere. Although she started as a pioneering woman active and expressive on social and political fronts, she gradually reoriented her life around nonradical and less socially engaged interests such as traveling in Europe and the United States and promoting animal rights and religious participation. In particular, Buddhism became a major interest in her late years.

It is noteworthy that reconfiguring the conventional poetic space of the *gui* also projects such a "nonpolitical" stance, a strategy apparent in the group of poems titled "Random Thoughts from the Spring Boudoir: Harmonizing with Ms. Kang Tongbi's Rhyme." As the title indicates, Lü's rhyme is derived from Kang Tongbi's poem. The second daughter of Kang Youwei (1858–1927), Kang Tongbi was also a leading figure in the women's liberation movement. In 1902, Kang visited her father, who was in exile after the failure of the 1898 reform, and accompanied him to India, where they explored Buddhist history. She recorded this experience as well as her reflections on the decline of Buddhism in India in two poems, in which she also proudly asserts: "Speaking of women traveling to the West, / I'm the first one from China."[85] Echoing Kang, Lü Bicheng made a similar claim in another poem about her pioneering travel to Europe, but in this group of poems she engages instead with questions of self-perception and cultivation.[86] Although it is difficult to determine when Lü's poems in response to Kang were written and if Kang read them, it is safe to say that they must have been written after Lü became well known and established, since she addresses many issues resulting from these experiences.

It is necessary to note that Lü names this group of five quatrains "Random Thoughts from the Spring Boudoir." Although one cannot determine the orientation of her speaking position in relation to the prevalent meanings of the *gui* before reading the poems, the presence of the term in the title suggests her intention to situate her poems in the larger discursive space of the *gui*. The fifth poem of the group, in which the theme of the poet's assertion of self-cultivation culminates, illustrates the meaning she intends to bring into this space:

倦繡惟求物外因，	Tired of embroidering, I seek only the reason beyond the material world;
自鋤瑤草傍雲根。	Hoeing jasper grass by myself, I lean against the root of clouds.
而今蕙帶荷衣客，	Now the sojourner is clothed in lotus leaves and belted with orchids.
誰識天花散後身。	Who would recognize this body rising from the fall of heavenly flowers?[87]

"Tired of embroidering" or "tired by embroidering" (*juan xiu*) is one of the common motifs associated with the boudoir space. In the older literati tradition, the moment when a woman becomes exhausted from embroidering can be depicted as a typical boudoir scenario in which a woman pauses in her work and is caught up in thinking of her distant lover and/or displaying her enticing and fragile beauty. The following lines by Yuan Jue (1266–1327) exemplify this conventional portrayal of a boudoir woman: "The ivory bed thickly fragrant, green curtains bring the spring; / Tired by embroidering, the beauty lies down stretching."[88] This sensuous and amorous depiction of the moment of becoming tired from embroidering, however, was reinscribed by *guixiu* poets as a moment devoted to moral and intellectual activities such as meditation, reading, and writing. This is exemplified by many of the authors anthologized in *The Anthology of Correct Beginnings*. In the above poem, Lü Bicheng's line "Tired of embroidering, I seek only the reason beyond the material world" also falls into this category of rewriting the literati convention. Just as implied in the poems of many of her women predecessors, Lü's persona's weariness with embroidering may not actually be caused by the activity but may be instead a symbolic rejection of the womanly work.[89] She may have no interest in embroidery at all. She claims that what she intends to pursue is nothing but exploring "the reason beyond the material world," an ambitious philosophical engagement. The succeeding lines go on to emphasize the philosophical and religious enlightenment the poet attempts to pursue. Given its different uses in previous texts, the term "the root of clouds" (*yungen*) can refer specifically to deep mountains where clouds are generated, rocks, or monasteries and temples. In figuratively portraying herself "hoeing jasper grasses" next to "the root of clouds," Lü's use of the term in this line can be understood as a trope encompassing all these meanings: she is cultivating her self not only in imagined nature but also in religious realms. Although the mention of the heavenly flowers in the last line indicates her Buddhist tendency, she is in general crafting a space for her self, a transcendent site distant from the secular or material world. Whether it is a hermit's dwelling, an immortal's abode, or a Buddhist temple, it is certain that the enlightening clouds are rooted in the inner world of her self. Moreover, in inscribing her enlightenment in the corner of her "spring boudoir," where she is "tired of embroidering," she turns the boudoir into a spiritual sanctum for herself.

In a way, her reconstruction of the boudoir into a space of self-enlightenment is no different from what the *guixiu*'s literary culture accomplished in the Qing. But given the different historical and personal contexts, the significance of her transformed poetics should be evaluated in a different light. While the rewriting strategy of the women authors in Yun Zhu's anthology could be understood as an attempt to conform to contemporary literary trends and ideological conditions, Lü Bicheng's continuous reinscription of the boudoir as a personal poetic device represents her counterreaction to the process of universal modernization. Her vigorous insistence on an essentialist feminine poetics that is sentimental and personal is not simply a return to the traditional but reserves the *gui* as a private corner from which to cope with the tumultuous, external world.

Qiu Jin's life was virtually a performance of the new-woman persona constructed by male political activists such as Jin Tianhe, and her revolutionary writings are characterized by intertextual echoes with her contemporary discourses. However, a further comparison between Qiu and Lü Bicheng shows that different women did make different choices in reacting to the processes of modernization. While Qiu "entered the sphere of high politics" at the expense of her life, Lü was finally able to "subordinate political action to professional, educational, or feminist activities."[90] Having discarded the subject position in the inner chambers and adopted literary cross-dressing, Qiu Jin's transformed poetic employment of the *gui* topos represents a discontinuity of the feminine poetic tradition. Lü, however, continuously modified the spatial trope of *gui* into a space of self-expression even after the mainstream literary scene had become dominated by a new concept of literature. Lü's case suggests the legacy of the *gui* as a poetic space that retains the potential be revitalized. It continues to provide a space for expressing gender-related concerns and can always be written anew.

Conclusion

Multiple strata of social and cultural forces have shaped the meaning of texts written by late imperial Chinese women, but their distinctive approach to poetry writing lies in the ways in which each writing subject interacted with the sociocultural domain to which she belonged. It is essential to ask, then, what was their relationship to the preexisting poetic tradition? When they inevitably brought their subjective experiences and perspectives to their writing, what areas were particularly subject to rewriting? What topical areas were they interested in developing? Scholars have raised similar questions that are crucial to understanding the nature of Ming-Qing women's poetic practice more broadly.[1] The poetic space centered on the *gui*, a tradition originally established by male literati and then taken over by women poets in the late imperial era, provides a productive area for exploring the critical issues of women's ways of participating in literary practice with greater focus and depth.

An analysis of women writers' depiction of the *gui* well illustrates the distinctiveness of the female territory of textual production and its connection to the so-called general culture and mainstream literary tradition. As a conceptual anchor, the *gui* illustrates a poetics of women in late imperial China that can account for their collective experience as well as their individual poetic expression. While their writings are connected to the literati tradition of feminine poetics associated with the boudoir, they simultaneously reconceived the spatial topos as a distinctive textual territory encoded with their subjective perspectives and experiences.

Social, cultural, and literary processes underlay their poetics, and their subjective experiences with the *gui* influenced the ways in which they transformed the boudoir topos. Two interconnected critical issues are at play here: the effect of language on gender and the effect of gender on language. The boudoir as an inherited poetic space was the property of male literati for centuries. The boudoir in its conventional sense, a space evoking feminine beauty and sentiments, assumed a significant place in both *shi* and *ci* poetry. This long-standing literary tradition established a culturally recognized mode of women's (or womanly) experience. The performance of conventional textual positions and artistic effects associated with the boudoir is a commonplace in late imperial women's poetry. Some of these poems have no marked references to the poet's actual life and experience but read as merely inspired by the literary past. They reveal a predetermined textual construction of feminine subjectivity and its influence on women's entry into the literary tradition.

However, women also lived outside of the poetic convention. When they became writing subjects, they projected in their poetry subjective perspectives and experiences determined in part by the social and historical conditions under which they lived. They not only wrote the tradition anew but also bestowed on the cultural signifier of the *gui* much broader and richer meanings emerging from their own social and cultural lives. They rendered the *gui* a discursive space whose scope extended beyond the sensual and emotive space that had been constructed in poetic convention.

Women's depictions of the boudoir constructed a textual territory distinct from poetic convention and were themselves diverse: different women writers or the same writer under different circumstances perceived and represented this space differently. Their writing on boudoir life drew nuance from their experiences and self-perceptions even as it was influenced by their socially gendered consciousness and shared ideals. Some women chose to embrace the expression of personal interests whatever the risk to ideals of female propriety. Indeed, the boudoir as inscribed in women's texts is far more complex than the cultural ideal in dominant discourses. Sometimes it appears to be a peaceful environment in which women enjoy their everyday lives; sometimes a prison in which women find themselves confined; sometimes a lost paradise that women persistently pursue in memories and dreams. The *gui* is a space full of ambivalent inscriptions, a site of struggle over the meaning of life as a woman, of female subjectivity.

Conclusion

In its search for self-meaning and exploration of the affects evoked in this symbolic space, the writing late imperial Chinese women produced on the *gui* reveals a complex process of self-understanding. The nuances of women's perspectives on and perceptions of gendered boundaries resulted in rich poetic expressions and strategies.

This study has put women's writing at the center of analysis, bringing forth the significance of their participation in and contribution to literary practice. It is important to note, however, that the dynamic relationship between the literary tradition and the creativity of an individual writer was by no means exclusive to women. Although men in general tended to perpetuate stereotyped images of women and the boudoir that were established in the poetic tradition, a few avant-garde male writers such as He Guochen and Zhou Shi fashioned a new style of boudoir poetics in a woman's voice that reflected the spirit of their time. These writings by male authors could have been inspired by the new modes of self-representation created by women writers or intended as a call for women to take up new subject positions. Their writings suggest that any mode of poetic expression can be after all a textual performance, which does not require the author's gender as an essential factor.

However, the gender status of authors remains germane. Women writers, rather than men, were the collective force that brought the innovative poetics of the boudoir into relief. While the relationship between the author's gender and what is represented in the text should not be essentialized, it is important to acknowledge the concurrent development of late imperial Chinese women's literary culture and the vibrant site of their representations of boudoir life. This does not imply that only women can "truly" represent themselves. Rather, the difference emerged from the different subject positions and experiences of men and women in relation to the *gui*.

A gendered location particularly associated with women, the *gui* influenced women authors more directly as both social and writing subjects. It was imperative for them to reconstruct the poetic genre in accord with their subjective experience and vision. Boudoir poetry in the literati tradition focused on the image and emotions of women, yet it had a problematic relationship to the historical subject positions and experiences of women in the late imperial era. Specifically, there were discrepancies between the abandoned-woman persona and the *guiren* or *guixiu* identity that orthodox gender ideology calls on women to claim. Thus, the revisionary impulse of the women authors examined in this study came from their foremost interest in rewriting the stereotypical images and feminine codes that could not adequately represent them in light of normative gender ideology and alternative self-conceptions. As poems by many authors included in *The Anthology of Correct* Beginnings illustrate, women's attempts to seek a coherent subject-position within contradictory discourses, in order to conform to normative ideological and aesthetic standards, played an instrumental role in their transformation of conventional boudoir poetics and aesthetics.

The transformative power of writing that women demonstrated in boudoir poetics was also due to the unprecedented development of a larger women's literary culture in the late imperial period. This culture not only encouraged more and more women to participate in literary practice but also cultivated new feminine ideals—such as the *guixiu* image—and lifestyles with which women could align themselves. Although different qualities of a *guixiu* were emphasized and the cultural activities that enriched their depictions of boudoir life were varied, literary talent remained an essential component. The image of a devoted woman poet, for example, established an unprecedented persona in the boudoir setting.

Literate women's culture was not merely limited to the women's sphere. It is evident that many women read extensively rather than focusing on female-centered literatures. Their exposure to broader and richer cultural traditions and trends took their vision beyond the inner chambers. Many were inspired to embrace ideals and values that transcended gendered roles and concerns. Importantly, they projected this broader vision in their depiction of boudoir life. Although the boudoir is still explicitly or implicitly depicted in their poetry, the sentiments associated with it fundamentally change the tone of the boudoir as a poetic space.

Beginning in the late Ming, as social upheavals increasingly pushed women to the forefront of historical change, some women poets cast a gaze outward from the "small window" of their boudoir, offering their perspectives on history and society. During the reformist movements of the late Qing and early Republican era, some pioneering women used poetry to connect the women's *gui* to political and cultural reforms. Their inscriptions of political sentiments such as loyalism and ideas of modernity into the boudoir space are remarkable.

Because the *gui* defined women's place in society, some women writers consciously invoked this conception of the *gui* in order to reflect on their gender roles. They used it as the symbol of their gender status but questioned and resisted their subjection as women. In reacting to social disorder as a woman who had no way to play an active role, Chen Yunlian's lines "Women located in the inner chambers, / Their ambitions cannot be fulfilled" are representative. In her understanding, the *gui* places restrictions on women, but is a normative gender location. Echoing Chen, yet taking a more radical stance, Gu Zhenli schematically subverted gender conventions associated with the *gui*. As the author, she demonstrates agency in moving across different subject-positions by strategies of deconstruction and construction. Her self-displacement from the conventional feminine subject constitution and her self-representation as an eccentric are a significant transformation of gendered identities associated with the *gui* space.

Ironically, it is because the thematics and stylistics of their writing go beyond the inner chambers that women such as Gu Zhenli won high compliments from their contemporary male critics. Like the sex-segregation ideology that consigned women to the *gui*, many critics in the Ming and Qing presumed that women's writing was predetermined by their gender status. Thus, they often showed their amazement when encountering women who were able to transcend the conventions of femininity and perform poetics that supposedly belonged to the men's domain. For example, in commenting on a poem by Zhou Qiong, which presents a self-image challenging the conventional role of women, the anthologist Deng Hanyi notes: "This is a poem by a lady from the inner chambers, but it bears the air of tragedy and grandeur. The author is indeed not an ordinary woman."[2] Contrasting the poetic style and gender of the poet, Deng's comment represents the recognition of women's transcendence of gender conventions associated with the *gui*, not only in terms of poetics, but also in terms of cultural assumptions about women's creativity.

These women writers may be viewed as revisionists. In reconstructing their image and the space of the boudoir, they demonstrated a creative mobilization of available discourses that accorded with their various expressive needs. Through adjusting and refashioning "the scripted voices and conventional scenarios of tradition," they discursively transformed the traditional feminine space associated with the boudoir.[3] Their literary agency manifests itself in the active interactions between the literary past and present, textual and historical experiences, ideology and literature, and negotiations with binary gendered categorizations. As Sabine Sielke puts it, "As we acknowledge subjectivity as a partly predetermined, partly self-determined interrogation of discourses, history turns out to be a dialogue and process mediating between past and present (texts)."[4] Taking into account social and cultural determinants in late imperial Chinese women's discursive practice as well as their individual literary agency makes it clear that, as both recipients and agents of their broader culture, women adopted in their writing variable positions and strategies in internalizing, reflecting, modifying, or criticizing prevalent ideas and conceptions about their gender.

A remarkable transformation of boudoir poetics brought about by the emergence of this critical mass of women authors is evident in the late imperial era, especially in the Qing period. Their reconstructions of images of women and the boudoir were meaningful to both themselves and their society and were definitely not merely discourses or enunciations, evacuated of their role as productive historical subjects.

The Western concept of "minority literature" is useful for examining Ming-Qing women's writing, in reference not only to the marginal status of the minority writers but also to their potential for bringing about historical change.[5] As a socially subordinate group, Ming-Qing writing women can be considered minority writers. They did not originally have a legitimate place in language from which to articulate their positions but had to use the language long developed in literati culture, "the language of the dominant." However, because of their problematic relationship to this language, it was necessary for them to "implicitly change the meaning of the established majority canon, with the intrusion and existence of 'difference from.'"[6]

With the body of their work, Ming-Qing women poets formed "China's late imperial minor tradition," one accorded wide recognition by both men and women of their time.[7] As *The Anthology of Correct Beginnings* shows, Yun Zhu and like-minded supporters sought to elevate women's writing to an unprecedented status. They moved beyond a claim for the legitimacy of women's writing toward an attempt to establish authority over women's literary production. Their efforts suggest, in fact, that the minor desired to become major. Judging from the rhetoric and strategies adopted in the making of the anthology and its legacy in later years, one could argue that Qing women's writing had indeed come to occupy "a crucially important place in Chinese literary history."[8]

How might this *guixiu* tradition have further evolved if it had not had been abruptly undermined by new cultural reforms in the late Qing and those of the May Fourth Movement? Disparaging this tradition as the product of "the woman of talent" who "teased the wind and fondled the moon," Liang Qingchao disqualified it as serious literature and learning. Following Liang, Hu Shi also deemed it useless because of its association with the inner chambers. This determined misreading for the purpose of advancing their own political agendas obscured a remarkable transformation of the literati tradition by late imperial women poets, a major development in Chinese literary history that is only now regaining its place in the limelight.

NOTES

INTRODUCTION

1. Hu Shi, "Sanbai nian zhong nü zuojia," 587–88.
2. Hu Shi's dismissal of Qing women's poetry followed the critical trend set by late Qing reformists such as Liang Qichao (1873–1929) that was against traditional feminine poetics in general. For more details, see chapter 5.
3. Among the most active scholars in this area are social historians such as Dorothy Ko, Susan Mann, and Paul Ropp and literary scholars such as Kang-i Sun Chang, Grace S. Fong, Beata Grant, Wilt Idema, Maureen Robertson, and Ellen Widmer, whose major studies are listed in the bibliography.
4. See, for example, David Palumbo-Liu's discussion of the Song poet Huang Tingjian (1045–1105) in his *The Poetics of Appropriation*.
5. For example, see Ko, *Teachers of the Inner Chambers*, and Ko, "Lady-Scholars." See also Mann, *Precious Records*, chapter 4.
6. Robertson, "Voicing the Feminine" and "Changing the Subject"; Fong, "Engendering the Lyric."
7. Robertson, "Changing the Subject," 200–204.
8. Viewing women's writings as "particularized by gendered subformations," Grace S. Fong shows the literary agency of women writers from their "differential positioning within a normative female hierarchy as daughters, mothers, wives, concubines, maids, etc." See Fong, *Herself an Author*.
9. Xu Shen's (58–147) *Shuowen jiezi* defines the *gui* as a gate specially set. See Xu Shen, *Shuowen*, 12.102.
10. For *guige*, for example, see Sima Qian, *Shi ji*, 120.262, For *guikun*, for example, see Ban Gu, *Bai hu tong*, 4.266. For *guifang*, for example, see Ban Gu, *Han shu*, 76. 264.
11. Ruan Yuan, *Shisanjing*, 28.533, 28.538, 28.538–39. All translations, unless otherwise indicated, are my own.
12. Song Ruozhao, *Nü lunyu*, 70. 3291.
13. Sima Guang, *Zhi jia*, 22952. For a quotation and discussion of this passage by Sima Guang, see Ebrey, *The Inner Quarters*, 23–24.
14. Ruan Yuan, *Shisanjing*, 27.520.
15. For a book-length biography and study of Ban Zhao, see Swann, *Pan Chao*. For discussions of Ban Zhao's *Nü jie*, see Lily Xiao Hong Lee, *The*

Virtue of Yin, 11–24; Chen Yu-shih, "The Historical Template of Pan Chao's *Nü chieh,*" 229–57. See also, Idema and Grant, *The Red Brush,* 11–43.

16. According to Huang Liling, there were two versions of *Nü si shu,* the Chinese and Japanese versions. The set of four books that circulated in Japan does not include the *Nüfan jielu* but the *Nü xiaojing* by Chen Miao of the Tang period instead. The other three are the same. See Huang Liling, *Nü sishu,* 3. The author of *Nüfan jielu* is also known as Liu shi.

17. Mann, *Precious Records,* 80.
18. Bray, *Technology and Gender,* 55.
19. Ibid.
20. For a discussion of Chen Hongmou's thought on women and family, see Rowe, *Saving the World,* 313–22.
21. Chen Hongmou, *Wuzhong yigui,* 100.
22. Rowe, *Saving the World,* 314.
23. Furth, "The Patriarch's Legacy," 196.
24. In this regard, I agree with William Rowe, who points out that "[n]o elite commentary in late imperial China, no matter how self-consciously reformist on gender issues, challenged the view that women fundamentally were not, could not be, and indeed morally should not be identical with men, or assume the same functions in society." See Rowe, "Women and the Family," 495.
25. Handlin, "Lü K'un's New Audience."
26. Ko, "Lady-Scholars." It is noteworthy that these women poets were active in the same period as Chen Hongmou.
27. Lü Kun, *Gui fan,* "Xu," 1a-b.
28. Ibid., "Yuanqi," 1a.
29. Ibid., "Xu," 1, 3.
30. Lü Kun, *Gui fan,* "Yuanqi," 1a.
31. Lü Kun, *Gui fan,* "Xu," 1a, 2a.
32. Handlin, "Lü K'un's New Audience," 26.
33. Borrowing the Freudian term "scopophilic instinct," Maureen Robertson offers an analysis of the aesthetic end of the poems in the *Yutai xinyong* as intended to satisfy male readers' "desire for specular pleasure." See Robertson, "Voicing the Feminine." For a study of the complicated history involved in Palace-Style poems about women, see Miao, "Palace-Style Poetry." For a recent interpretation of male authors' use of women's image and sexuality as a form of power struggle and social interaction, see Rouzer, *Articulated Ladies.*
34. Hu Ying, "Re-Configuring Nei/Wai," 87.
35. Having said that, I am indebted to Catherine Belsey's understanding of ideology as "both a real and an imaginary relation to the world—real in that it is the way in which people really live their relationship to the social relations which govern their conditions of existence, but imaginary in that it discourages a full understanding of these conditions of existence and the ways in which people are socially constituted within them." See Belsey, "Constructing the Subject," 46.

36. On the *querelle des femmes* between Zhang Xuecheng and Yuan Mei, see Mann, "Classical Revival and Gender Question," and Mann, "'Fuxue' (Women's Learning." For other discussions of the debate on women's talent, see also Chang, "Ming-Qing Women Poets," and Ho, "The Cultivation of Female Talent."

37. Gilbert and Gubar, *The Madwoman in the Attic*, 45–46.

38. For a discussion of the nonfictional nature of traditional Chinese poetry, see Owen, *Traditional Chinese Poetry and Poetics*, chapter 2.

39. Bray, *Gender and Technology*, 142.

40. My view of the paradox of a woman being both a "subjected being" and a "free agent" is indebted to Louis Althusser's view of the autonomy of the subject: individuals are subjected beings but "free" in the sense of their willingness to participate in the process of subject formation. See Althusser, *Lenin and Philosophy*, 169.

41. Drawing on Lacan's theory of the subject, Belsey provides an apt description of the situation these women faced: "The subject is thus the site of contradiction, and is consequently perpetually in the process of construction, thrown into crisis by alterations in language and in the social formation, capable of change." See Belsey, "Constructing the Subject," 50.

42. Robertson, "Changing the Subject," 200.

43. Gilbert and Gubar, *The Madwoman in the Attic*, "Preface to the First Edition," xi.

44. See, for example, Moi, *Sexual/Textual Politics*, 61–66.

45. Ibid., 75–80.

46. Gilbert and Gubar, *The Madwoman in the Attic*, "Preface to the First Edition," xi.

47. Felski, *Beyond Feminist Aesthetics*, 45.

48. Showalter, "Feminist Criticism," 260.

49. Counted by Ellen Widmer, in Widmer, "The Rhetoric of Retrospection," 193.

50. Cases of women of the working classes publishing in classical language and forms are rare. The most famous is that of He Shuangqing, the wife of a farmer, but her existence has been questioned. For a book-length study on this subject, see Ropp, *Banished Immortal*. For an introduction and English translation of works by peasant women in a script known as "women's script" (*nüshu*), unique to Jiangyong, Hunan, see Idema, *Heroines of Jiangyong*.

51. My observation here is based on examples in Grant, *Daughters of Emptiness*, 67, 133.

CHAPTER 1. THE GREEN WINDOW

1. Decades ago, Michael E. Workman proposed the term "boudoir/bedchamber topos" as a major convention of the *ci* genre. Although Workman, sampling early lyrics, focuses only on one conventional theme, the grief of separation associated with the women's chambers, his concept of topos in

theory is multidimensional and dynamic. See Workman, "The Bedchamber Topos," 7.

2. For an English translation of and introduction to the anthology, see Birrell, *New Songs*. Birrel also discusses this anthology with regard to postmodernist issues such as transgressive writing and homoerotics. See Birrell, *Games Poets Play*. For a more recent study of the anthology in the context of Liang literary culture, see Tian, *Beacon Fire and Shooting Star*, chapter 4. For a discussion of this anthology from the perspective of male literati's homosocial community, see also Rouzer, *Articulated Ladies*, chapter 4.

3. On Xiao Gang's literary salon and practice, see Marney, *Liang Chien-wen Ti*. See also Wu, *The Poetics of Decadence*, chapters 1 and 2; Miao, "Palace-Style Poetry"; Tian, *Beacon Fire and Shooting Star*, 144–50, 260–309.

4. The anthology was reprinted in many different editions during its long circulation history. Editors of the anthology from the Song onward tended to expand it by adding their own selections. Scholars hold different opinions about the number of poems. Ronald Miao and Anne Birrell claim that there are more than six hundred. Wu Zhaoyi and Cheng Yan's edition (1774) includes 870 poems. Wu notes that Song editions of the anthology were shorter, consisting of 691 poems. See Xu Ling, *Yutai xinyong*, 535–36.

5. For a review of previous major studies on the Palace Style and a view of the Palace Style as "a new poetics of seeing" illuminated by Buddhist teachings, see Tian, *Beacon Fire and Shooting Star*, 175–85, 211–59.

6. For the former view, see Miao, "Palace-Style Poetry," 8. For the latter point of view, see Tian, *Beacon Fire and Shooting Star*, 211–59. The term *xinti* is used by the compiler of the *Liang shu* as quoted in Tian, *Beacon Fire and Shooting Star*, 175.

7. Xiaofei Tian argues for a more fluid and diverse nature of Palace-Style poetry. The phrase "a poetry of images" is quoted from her. See Tian, *Beacon Fire and Shooting Star*, 202.

8. As quoted and translated by Xiaofei Tian, in ibid., 182.

9. As quoted in Mu Kehong, in Xu Ling, *Yutai xinyong*, 2.

10. As Xiaofei Tian points out, the term *ti* should not necessarily be understood as the subject matter of poetry but as the style or form. It seems fitting to take the *ti* of the boudoir as observed by Hu Yinglin in this light as well. See Tian, *Beacon Fire and Shooting Star*, 175.

11. Xu Ling, "Xu," in *Yutai xinyong*, 12–13.

12. The figuration of a female audience here has elicited different interpretations. While Anne Birrell and Paul Rouzer take it as a rhetorical prop that is not indicative of an actual female readership, Xiaofei Tian argues that the female figure indeed represents the anthology's targeted audience, literary women in the Liang palace. See Birrell, *New Songs*, 6; Rouzer, *Articulated Ladies*, 136; Tian, *Beacon Fire and Shooting Star*, 189–95.

13. In her recent book, Birrell attempts to show the distinctiveness of the voices of a few women authors, arguing that, to varying degrees, these women inscribe their female selves into their verses. See Birrell, *Games Poets Play*, 176–208.

14. Rouzer, *Articulated Ladies*, 289.

15. Birrell, *New Songs*, 9.
16. Kang Zhengguo, *Fengsao*, 167.
17. Xu Ling, *Yutai xinyong*, 385.
18. See, for example, Marney, *Liang Chien-wen Ti*, 103. See also Miao, "Palace-Style Poetry," 13–14.
19. For a discussion of "Nineteen Old Poems" and an English translation and annotation of seventeen of the poems, see Watson, *Chinese Lyricism*, 15–32. Wu Zhaoyi and Cheng Yan's edition, the version I use, includes nine poems considered to have been authored by the Han writer Mei Cheng (d. 140 BCE).
20. Xu Ling, *Yutai xinyong*, 1.19–20. Translation by Anne Birrell, in Birrell, *New Songs*, 39.
21. Xu Ling, *Yutai xinyong*, 1.21. Translation by Anne Birrell, in Birrell, *New Songs*, 40.
22. Samei, *Gendered Persona*, 57.
23. Lady Li was a Han palace woman famous for her beauty and singing talent. After she died, the Han emperor's necromancer tried to make her soul return. See Wu Zhaoyi's annotation in Xu Ling, *Yutai xinyong*, 2.87. Adopting this allusion, the poet expresses his wish to see his late wife.
24. Xu Ling, *Yutai xinyong*, 2.86–87. Translation by Anne Birrell, in Birrell, *New Songs*, 83.
25. Chang, *Six Dynasties Poetry*, 154–56. On the court poets' particular ways of seeing and treating things in their *yongwu* poetry, see also Tian, *Beacon Fire and Shooting Star*, 211–59.
26. Chang, *Six Dynasties Poetry*, 155.
27. Xu Ling, *Yutai xinyong*, 5.191–92.
28. Birrell, *New Songs*, 10.
29. Xu Ling, *Yutai xinyong*, 7.299. Translation by Anne Birrell, in Birrell, *New Songs*, 199.
30. Birrell, *New Songs*, 11.
31. For these poems, see, respectively, Xu Ling, *Yutai xinyong*, 7.298, 8.346, 8.376.
32. Rouzer, *Articulated Ladies*, 139.
33. The original title is "To harmonize with Xu Lushi's Poem on Seeing His Wife Making Bedding." I follow Birrell's translation of the title, "Her Hidden Room."
34. Xu Ling, *Yutai xinyong*, 7.289. Translated by Anne Birrell, with modification of line 11. See Birrell, *New Songs*, 193–94.
35. For this poem attributed to Ban Jieyu, see Xu Ling, *Yutai xinyong*, 1.25–26.
36. Ibid., 8.376.
37. Ibid., 8.346. Translation by Anne Birrell, in Birrell, *New Songs*, 220. For another translation and discussion of this poem, see Robertson, "Voicing the Feminine," 70.
38. Birrell, *New Songs*, 15. For an early example linking human aging with seasonal changes, see lines 7–10 in Qu Yuan's (340–278 BCE) "Li sao," in *Chu ci*, 2. For a thematic analysis of lamentation over human transience

expressed in Han *yuefu* poetry such as those in "Nineteen Old Poems," see Cai Zongqi, *The Matrix of Lyric Transformation*, 69–74.

39. Birrell, *New Songs*, 15.
40. Xu Ling, *Yutai xinyong*, 8.366.
41. Ibid., 5.214. Translation by Anne Birrell, in Birrell, *New Songs*, 158–59.
42. Many scholars have noted the immorality associated with Palace-Style writing. For an early study making such an observation, see Marney, *Liang Chien-wen Ti*, 115–17. Fusheng Wu views "decadent poetry" as a subgenre, arguing that the poetry poses a challenge to the orthodox poetic canon. See Wu, *The Poetics of Decadence*, 33–36.
43. See, for example, Rouzer, *Writing Another's Dream*; Wu, *The Poetics of Decadence*, chapters 3–5; Owen, *The Late Tang*, 168–82.
44. Rouzer, *Writing Another's Dream*, 70.
45. There are many debates regarding the origin of the *ci*. My argument focuses on the literati practice. For a review of the evolution of the genre in its broader social and cultural contexts, see Chang, *The Evolution of Chinese Tz'u Poetry*, introduction. See also Lin, "Formation of a Distinct Generic Identity," 375–91.
46. It includes a few Tang poets.
47. Fusek, *Among the Flowers*, 12.
48. Fong, "Persona and Mask," 460.
49. Quoted in Ouyang Jiong, *Huajian ji*, 221.
50. Ibid.
51. Yu, "Song Lyrics and the Canon," 75.
52. There are a few poems in which love sentiments are expressed from the perspective of the male lover. Although the male perspective can be identified through some specific referential information, the sentiments are not significantly different from those expressed from the perspective of the female persona. For a discussion of the male voice in the *Huajian ji*, see Samei, *Gendered Persona*, 176–81.
53. Ouyang Jiong, *Huajian ji*, 1.4.
54. Ibid., 1.2. Translation by Paul Rouzer, in Rouzer, *Writing Another's Dream*, 64–65.
55. Ouyang Jiong, *Huajian ji*, 1.8. Translation based on Paul Rouzer's in Rouzer, *Writing Another's Dream*, 66–67.
56. See, for example, Gao Feng, *Huajian ci yanjiu*, 47–50.
57. Ibid., 49.
58. Hong Huasui, "Huajian ci," 218–73.
59. Ouyang Jiong, *Huajian ji*, 9.167. Translation by Lois Fusek, in Fusek, *Among the Flowers*, 165.
60. Yeh, "Ambiguity," 121.
61. Here, I use the concept of canon in Wendell Harris's sense of "nonce canon," which promotes a body of texts embracing an emerging new literary style or taste. See Harris, "Canonicity," 112, 116.
62. Egan, *The Literary Works of Ou-yang Hsiu*, 133.

63. For a discussion of this *ci* and the anecdote describing the circumstances under which the poet wrote it, see ibid., 135–37.
64. *Quan Song ci*, 1.140. Translation by Ronald Egan, in Egan, *The Literary Works of Ou-yang Hsiu*, 136.
65. *Quan Tang shi*, 541.6222
66. Egan, *The Literary Works of Ou-yang Hsiu*, 156.
67. Ibid., 154.
68. As quoted in Fong, *Wu Wenying*, 50.
69. This *ci* has also been attributed to Feng Yansi (903–960), but scholars such as James Liu think that its style is closer to Ouyang Xiu's. See Liu, *Major Lyricists*, 43. The authorship of this *ci* does not matter for my discussion of the development of boudoir poetics by literati authors.
70. Ouyang Xiu, *Ouyang Xiu quanji*, 231–32. Translation by James Liu, in Liu, *Major Lyricists*, 43, with modifications.
71. For these lyrics, see Li Qingzhao, *Li Qingzhao ji*, 105–10.
72. Fong, "Engendering the Lyric," 121.
73. Ibid.
74. Li Qingzhao, *Li Qingzhao ji*, 59–60. Translated by Wilt Idema and Beata Grant, with modifications. See Idema and Grant, *The Red Brush*, 225–26.
75. For Xie Yi's and Liu Yong's lines, see, respectively, *Quan Song ci*, 2.649, 1.25.
76. "Three Times Five" refers to the First Night Festival.
77. Li Qingzhao, *Li Qingzhao ji*, 150. Translation by Wilt Idema and Beata Grant, in Idema and Grant, *The Red Brush*, 232.
78. Ibid. 111. Translation by Wilt Idema and Beata Grant, with minor modifications, in Idema and Grant, *The Red Brush*, 233.
79. For this lyric to the tune "Pride of Fisherman," see Li Qingzhao, *Li Qingzhao ji*, 8.
80. Ibid., 1.94.
81. In addition to the view at night, Yan Shu's *ci* describes a longer process of time change, from night to early morning.
82. *Quan Song ci*, 1.89.
83. For a discussion of Li Yu's manipulation of the boudoir convention, see Workman, "The Bedchamber Topos." See also Samei, *Gendered Persona*, 83–84.
84. Long before *ci* practice, literati authors had invoked daily life in the home setting as a rich source of representational codes in the *shi* genre. Early examples can be traced back to Tao Qian (365–427), but mid-Tang poets such as Yuan Zhen (779–831) and Bai Juyi (772–846) brought forth the literati's private, domestic life as popular subject matter. See Liu Ning, *Tang Song zhi ji shige*, especially 3–10. Representation of the literati's everyday lifestyle in the *shi* genre may have influenced *ci* writers in choosing the subject matter, but the two genres are different in aesthetic style.
85. Egan, *Word, Image, and Deed*, 312.
86. Fong, "Engendering the Lyric," 121.

87. Poetry with erotic themes has been thought to resist allegorical reading because of its particular attention to the evocation of "glamour and charm" by means of sensual details. See Miao, "Palace-Style Poetry," 31.

88. On the theory and practice of this school, see Yeh, "The Ch'ang-chou School."

89. Zhang Jian, *Qindai shixue*, 203.

90. See Wang Yanhong, *Wang Cihui shi ji*.

91. Shen Deqian, *Qingshi biecai*, "Fanli," 2.

92. Ibid, 7.132.

93. Ibid.

94. For a study of the seventeenth-century *ci* revival, see Chu, "Interplay between Tradition and Innovation."

95. Ibid., 74.

96. On different *ci* schools in the Qing period, see Wang Yunxi and Gu Yisheng, *Zhongguo wenxue piping shi*, chapter 4. See also Zhang Hongsheng, *Qingdai cixue*, chapter 6.

97. Yeh Chia-ying thinks that the autobiographical and symbolic elements of Chen Zilong's love lyrics make them excellent candidates for allegorical readings, particularly as the expression of patriotic sentiment. See Yeh, "Ch'en Tzu-lung." Kang-i Sun Chang's book-length study of Chen Zilong and Liu Rushi takes the perspective that Chen's political poetry was inspired by his love poetry addressed to Liu. See Chang, *The Late-Ming Poet Ch'en Tzu-lung*.

98. For a study of Zhu Yizun's love lyrics in the *Jingzhiju qinqu*, see Fong, "Inscribing Desire."

99. It is believed that he composed the lyrics to record his love affair with his wife's sister. See Fong, "Inscribing Desire," 448.

CHAPTER 2. A NEW FEMININE IDEAL

1. Fong, "Engendering the Lyric," 118–19.

2. Idema and Grant, *The Red Brush*, 7; Widmer, *The Beauty and the Book*, 28.

3. This term is borrowed from Stephen Owen; see Owen, "The Self's Perfect Mirror," 79. I find it useful because women's boudoir poetry was often produced and received as a more realistic depiction of their life experience. There are cases in which the author claims distance from what she presents, signaling it with titles such as "I Wrote This Poem on Behalf of Others." Poems in these cases are written mostly in conventional modes such as the boudoir plaint and the appreciation of feminine beauty.

4. For an article focused on the literary milieu of the anthology and its textual politics as a case study of literary women seeking legitimacy and authority for their discursive practice, see Li Xiaorong, "Gender and Textual Politics." Here I only reiterate some major points so as to contextualize the textual transformation to be discussed in the remainder of this chapter.

Materials for pages 86–92 in this chapter are derived from ibid., 77, 81–83, 91–93, and 96, with the permission of the editors.

5. Wang Qishu's *Xiefang ji* (printed 1773) and Huang Zhimo's *Guochao guixiu liuxu ji* (printed 1853), two anthologies compiled by male scholars, include more poems and authors than *The Anthology of Correct Beginnings*. Given the large number of copies extant in libraries around China and in present-day book markets in the Jiangzhe region, it is likely that Yun Zhu's anthology was widely published and circulated.

6. Qian Zhonglian, "Xu," in Xie Zhengguang and She Rufeng, *Qingchu ren xuan qingchu shi huikao*, 2–3.

7. Here, I translate the term *zheng*, used by Shen Deqian, Yun Zhu, and other Qing poets and anthologists, as "orthodox" (or, occasionally, "correct"). Kwang-Ching Liu notes that "orthodoxy" is almost synonymous with "Confucianism"; see his "Introduction: Orthodoxy in Chinese Society," in Kwang-Ching Liu, *Orthodoxy in Late Imperial China*, 1.

8. On Shen Deqian's poetic theory and practice, see Zhang Jian, *Qingdai shixue*, 511–70.

9. Ibid., 533.

10. Ibid., 570.

11. Shen Deqian, *Qingshi biecai ji*, "Fanli," 2.

12. Ibid. "The green bower," not to be confused with "the green window," refers to the dwellings of prostitutes and courtesans.

13. Yun Zhu, *Guochao guixiu zhengshi ji*, "Liyan," 5a.

14. Ibid.

15. Ibid., "Fulu," 8b–21a.

16. Mann, *Precious Records*, 216.

17. Yun Zhu, *Guochao guixiu zhengshi ji*, "Liyan," 5a.

18. Kong Yingda, *Maoshi zhengyi*, in Ruan Yuan, *Shisanjing zhushu*, 2:19.

19. Mann, *Precious Records*, 116.

20. Yun Zhu, *Guochao guixiu zhengshi ji*, 16.23b.

21. Ibid., 2a. Translation by Susan Mann in Mann, *Precious Records*, 96, with a minor modification.

22. Robertson, "Changing the Subject," 200.

23. Yun Zhu, *Guochao guixiu zhengshi ji*, 20.24b.

24. Xu Ling, *Yutai xinyong*, 7.285. Translation by Anne Birrell, in Birrell, *New Songs*, 191.

25. Gao Jingfang, *Hongxuexuan gao*, 3.17b–18a.

26. On the *Langui baolu*, see Mann, *Precious Records*, 208–14.

27. Yun Zhu, *Langui baolu*, 6.15b.

28. Yun Zhu, *Guochao guixiu zhengshi ji*, 8.11b. The copy I consulted is held in the Library of the Chinese Academy of Sciences and contains six *juan*. Hu Wenkai also points out this mistake made by Yun Zhu. See Hu Wenkai, *Lidai funü zhuzuo kao*, 499.

29. Yun Zhu, *Guochao guixiu zhengshi ji*, 8.13b.

30. The term *qin* in line 4 is ambiguous; it can refer to her natal parents or to her parents-in-law.

31. Men also wore hairpins, but the type of hairpin called *chai* was specially used by women.

32. Yun Zhu, *Guochao guixiu zhengshi ji*, 1.14a.

33. Robertson suggests that women's rewriting of coded images is not conducted in "any programmatic way." According to her, only in a few cases was their employment of established codes the result of discursive positions different from those in conventional models. See Robertson, "Voicing the Feminine," 82.

34. Yun Zhu, *Guochao guixiu zhengshi ji*, "Buyi," 15b.

35. *Quan Tang shi*, 227.2451.

36. Yun Zhu, *Guochao guixiu zhengshi ji*, 12.1.

37. *Quan Tang shi*, 683.7911.

38. Robertson, "Voicing the Feminine," 83.

39. Ko, *Teachers of the Inner Chambers*, 160.

40. Meng Guang's husband, Liang Hong (courtesy name Boluan), wrote "Song of Five Sighs," which criticizes the Han court's decadent lifestyle, and was forced to go into exile to escape the emperor's persecution. For Liang Hong's biography, see Fan Ye, *Hou Han shu*, 83. 2765–68.

41. Yun Zhu, *Guochao guixiu zhengshi ji*, "Buyi," 43b.

42. Xu Ling, as mentioned in chapter 1, was the compiler of the *Yutai xinyong*. Yu Xin was also an important poet in the practice of the Palace Style. See Chang, *Six Dynasties Poetry*, 146–84.

43. The bureaucratic practice of posting officials away from their native places started in the Qin dynasty (221–206 BCE), but the Ming and Qing developed the system of avoidance. For a study of the avoidance system of the Qing and its predecessors, see Wei Xiumei, *Qingdai zhi huibi zhidu*, 5–56.

44. It was also common practice for a husband to go to his post accompanied by his concubine and leave his wife behind to take care of the household.

45. *Yujian* (fish letter) is a special term referring to a letter carried by a carp to a loved one, derived from the Han *yuefu* "Watering Horse at a Long Wall Hole," in Xu Ling, *Yutai xinyong*, 1.33–34. For an English translation of this poem, see Birrell, *New Songs*, 47.

46. Yun Zhu, *Guochao guixiu zhengshi ji*, 17.4.

47. Robertson, "Voicing the Feminine," 69.

48. Yun Zhu, *Guochao guixiu zhengshi ji*, 9.23b.

49. *Quan Tang shi*, 143.1446.

50. Xu Zhen'e, *Shishuo xinyu jiaojian*, 17.4, 349. Translation by Richard B. Mather, in Mather, *A New Account*, 324.

51. For a study of the various implications of the cult of *qing* in Ming-Qing literature, see Martin Huang, "Sentiments of Desire."

52. Yun Zhu, *Guochao guixiu zhengshi xuji*, "Fulu," 13b.

53. Yun Zhu, *Guochao guixiu zhengshi ji*, 14.5b-6a.

54. Yun Zhu, *Guochao guixiu zhengshi xuji*, "Buyi," 9b.

55. Yun Zhu, *Guochao guixiu zhengshi ji*, 9.11a.

56. Ibid., 18.1b.

57. The second watch (7:00–9:00 P.M.), *er geng*, is the second of the five two-hour periods into which the night was traditionally divided.

58. Yun Zhu, *Guochao guixiu zhengshi ji*, 5.6b.
59. Mann, *Precious Records*, 99.
60. *Lunyu*, 3.20, 32.
61. Kang-i Sun Chang introduces the concept of "androgyny" into the discussion of Ming-Qing women's literary culture. See Chang, "Ming-Qing Women Poets and Cultural Androgyny."
62. Ibid., 14, 15.
63. For another study drawing on the concept of androgyny, see Zhou Zuoyan, *Androgyny*.
64. Yun Zhu, *Guochao guixiu zhengshi ji*, "Xu," 4b.
65. Ibid., 15.12b. For another English translation and brief note on this poem, see Robertson, "Changing the Subject," 204.
66. Chang, "Ming-Qing Women Poets and Cultural Androgyny," 17; Robertson, "Changing the Subject," 203.
67. Yun Zhu, *Guochao guixiu zhengshi ji*, 20.23b.
68. Xu Ling, *Yutai xinyong*, 2.68. Translation by Anne Birrell, in Birrell, *New Songs*, 71–72.
69. Birrell's translation does not have these last two lines, which are included in the version I use. Translation of the two lines is mine.
70. Yun Zhu, *Guochao guixiu zhengshi ji*, 6.19a-b.
71. Chang, "Ming-Qing Women Poets and Cultural Androgyny," 13.
72. For a study of the changing concept of the recluse in literature from antiquity to the late Qing, see Li Chi, "The Changing Concept of the Recluse," 234–47. For a book-length study of the evolution of the practice of reclusion from early China to the Six Dynasties, see Berkowitz, *Patterns of Disengagement*.
73. As noted in chapter 1, Yuan Zhen and Bai Juyi of the mid-Tang had begun a trend of using daily life in the home setting as a rich source of poetic inspiration.
74. Ko, *Teachers of the Inner Chambers*, 152.
75. Yuan Hongdao, *Yuan Zhonglang quan ji*, 77.
76. On Yuan Hongdao and the Gong'an school, see Chou, *Yuan Hung-tao*.
77. Lu You (1125–1210) has a number of poems titled "Late Spring," yet none of them uses the same rhyme as Bing Yue's poem. He has only one pentasyllabic poem, "Families in Late Spring Mountains," that adopts the same category of rhymes. See *Quan Song shi* 39, 2177.24771. Presumably, Bing Yue is referring to this poem. However, there is no thematic similarity between the two.
78. Yun Zhu, *Guochao guixiu zhengshi xuji*, 6.2b.
79. Yun Zhu, *Guochao guixiu zhengshi ji*, 6.3a-b.
80. Translation by Herbert Giles, in Minford and Lau, *An Anthology of Translations*, 1009.
81. Yun Zhu, *Guochao guixiu zhengshi ji*, 6.2a-b.
82. Ibid., 6.2a.
83. Ibid., 3.16b.
84. *Lunyu*, 15.1.

85. Relating Tao Qian's philosophy of life to Confucianism, Buddhism, and Daoism is a complex issue in Chinese scholarship. A popular theory is that he was a Confucian in his early years but turned to the philosophy of Lao-Zhuang and Buddhism in his late years. For a study of Tao Qian's influence in the Chinese literary tradition, see Charles Kwong, *Tao Qian*. For a study of Tao Qian's image and legacy as a recluse, see Berkowitz, *Patterns of Disengagement*, 215–26. On the construction of Tao Qian as a perfect recluse by his early biographers, see Wendy Swartz, "Rewriting a Recluse." For a study of how the cultural icon Tao Qian was produced in the context of manuscript culture, see Xiaofei Tian, *Tao Yuanming and Manuscript Culture*.

86. Tao Qian, *Tao Yuanming ji*, 123–28.
87. Ibid., 126.
88. Yun Zhu, *Guochao guixiu zhengshi ji*, 6.12a.
89. Ibid., 8.19a.
90. Li Chi, "The Changing Concept of the Recluse," 241.
91. Tao Qian, *Tao Yuanming ji*, 89.
92. Chang, "Ming-Qing Women Poets and Cultural Androgyny," 11.
93. *Lunyu*, 17.9, 192.
94. Owen, *Readings in Chinese Literary Thought*, 43.

CHAPTER 3. CONVENTION AND INTERVENTION

1. For a general evaluation of Gu Zhenli's life and lyrics, see Deng Hongmei, *Nüxing ci shi*, 257–70. For discussions and English translations of her lyrics, see also Chang and Saussy, *Women Writers of Traditional China*, 426–29; Li Xiaorong, "Engendering Heroism," 30–34; and Wai-yee Li, "Early Qing to 1723," 183–84.
2. See Yun Zhu, *Zhengshi xuji*, 2.13b–24a.
3. Deng Hongmei, *Nüxing ci shi*, 258.
4. Chen Weisong, *Furen ji*, 56–57.
5. For examples of comments on Gu Zhenli's lyrics by critics of later generations, see You and You, *Qing ci jishi*, 288–89.
6. Hou Jian, "Postscript to the *Qixiangge ci*." Quoted from You and You, *Qing ci jishi*, 288.
7. Her voice in the *shi* poems is not as distinctive as that in her song lyrics.
8. The edition more accessible to scholars today is not this first version published in 1823 but the one reprinted in 1896 in Xu Naichang's *Xiaotanluanshi guixiu huike ci*. I have not been able to find the 1823 version. None of the major libraries in China hold it. I know of its existence only through Hu Wenkai's *Lidai funü* and the *Qing ci jishi huiping*. The latter includes several excerpts from the prefaces and postscript to the 1823 version *Qixiangge ci*. See Hu Wenkai, *Lidai funü*, 804; You and You, *Qing ci jishi*, 288.
9. *Quan Qing ci*, 7.3759.
10. *Quan Tang shi*, 768.8724.
11. For an example in which the poet uses this motif, see Meng Haoran's (689–740) poem "A Spring Dawn," in *Quan Tang shi*, 160.168.

12. Li Qingzhao, *Li Qingzhao ji*, 67.
13. For a study on the influence of Li Qingzhao on Ming-Qing women's *ci* writings, see Zhang Hongsheng, "*Jingdian queli yu chuangzuo jiangou.*"
14. *Quan Qing ci*, 7.3759.
15. Ibid., 7.3769.
16. A kind of paper created by the Tang courtesan poet Xue Tao that was specially used for the writing of poetry.
17. *Quan Qing ci*, 7.3769.
18. Ibid., 7.3779.
19. Jiang Zhu (1764–1804) provides an example of a woman poet who struggled with the dilemma of having to give up her poetic engagement for Buddhist practice. See Grant, "Little Vimalakirti," 286–307.
20. For her appropriation of the heroic mode in the form of *Man jiang hong* in order to protest gender inequality, see Li Xiaorong, "Engendering Heroism," 30–34.
21. You and You, *Qing ci jishi*, 288. As Gu Zhenli addresses Hou Jin as Rongbin in a lyric discussed below, presumably it is his courtesy name.
22. *Quan Qing ci*, 7.3785.
23. Ibid., 7.3766.
24. Ibid., 7.3768. Translated by Kathryn Lowry, with modifications in lines 2 and 6. See Chang and Saussy, *Women Writers of Traditional China*, 428. Note that the crucial difference in line 6 is my use of the verb "exchange" (*huan* 換) instead of "soak" in Lowry's translation. Her rendition might be based on another similar character (渙), but the original texts included in both *Qu* and Xu Naichang's *Xiaotanluanshi guixiu huike ci* use the character 換.
25. Bray, *Technology and Gender*, 265.
26. For an example of a woman who portrays the moral gesture of donating her dowry to her husband's family, see Hang Wenru, "Handing in My Treasure Box," in Yun Zhu, *Guochao guixiu Zhengshi ji*, 8.19b–20a.
27. Sima Xiangru's authorship of "Changmen fu" is debatable. For a discussion and an English translation of this *fu*, see Knechtges, *Court Culture*, 47–64.
28. Ibid., 50.
29. *Quan Qing ci*, 7.3758.
30. *Quan Tang shi*, 182.1853. Translation by Stephen Owen, in *The Great Age of Chinese Poetry*, 138.
31. In populating his surroundings, Stephen Owen argues, Li Bai demonstrates his "creative self-sufficiency" rather than loneliness. See Owen, *The Great Age of Chinese Poetry*, 138. My reading, however, differs from Owen's.
32. Translation by Stephen Owen, in ibid., 138.
33. For the poem, see *Quan Tang shi*, 890.10051.
34. *Quan Qing ci*, 7.3758.
35. See Deng Hongmei, *Nüxing ci shi*, 262. However, she does not provide a source of information or explain why she thinks so.
36. *Quan Qing ci*, 7.3759.

37. For an example in which a male poet uses the same word in order to create an unconventional, masculine style, see the well-known line by Li He "The Eastern Pass's acid wind shoots the apple of the eye." On Li He's poem, see Tu Kuo-Ch'ing, *Li Ho*, 58–59.

38. *Quan Qing ci*, 7.3760.

39. The phrase "the Three Star entering the door" is derived from the poem "Chou mou," in *Shi jing* (*Maoshi* no. 118). For an English translation of this poem, see Waley, *Book of Songs*, 87. The phrase, "bearing fruit to benefit the house" is borrowed from "Tao yao," *Shi jing* (*Maoshi* no. 6). For an English translation of this poem, see Waley, *Book of Songs*, 106.

40. *Quan Qing ci*, 7.3760.

41. Ibid., 7.3771.

42. Chen Weisong, *Furen ji*, 56–57.

43. These two lines allude to "The Biography of Li Mi," discussed in text below.

44. *Quan Qing ci*, 7.3761–62.

45. Another example is Shen Cai (b. 1732), who was born much later than Gu Zhenli and also expresses her negative attitude toward bound feet in poetry. See Fong, *Herself an Author*, 79–80. *The Anthology of Correct Beginnings* also includes a poem by Li shi criticizing this bodily practice; see "Bow Shoes," in Yun Zhu, *Zhengshi xuji*, 6.25b.

46. *Quan Qing ci*, 7.3762.

47. Ibid., 20.3785.

48. See Fan Ye, comp., *Hou Han shu*, 23.3270–71.

49. For a recent study of women's poetry on illness in late imperial China, see Fong, "Writing and Illness." See also Yang, "Women and the Aesthetics of Illness."

50. Fong, "Writing and Illness," 30.

51. Liu Yiqing, *Shishuo xinyu*, 19.26, 697. For a discussion of this story, see Qian, *Spirit and Self*, 146–48.

52. Qian, *Spirit and Self*, 147.

53. Wei Shou, *Wei shu*, 90.1938.

54. *Quan Qing ci*, 7.3785. (Xu) Feiqiong is a female immortal who lives in Jasper Terrace (Yaotai) and can bring people to the immortals' land through dreams. For the record of Xu Feiqiong, see Li Fang, *Taiping guang ji*, 70.433.

55. Tao Qian, *Tao Yuanming ji*, 90–91. Translated by James Hightower, with one modification. I translate the term *xiao'ao* as "unrestrained and haughty" instead of "complacent," in his original translation. See Hightower, *The Poetry of Tao Qian*, 134.

56. Xin Qiji (1140–1207), for example, is known as a creator of these images. For a study analyzing the images of the self constructed in Xin Qinji's lyrics, see Lian, *The Wild and Arrogant*.

57. *Quan Song ci*, 3.1583.

58. Many scholars note the influence of these late Ming trends on women's literary culture. See, for example, Ko, *Teachers of the Inner Chambers*, 59–60. See also Zhong Huiling, *Qingdai nü shiren yanjiu*, 5–21.

59. For a discussion of Zhou Qiong's poetic voice, see Wai-yee Li, "Women Writers and Gender Boundaries," 201–3.
60. "In Reply to Zhang Cichen in His Rhyme," in Deng Hanyi, *Shiguan*, 449.
61. Green Creek is located in present-day Nanjing, Jiangsu.
62. Lone Hill is located in present-day Hangzhou, Zhejiang.
63. *Quan Qing ci*, 7.3762.
64. Ibid., 7.3772.
65. *Quan Song shi* 2, 106.1217–1218.
66. *Quan Qing ci*, 7.3763.
67. Sielke, *Fashioning the Female Subject*, 34.
68. My use of the word "deconstruction" here refers to Gu's sweeping attacks on conventions of femininity and normative womanhood in her lyrics.
69. Sielke, *Fashioning the Female Subject*, 22.
70. Ibid., 220.
71. Ibid.
72. Ibid., 108.

CHAPTER 4. INSIDE OUT

1. Chang, "Women's Poetic Witnessing," 505.
2. For studies in this regard, see, for example, Fong, "Writing from Experience," and Wai-yee Li, "History and Memory in Wu Weiye's Poetry." For a general review of history and memory in early Qing literature by both men and women, see also Wai-yee Li, "Early Qing to 1723," 168–200.
3. In her study of "poems of witness" by women during the Ming-Qing era, Chang calls attention to the significant roles women played in recording their experiences in times of war and chaos. See Chang, "Women's Poetic Witnessing."
4. See, for example, Wakeman, *The Great Enterprise*, 1.
5. Struve, *Voices from the Ming-Qing Cataclysm*, 2.
6. Twitchett and Fairbank, *The Cambridge History*, 264.
7. Reilly, *The Taiping Heavenly Kingdom*, 3.
8. Dong Baohong, *Yinxiangge shichao*, 11a.
9. Several rebellions involved armies called the "Red Turbans" in earlier times. Given her time and region, the author presumably means the Taipings because they also wore red turbans as typical rebel head coverings.
10. Yizheng was also referred to as Zhenzhou in ancient times.
11. *Qing shi gao*, 20.727.
12. For a discussion of songs centered on the image of Luofu, see Allen, "From Saint to Singing Girl."
13. For the poem, see Xu Ling, *Yutai xinyong*, 1.6–9.
14. "Orally Composed the New Year's Day," in Dong Baohong, *Yinxiangge shichao*, 10a–b.
15. Dong Baohong, *Yinxiangge shichao*, 1b–2a. "Facing the pond" means to learn calligraphy.

16. "Sigh over My Life," in Dong Baohong, *Yinxiangge shichao*, 12a.
17. Dong Baohong, *Yinxiangge shichao*, 19a–b.
18. "Rhapsody on My Life's Encounters," in Dong Baohong, *Yinxiangge shichao*, 19a, 20b.
19. Ibid. 19a.
20. Dong Baohong, *Yinxiangge shichao*, 11b.
21. For a biography of Cai Runshi, see *Guangxu Zhangzhou fuzhi*, 34.742–743.
22. Huang Daozhao and Cai Runshi, *Huangshizhaigong kangli weikangao*, 42.
23. For a biography of Huang Daozhou, see *Ming shi*, 255. 6592–6601, and *Guangxu Zhangzhou fuzhi*, 31. 638–41. For Huang Daozhou's loyalist activities in the last years of his life and for an account of his death, see also Struve, *The Southern Ming*, 89–92, and Mote, *Imperial China*, 835–36.
24. *Guangxu Zhangzhou fuzhi*, 34.742.
25. Mote, *Imperial China*, 835.
26. Ibid., 836.
27. *Guangxu Zhangzhou fuzhi*, 34.742.
28. The poem mentions Huang's death. See Huang Daozhou and Cai Runshi, *Huangshizhaigong kangli weikangao*, 43.
29. This allusion is derived from Tao Qian's "The Peach Blossom Spring," for which see Tao Qian, *Tao Yuanming ji*, 165–68. For an English translation, see Hightower, *The Poetry of Tao Qian*, 254–58.
30. In Tao's writing, people in the Peach Blossom Spring had fled to avoid troubles at the time of the Qin dynasty. It is particularly relevant for Cai to allude to this story in her poem.
31. See Ko, *Teachers of the Inner Chambers*, esp. 117–22.
32. "An Autumn Day on the Lake." See Gong Xianzong, *Nüxing wenxue bai jia zhuan*, 366.
33. Gong Xianzong, *Nüxing wenxue bai jia zhuan*, 367.
34. Wu Chai, *Peiqiuge yigao*, "Xu," 10a–b.
35. Ibid., 1.12a.
36. The original poem in the *Shi jing* (*Maoshi* no. 57) celebrates the wedding of the daughter of the Lord of Qi. As Waley suggests, this song may have also been sung at ordinary people's weddings. See Waley, *Book of Songs*, 81. For an English translation of the poem, see ibid., *Book of Songs*, 80.
37. Wu Chai, *Peiqiuge yigao*, 1.12a.
38. *Quan Tang shi*, 285.49
39. For a historical record mentioning Ban Zhao completing the *Han shu*, see her biography in Fan Ye, *Hou Han shu*, 84.2784.
40. See, for example, "In the Fifth Month of the Year Guihai [1863] When Bandits Are Fleeing into the Mountains, I'm Going to Haimen to Escape Calamity. Stirred by the Situation, I Write These Four Regulated Verses," in Wu Chai, *Peiqiuge yigao*, 2.3a–4a; "Crossing Lake Tai," ibid., 2.4a–b; "Temporarily Dwelling in Meili," ibid., 2.5a; "Chatting with Lansheng in the Night at the Qinchuan Lodge, I Present a Poem of Thirty-Two Rhymes to

Her. At the Time I'm About to Go to Loujiang," ibid., 2.6b–7b; "My Impression When Traveling in Yinxi," ibid., 2.8a; and "I Encountered a Snowstorm When My Boat Landed at the Pond of Baimao. Upon Arriving at Meili, I Hear of the Success of Taking Back the Provincial Capital. It is the Twenty-Fifth Day of the Tenth Month in the Winter of Guihai," ibid., 2.9b–10a.

41. Wu Chai, *Peiqiuge yigao*, 2.10b.

42. Wu appended Yu's poems after her reply, "Yu Menghua Painted a Picture for Me and Inscribed Wonderful Poems. I Write These Poems as a Reply." See Wu Chai, *Peiqiuge yigao*, 2.14a.

43. Wu Chai, *Peiqiuge yigao*, 2.14a.

44. Ibid., 2.14a.

45. "Poem Sent to Yu Menghua (Zhen)," in ibid., 2.11a.

46. In her examination of Zuo Xixuan's lyrics, Deng Hongmei points out that "the sentiments expressed in Zuo's lyrics extend from the realm of the inner chambers to the larger human world." See Deng Hongmei, *Nüxing ci shi*, 531.

47. Chen Weisong, for example, makes such comment. See You and You, *Qing ci jishi*, 65. The term "loyalist lyrics" is borrowed from Kang-i Sun Chang's discussion of Xu Can's lyrics. See Chang, "Liu Shih and Hsü Ts'an," 169. For recent studies of Xu Can, see Chang, "Liu Shih and Hsü Ts'an"; Chen Bangyan, "Ping jie nü ciren," 1–25; and Deng Hongmei, *Nüxing ci shi*, 271–91. See also Li Xiaorong, "Engendering Heroism," 15–21.

48. Judging from her extant writings, Li Qingzhao did write some lyrics that can be characterized as in the *haofang* style, but she touched on the subject of loyalism only in her *shi* poetry. Moreover, in her "Ci lun" (On the lyric), Li Qingzhao insists on the orthodox feminine, gentle-and-restrained, or *wanyue*, quality of the *ci* genre.

49. Zhu Zhongmei, *Jingge xinsheng*, 6a–b. The source of Zhu Zhongmei's *ci* cited here is Xu Naichang, *Xiaotanluanshi huike guixiu ci*. However, Zhu Zhongmei also had a *shi* collection titled *Jingge xinsheng* that is included in Li Yuanding's *Shiyuan quanji*. See Li Yuanding, *Shiyuan quanji*, 102–9.

50. Deng Hongmei has offered a brief introduction to the life and lyrics of Zhu Zhongmei. See Deng Hongmei, *Nüxing ci shi*, 239–42.

51. Zhu Zhongmei, *Suicao xubian*, 111.

52. "Shu li," in *Shi jing* (*Maoshi* no. 65). For an English translation of this poem, see Waley, *Book of Songs*, 306.

53. For the poem "The Lane of Black Robes," see *Quan Tang shi*, 365.4117. Wang and Xie refer to the two ministers in the Jin period (265–420), Wang Dao (276–339) and Xie An (320–385), who are believed to have lived on the Lane of Black Robes in Nanjing.

54. For "Yu fu," see Wang Yi, *Chu ci*, 7.298. For the citation in *Mencius*, see *Mengzi zhushu*, 7A: 55, 2719. Translation based on James Legge's, in Legge, *The Book of Poetry*, 299.

55. Zhu Zhongmei, *Suicao*, 97.

56. See Samei, *Gendered Persona*, 146–48, 188–89.

57. Yeh, "Chen Tzu-lung"; Chang, *The Late Ming Poet Ch'en Tzu-lung*.

58. *Quan Qing ci*, 7. 3761.

59. Many scholars have noted this. For a study focusing on women's appropriation of the form for expressing their gendered concerns, see Li Xiaorong, "Engendering Heroism."

60. "The melody of singing girls" is derived from the lines "Singing girls do not know the sorrow of the fallen state; / They are still singing the 'Flowers, of the rear courtyard'" by the Tang poet Du Mu (803–ca. 852). See *Quan Tang shi*, 35.1245. "Flowers, of the rear courtyard" was the title of a tune created by the last emperor of the Chen dynasty (557–89), which became a convention referring to the music of a fallen dynasty. See *Quan Tang shi*, 35.1245.

61. On Liu Shu's life and lyrics, see Deng Hongmei, *Nüxing ci shi*, 214–19. See also Wai-yee Li, "Women Writers and Gender Boundaries," 188–95. For a biography of Qin Liangyu, see Hummel, *Eminent Chinese of the Ch'ing Period*, 68.

62. Chen Yunlian, *Xinfangge shicao*, 2.2a.

63. Ouyang Xiu, *Xin Tang shu*, 102.3796.

64. Chen Yunlian, *Xinfangge shicao*, 2.2a–b.

65. "In the Autumn of the Year Dingyou [1837] Sending My Husband Off to the North," in Chen Yunlian, *Xinfangge shicao*, 2.14b–15b.

66. "Saying Good-bye to My Mother When I'm About to Go to Tianjin," in Chen Yunlian, *Xinfangge shicao*, 2.17a–b.

67. Twitchett and Fairbank, *The Cambridge History*, 196.

68. Chen Yunlian, *Xinfangge shicao*, 3.17b.

69. Translation by Xinda Lian with modifications. Original lines are also quoted from him. See Lian, *The Wild and Arrogant*, 82.

70. For a discussion of different meanings of the sword in other women's poems, see Wai-yee Li, "Women Writers and Gender Boundaries," 196–201.

71. Twitchett and Fairbank, *The Cambridge History*, 199.

72. *Qing shi gao*, 20.727.

73. For a biography of Xie Zicheng, see ibid., 491.13583–5.

74. Chen Yunlian, *Xinfangge shicao*, 5.2b–4a.

75. Ibid., 5.2b.

76. Sima Qian, *Shi ji*, 84.2486–90.

77. In her examination of suicide writings by several exemplary Ming-Qing women, Grace S. Fong aptly illustrates the cultural significance behind these women's choice of suicide. See Fong, "Signifying Bodies."

78. He Huisheng, *Meishenyinguan shi*, "Ba," 1a. For a biography of Long Qirui, see *Qing shi gao*, 82.13291–2.

79. *Qing shi gao*, 82.13291.

80. Ibid., 82.13292.

81. He Huisheng, *Meishenyinguan shicao*, 4a.

82. Ibid., 2a–b.

83. Ibid., 4a–b.

84. Susan Mann has also briefly discussed this poem; see Mann, "The Lady and the State," 301–2.

85. He Huisheng, *Meishenyinguan shicao*, 5a.
86. See "The Biography of Mme. Qiaoguo," in Wei Zheng, *Sui shu*, 80.1800–1803.
87. Wei Zheng, comp., *Sui shu*, 80.1801–2.
88. He Huisheng, *Meishenyinguan shicao*, 5a.
89. For a biography of Ban Chao, see Fan Ye, *Hou Han shu*, 47.1571.
90. See, for example, the lines attributed to Huarui furen (Lady Huarui), in the Later Shu (930–65), "A hundred and forty thousand troops laid down their weapons, / Among them not a single one worthy of being called a man." As quoted and translated by Idema and Grant, in Idema and Grant, *The Red Brush*, 296. On Lady Huarui, see also Idema and Grant, *The Red Brush*, 293–97.
91. He Huisheng, *Meishenyinguan shicao*, 5a.
92. See Xu Ling, *Yutai xinyong*, 1.30–32.
93. Presumably, "Wencheng" refers by his posthumous title to Wang Yangming (1472–1529), who suppressed the rebellions of Prince Ning in Jiangxi and non-Chinese people in Guangxi. See Israel, "To Accommodate or Subjugate," and Israel, "The Prince and the Sage." I thank an anonymous reader for bringing this to my attention.
94. He Huisheng, *Meishenyinguan shicao*, "Ba," 1a.
95. Ibid.
96. Ibid.
97. Ibid, "Tici," 1a.
98. Ibid., "Xu," 1a.
99. For the story recording Xie Daoyun's poetic talent and this poetic line by her, see Liu Yiqing, *Shishuo xinyu*, 131.
100. He Huisheng, *Meishenyinguan shicao*, "Xu," 1a.
101. Ibid., "Tici," 1b.
102. Great Preface, quoted from Owen, *Readings in Chinese Literary Thought*, 43.
103. Wang Caiping, *Duxuanlou shigao*, "Xu," 1a. Wang Caipin is another woman poet who lived through the Taiping Rebellion. Her *Duxuanlou shigao* contains ten *juan* of *shi* poetry produced from 1840 to 1891, including a number of poems written about her experience escaping the war. I do not discuss her poems in this chapter because they are not related to my theoretical focus, the *gui*, but her collection deserves an in-depth study from the perspective of the influence of social disorder on women's life courses and their approaches to the writing of poetry. For a discussion of the political concerns expressed in Wang Caiping's poems, see Mann, "The Lady and the State," 287–90. On Wang Caiping, see also Mann, *Talented Women of the Zhang Family*, 130–64.

CHAPTER 5. THE OLD BOUDOIR AND THE "NEW WOMAN"

1. On Qiu Jin's life and political activities as a "new woman," see Rankin, "The Emergence of Women." On Qiu Jin's lyrical voice, see Fong, "Engendering the Lyric." For a study of Qiu Jin's writing from the perspective of

autobiographical narrative, see Wang Lingzhen, *Personal Matters*, 27–60. For English translations of Qiu Jin's writing in various genres, see Idema and Grant, *The Red Brush*, 767–808; Dooling and Torgeson, *Writing Women in Modern China*, 39–78; Chang and Saussy, *Women Writers of Traditional China*, 632–57.

2. On the role of missionary schools in popularizing modern education for women, especially those from lower classes, see Liu Ningyuan, *Zhongguo nüxing shi leibian*, 235–38.

3. Liao Xiuzhen, "Qingmo nüxue," 220. On the transformation of women's education in the late Qing, see also Cong, "From 'Cainü' to 'Nü jiaoxi'."

4. Weikang Cheng, "Going Public through Education," 119.

5. Ibid., 117.

6. Chen Dongyuan, "Zhongguo de nüzi jiaoyu," 251.

7. However, some schools, even among the earliest ones, consciously recruited girls from poor families to audit classes. There were also programs and workshops especially designed for girls from the lower classes. See Weikang Cheng, "Going Public through Education," 121, 126.

8. Luo Suwen, *Nüxing yu jindai zhongguo shehui*, 83.

9. Liu Ningyuan, *Zhongguo nüxing*, 243.

10. "Shanghai xinshe zhongguo nüxuetang zhangcheng," 103.

11. Pan Xuan, "Shanghai nüxuebao," 136.

12. Dooling and Torgeson, *Writing Women in Modern China*, 8.

13. Fan Wei, "Lun Zhongguo bodai funü zhi zhidu," 199.

14. Guanxuehui shuji, "Shanghai chuangshe zhongguo nü xuetang ji," 125.

15. As quoted in Huang Yanli, "Zhongguo funü jiaoyu zhi jinxi," 271.

16. See, for example, Judge, *The Precious Raft of History*, 110–15.

17. Lu Cui, "Nüzi ai guo shuo," 143.

18. Liang and Kang had launched a "public vehicle petition"(*gongche shangshu*).

19. Quote from Pao Chia-lin, "Minchu de funü sixiang," 323.

20. Barlow, "Theorizing Woman," 265.

21. Jin Tianhe, *Nüjie zhong*, 22–23.

22. See Wang Zheng, Dorothy Ko, and Lydia Liu, "Cong *Nüjie zhong* dao 'nanjie zhong,'" 1–4.

23. On reformists' criticism of the Chinese female literary heritage as part of their agenda to usher in radical cultural changes, see Judge, *The Precious Raft of History*, chapter 3.

24. Liang Qichao, "Lun nüxue," 76.

25. For other examples of men and women echoing Liang Qichao's condemnation of the woman of talent, see Judge, *The Precious Raft of History*, 87–95.

26. "The pepper Flowers" refers to a work by the wife of Liu Zhen of the Jin period. See *Jin shu*, 96.260.

27. Liu Renlan, "Quan xing nüxue qi," 97.

28. Jin Tianhe, *Nüjie zhong*, 8.

29. David Der-wei Wang, "Chinese Literature from 1841 to 1937," 442.

30. Judge, *The Precious Raft of History*, 90.
31. This term was coined by Liu Na. For her discussion of this movement, see Liu Na, *Shanbian*, 85–99.
32. As quoted in ibid., 98.
33. Translated by Shengqing Wu, in Wu, "'Old Learning,'" 8.
34. All these three poems are quoted from Liu Na, *Shanbian*, 97.
35. As Joan Judge points out, "The subjectivities of women and the representations of women that emerged out of... various imaginings were not exclusively the product of new nationalist discourses but also of the articulation between these new discourses and existing cultural forms." See Judge, "Talent, Virtue, and the Nation," 768.
36. Wang Lingzhen, *Personal Matters*, 30.
37. Qiu Jin, *Qiu Jin quanji*, 284. Translation by Wilt Idema and Beata Grant, in Idema and Grant, *The Red Brush*, 771.
38. Ibid., 289.
39. Ibid., 290.
40. Ibid., 291.
41. Ibid., 40.
42. Ibid., 297.
43. Ibid., 312.
44. Ibid., 149.
45. Xu Ling, *Yutai xinyong*, 1.1–2. For an English translation of this poem, see Birrell, *New Songs*, 30.
46. "Breaking a Willow Branch" is the title of some Han *yuefu* songs, but there are no extant poems. Its association with the theme of separation was not established until the Six Dynasties and Tang periods. In the Tang, the theme "breaking a willow branch" became a well-known subgenre in the new *yuefu*. Liu Yuxi's "Songs of Willow Branches" (Liuzhi ci) have been celebrated as the exemplary works.
47. Qiu Jin, *Qiu Jin quanji*, 158.
48. Rankin, "The Emergence of Women," 53.
49. Jin Tianhe, *Nüjie zhong*, 44.
50. The phrase "swallows in a dangerous nest" (*weichao yan*) is derived from the line "It is like swallows nesting on curtains," in *Zuozhuan*, vol. 3: 29.13, 1167.
51. An allusion to the story of Suo Jing of the Jin period. Having realized the imminent fall of the Jin dynasty, Suo Jing points to the bronze statues of camels and says, "I will see you standing in thrones." See *Jin shu*, 60.170.
52. According to Lü Bicheng's recollection of their first and only meeting, Qiu was still using "Qiu Guijin" on her business card when they met in 1904. She removed the character after she went to Japan.
53. Qiu Jin, *Qiu Jin quanji*, 189.
54. "The peach-flower horse" alludes to the horse of the woman general Qin Liangyu.
55. Jin Tianhe, *Nüjie zhong*, 5.

56. According to the *Shi ji*, Guo Jie was a chivalrous man who had been hailed as a hero because of his bravery and generosity to local people but was persecuted by the government. See Sima Qian, *Shi ji*, 124.269.
57. Qiu Jin, *Qiu Jin quanji*, 216.
58. Wang Lingzhen, *Personal Matters*, 44.
59. Qiu Jin, *Qiu Jin quanji*, 274
60. Ibid.
61. Ibid.
62. Qiu Jin, "Nüzi ge," 221.
63. Liu Na, *Shanbian*, 72.
64. Qiu Jin, *Qiu Jin quanji*, 217.
65. See, for example, Fong, "Alternative Modernities" and "Reconfiguring Time, Space, and Subjectivity"; Wu Shengqing, "Old Learning"; Liu Na, *Shanbian*, 104–9.
66. Lü Bicheng, *Lü Bicheng ci jianzhu*, 499. Translation by Fong, in Fong, "Alternative Modernities," 20, with modifications.
67. Lü Bicheng, *Lü Bicheng shiwen jianzhu*, 6.
68. Jin Yi, *Nüjie zhong*, 18, 46.
69. Lü Bicheng, *Lü Bicheng shiwen jianzhu*, 1.
70. Ibid., 2.
71. As quoted in J. D. Schmidt, *Within the Human Realm*, 47.
72. Likewise Lü Bicheng in her later years did an equally excellent job of adapting the *ci* tradition in order to incorporate her European travels.
73. Liu Na, *Shanbian*, 85.
74. As quoted in J. D. Schmidt, *Within the Human Realm*, 208.
75. For an introduction of Chen Hengzhe and an English translation of this work, see Dooling and Torgeson, *Writing Women in Modern China*, 87–100.
76. Ibid., 87.
77. Both Fong and Wu have explored the question of what it meant to her to write in classical language and form. Their works have focused on the relation of Lü's writing to tradition and modernity.
78. The terms refer respectively to the philosophical arguments of Huishi and Gongsun Long of the Warring States period (475–221 BCE). While the former attempts to argue against the existence of difference, the latter uses the qualities of a rock, such as its hardness and white color, that can be independent of the rock to emphasize the difference between materials.
79. Lü Bicheng, *Lü Bicheng shiwen jianzhu*, 27.
80. Given that this essay was published in 1929 and some issues it addresses cannot be dated before Lü's second trip to United States and Europe in 1926, I agree with Wu Shengqing's dating. See Wu Shengqing, "Old Learning," 22.
81. Xue Shaohui (1866–1911) expressed a similar point of view; see Qian Nanxiu, "Xue Shaohui and Her Poetic Chronicle," 351–54.
82. Lü Bicheng, *Lü Bicheng shiwen jianzhu*, 476–77.
83. Wu Shengqing, "Old Learning," 22.
84. Ibid., 1.

85. Quoted from Li Baomin's annotation, in Lü Bicheng, *Lü Bicheng shi wen jianzhu*, 79–80.
86. For her claim, see Lü Bicheng, *Lü Bicheng ci jianzhu*, 250.
87. Ibid., 79.
88. Quoted from Li Baomin's annotation, in Lü Bicheng, *Lü Bicheng shi wen jianzhu*, 81.
89. Grace S. Fong points out that the term *juanxiu* is wonderfully ambiguous in Chinese, and women poets in the late imperial period often played with the ambiguity. See Fong, "Female Hands," 13.
90. Rankin, "The Emergence of Women," 65.

CONCLUSION

1. See, for example, Robertson, "Literary Authorship," 378.
2. Deng Hanyi, *Shiguan*, 449.
3. Robertson, "Changing the Subject," 217.
4. Sielke, *Fashioning the Female Subject*, 219.
5. My discussion here is indebted to Robertson, who borrows this concept from French philosopher-critics Gilles Deleuze and Felix Guattari. See her note in "Literary Authorship," 381–82.
6. Ibid., 383.
7. Ibid., 385.
8. Ibid.

GLOSSARY OF CHINESE CHARACTERS

ao 傲
Bai Juyi 白居易
Ban Chao 班超
Ban Zhao 班昭
Bao Linghui 鮑令暉
Bao Zhao 鮑照
bi 碧
"Bianyan" 弁言
bingluan 兵亂
Bing Yue 冰月
"Buyi" 補遺
buyuan buyin 不怨不淫
Cai Runshi 蔡潤石
Cao Rui 曹睿
chai 釵
"Changmen fu" 長門賦
Chen Hengzhe 陳衡哲
Chen Hongmou 陳宏謀
Chen Huanghou 陳皇后
Chen Meisheng 陳梅生
Chen Miao 陳藐
Chen Shulan 陳淑蘭
Chen Weisong 陳維崧
Chen Yingning 陳攖甯
Chen Yunlian 陳蘊蓮
Chen Zilong 陳子龍
chenmin 臣民
Chuci 楚辭

Ci xuan 詞選
Cihui 次回
Cui Wei 崔鶠
Deng Hanyi 鄧漢儀
Dong Baohong 董寶鴻
Dong Yining 董以寧
Du Fu 杜甫
Feng Bao 馮寶
fang 房
Furen ji 婦人集
Gao Jingfang 高景芳
Gongsun Long 公孫龍
gu qiong 固窮
Gu Xiangquan 顧響泉
guan 觀
"Guanju" 關雎
gui 閨
guifang 閨房
guige 閨閣
guikun 閨閫
guimen zhong ren 閨門中人
guiren 閨人
guiren kouwen 閨人口吻
guiwa 閨娃
guixiu 閨秀
guiyan 閨艷
guiying 閨英
guiyuan 閨怨

"Guo feng" 國風
guomin 國民
guomin zhi mu 國民之母
gushi shijiu shou 古詩十九首
Hai Rui 海瑞
han gui 寒閨
Han Wo 韓偓
haofang 豪放
He Huisheng 何慧生
hongchuang 紅窗
Hou Jin 候晉
Hu Shi 胡適
Hu Wenkai 胡文楷
Hu Yinglin 胡應麟
Huang Daozhou
Huang Tingjian 黃庭堅
Huang Yuanjie 黃媛介
Huishi 惠施
Jiang Da 蔣達
Jiang Shumin 蔣淑敏
Jianwen 簡文
Jiaonü yigui 教女遺歸
jiju 寄居
jin 金
Jin Changxu 金昌緒
Jin Tianhe 金天翮
Jin Yi 金一
Jingzhiju qinqu 靜志居琴趣
Jishui 吉水
junzi 君子
Kang Guangren 康廣仁
Kang Tongbi 康同璧
Kang Youwei 康有為
kong chuang 空床
kong fang 空房
kong gui 空閨
kuang 狂
Langui baolu 蘭閨寶錄
Li Bai 李白
Li Duan 李端

Li He 李賀
Li ji 禮記
Li Qingzhao 李清照
Li Shangyin 李商隱
Li shi 李氏
Li Yingzhou 李瀛州
Li Yu 李煜
Li Yu 李漁
Li Zhi 李贄
Li Zhiling 李芝齡
Liang Hong 梁鴻
Liang Qichao 梁啟超
liangjia guixiu 良家閨秀
Liangxi shichao 梁溪詩鈔
Lin Bu 林逋
Lin Meirui 林梅蕊
Liu Ji 劉基
Liu Renlan 劉紉蘭
Liu Shi 柳是
Liu Shu 劉淑
Liu Wu 劉武
Liu Yong 柳永
Liu Yuxi 劉禹錫
"Liyan" 例言
Long Jidong 龍繼棟
Long Qirui 龍啟瑞
Lu Cui 盧翠
Lü Bicheng 呂碧城
Lü Kun 呂坤
lüchuang 綠窗
lüshi 律詩
Mao Huifang 茅慧芳
Mao Shuzhen 茅淑珍
Mei Cheng 枚乘
Meiguo guixiu 美國閨秀
minquan 民權
Nalan Xingde 納蘭性德
nannü pingdeng 男女平等
Nei xun 內訓
"Nei ze" 內則

Glossary of Chinese Characters

nu zhi nu 奴之奴
nuli 奴隸
nü guomin 女國民
Nü jie 女誡
Nü lunyu 女論語
Nü si shu 女四書
Nü xiaojing 女孝經
Nüfan jielu 女範捷錄
Nüjie 女界
Nüquan 女權
Ouyang Jiong 歐陽炯
Ouyang Xiu 歐陽修
Pan Xuan 潘璇
Pan Yue 潘岳
Peiqiuge 佩秋閣
pinshi 貧士
Qiaoguo 譙國
Qin Guan 秦觀
Qin Puzhen 秦璞貞
qing 青
qinglou shixing funü 青樓失行婦女
Qingshi biecai 清詩別裁
Qiu Jin 秋瑾
qun 群
renquan 人權
Rongbin 蓉濱
Rou putuan 肉蒲團
Ruan Ji 阮籍
Ruan Xian 阮鹹
Shan Shili 單士釐
Shanhua 善化
shangshu 上書
"Shao nan" 召南
She Yongning 佘永寧
Shen Deqian 沈德潛
Shen Yifu 沈義父
Sheng shi 盛氏
Shi yan zhi 詩言志
shijie geming 詩界革命

Shijing 詩經
Shizheng lu 施政錄
sifu 思婦
Sima Guang 司馬光
Sima Xiangru 司馬相如
Song of Five Sighs 五噫歌
Song Ruozhao 宋若昭
Tang Jingxian 唐靜嫻
Tang Qingyun 唐慶雲
Tao Qian 陶潛
ti 體
tianyuan 田園
Tiefei Daoren 鐵扉道人
Tong Feng 童鳳
tongxin 童心
Wang Caipin 王采蘋
Wang Changling 王昌齡
Wang Cihui 王次回
Wang Jiefu 王節婦
Wang Lang 王朗
Wang Wei 王煒
Wang Xizhi 王羲之
Wang Yanhong 王彥泓
Wang Yaofang 汪瑤芳
wanyue 婉約
Wei Chengban 魏承班
Wei Zheng 魏徵
Wei Zhuang 韋莊
Wei Yingwu 韋應物
Wen Tingyun 溫庭筠
Weng Guangzhu 翁光珠
wenrou dunhou 溫柔敦厚
wenxue 文學
Wenxue yanjiu hui 文學研究會
wo bei qing zhong 我輩情鍾
Wu Chai 吳苤
"Wu sheng" 吳聲
"Wu ti" 無題
Wu Weiye 吳偉業
Wudi 武帝

wuyan gushi 五言古詩
"Xi qu" 西曲
Xian 洗
Xiang fei 湘妃
xianggui 香閨
Xianglian ji 香奩集
xianglian ti 香奩體
xianqi liangmu 賢妻良母
xianyuan 賢媛
Xiao Gang 蕭綱
xiaojie 小姐
"Xiaoyin" 小引
Xie Daoyun 謝道韞
Xie Yi 謝逸
Xie Zicheng 謝子澄
xin qingnian 新青年
xin zhongguo zhi nüzi 新中國之女子
xing 興
xingling 性靈
xingqing zhenshu 性情貞淑
xinshi guiqing 新式閨情
xiuge 繡閣
xiuzhuan 修撰
Xu Can 徐燦
Xu Shu 徐淑
Xu Zaipu 許在璞
Xu Zhenyi 許振褘
Xu Zihua 徐自華
Xue Shaohui 薛紹徽
Xue Tao 薛濤
xuezheng 學政
Yan Shu 晏殊

Yang Sushu 楊素書
yanqing 艷情
"Yi ri" 一日
yin yu shi 隱於市
yinlü hexie 音律和諧
yishu 異數
Yizheng 儀徵
yongwu 詠物
yongxu cai 詠絮才
yu 玉
Yu Xin 庾信
yuan 怨
Yuan Hanhuang 袁寒篁
Yuan Hongdao 袁宏道
Yuan Jue 袁桷
Yuan Mei 袁枚
Yuan Zhen 元稹
Yun Zhu 惲珠
Zhang Huiyan 張惠言
Zhang Jinyong 張金鏞
Zhang Lingyi 張令儀
Zhang Xuecheng 章學誠
zheng 正
Zhi jia 治家
"Zhou nan" 周南
Zhou Qiong 周瓊
Zhou Shi 周實
Zhou Yao 周瑤
Zhou Zuoren 周作人
Zhu Yizun 朱彝尊
Zhu Zhongmei 朱中楣
Zuo Chen 左晨

BIBLIOGRAPHY

PRIMARY SOURCES

Ban Gu 班固. *Bai hu tong* 白虎通. Vols. 98–99 of *Congshu jicheng jianbian* 叢書集成簡編. Taibei: Shangwu yinshuju, 1966.

———. *Han shu* 漢書. Vol. 2 of *Er shi wu shi* 二十五史. Shanghai: Kaiming shudian, 1934.

Chen Hongmou 陳宏謀. *Wuzhong yigui* 五種遺規. Vol. 951 of *Xuxiu siku quanshu* 續脩四庫全書. Shanghai: Shanghai guji chubanshe, 1995.

Chen Weisong 陳維崧, comp. *Furen ji* 婦人集. Shanghai: Zhongyang shudian, 1935.

Chen Yunlian 陳蘊蓮. *Xinfangge shicao* 信芳閣詩草. 1859. In Ming-Qing Women's Writings Database, edited by Grace S. Fong. http://digital.library.mcgill.ca/mingqing/.

Deng Hanyi 鄧漢儀, comp. *Mingjia shiguan* 名家詩觀. 1672. Vols. 39–41 of *Siku quanshu cunmu congshu bubian* 四庫全書存目叢書補編. Jinan: Qilu shushe chubanshe, 1997.

Dong Baohong 董寶鴻. *Yinxiangge shichao* 飲香閣詩抄. 1851–61. Copy in the Shanghai Library.

Fan Ye 范曄, comp. *Hou Han shu* 後漢書. Beijing: Zhonghua shuju, 1965.

Fang Xuanling 房玄齡 et al., comps. *Jin shu* 晉書. Vol. 2 of *Er shi wu shi*. Shanghai: Kaiming shudian, 1934.

Gao Jingfang 高景芳. *Hongxuexuan gao* 紅雪軒稿. Preface date 1718. Copy in the Library of the Chinese Academy of Sciences, Beijing.

Guangxu Zhangzhou fuzhi 光緒漳州府志. Vol. 10 of *Zhongguo difangzhi jicheng* 中國地方志集成. Shanghai: Shanghai shudian; Chengdu: Bashu shushe; Nanjing: Jiangsu guji chubanshe, 2000.

Guanxuehui shuji 廣學会書記. "Shanghai chuangshe zhongguo nüxuetang ji" 上海創設中國女學堂記. In Xu Huiqi et al., *Zhongguo funü yundong lishi ziliao*, 125–26.

Guo Maoqian 郭茂倩, comp. *Yuefu shiji* 樂府詩集. Beijing: Zhonghua shuju, 2003.

He Huisheng 何慧生. *Meishenyinguan shicao* 梅神吟館詩草. 1878. Copy in the Shanghai Library.

Hu Xiaosi 胡孝思, comp. *Benchao mingyuan shichao* 本朝名媛詩鈔. 1766. Copy in the Harvard Yen-ching Library.

Huang Daozhou 黃道周 and Cai Runshi 蔡潤石. *Huangshizhaigong kangli weikangao* 黃石齋公伉儷未刊稿. Copy in the Cornell University Library, Ithaca, N.Y.

Ji Xian 季嫻, comp. *Guixiu ji* 閨秀集. Vol. 414 of *Siku quanshu cunmu congshu, Jibu* 四庫全書存目叢書, 集部. Jinan: Qilu shushe chubanshe, 1997.

Jiang Jixiu 蔣機秀, comp. *Guochao mingyuan shi xiu zhen* 國朝名媛詩繡鍼. 1797. Copy in the Capital's Library (Shoudu tushuguan), Beijing.

Jin Tianhe 金天翮. *Nüjie zhong* 女界鍾. Shanghai: Shanghai guji chubanshe, 2003.

Li Qingzhao 李清照. *Li Qingzhao ji [qian zhu]* 李清照集 [箋注]. Annotated by Xu Peijun 徐培均. Shanghai: Shanghai guji chubanshe, 2002.

Li Yuanding 李元鼎 and Zhu Zhongmei 朱中楣. *Shiyuan quan ji* 石園全集. Vol. 196 of *Siku quanshu cunmu congshu, Ji bu* 四庫全書存目叢書, 集部. Jinan: Qilu shushe chubanshe, 1997.

Liang Qichao 梁啟超. "Lun nüxue" 論女學. In Xu Huiqi et al., *Zhongguo funü yundong lishi ziliao*, 74–80.

Liu Renlan 劉紉蘭. "Quan xing nüxue qi" 勸興女學启. In Xu Huiqi et al., *Zhongguo funü yundong lishi ziliao*, 96–98.

Liu Yiqing 劉義慶. *Shishuo xinyu [jian shu]* 世說新語 [箋疏]. Edited by Yu Jiaxi 余嘉錫. Beijing: Zhonghua shuju, 1983.

Lu Cui 盧翠. "Nüzi ai guo shuo" 女子愛國說. In Xu Huiqi et al., *Zhongguo funü yundong lishi ziliao*, 143.

Lun yu [yi zhu] 論語 [譯注]. Edited and translated by Yang Bojun 楊伯峻. Hong Kong: Zhonghua shuju, 1984.

Lü Bicheng 呂碧城. *Lü Bicheng ci jianzhu* 呂碧城詞箋注. Annotated by Li Baomin 李保民. Shanghai: Shanghai guji chubanshe, 2001.

———. *Lü Bicheng shiwen jianzhu* 呂碧城詩文箋注. Annotated by Li Baomin 李保民. Shanghai: Shanghai guji chubanshe, 2007.

Lü Kun 呂坤. *Gui fan* 閨範. Shanghai: Shanghai guji chubanshe, 1994.

Ming shi 明史. Beijing: Zhonghua shuju, 1974.

Ouyang Xiu 歐陽修. *Ouyang Xiu quan ji* 歐陽修全集. Hong Kong: Guangzhi shuju, 1975.

———, comp. *Xin Tang shu* 新唐書. Beijing: Zhonghua shuju, 1975.

Pan Xuan 潘璇. "Shanghai nüxuebao yuanqi"上海《女學報》緣起. In Xu Huiqi et al., *Zhongguo funü yundong lishi ziliao*, 134–37.

Qian Zhonglian 錢仲聯, ed. *Qing shi jishi* 清詩紀事, vol. 2. Nanjing: Jiangsu guji chubanshe, 1987.

Qing shi gao 清史稿. Beijing: Zhonghua shuju, 1977.

Qiu Jin 秋瑾. "Nüzi ge" 女子歌. In Xu Huiqi et al., *Zhongguo funü yundong lishi ziliao*, 221.

———. *Qiu Jin quanji* 秋瑾全集. Edited by Guo Changhai 郭長海 and Guo Junxi 郭君兮. Changchun: Jilin wenshi chubanshe, 2003.

Quan Ming shi 全明詩. Shanghai: Shanghai guji chubanshe, 1990.

Quan Qing ci 全清詞 (*Shun Kang juan* 順康卷). Beijing: Zhonghua shuju, 2002.

Quan Song shi 全宋詩. Beijing: Beijing daxue chubanshe, 1991.

Quan Tang shi 全唐詩. Beijing: Zhonghua shuju, 1985.

Shen Deqian 沈德潛, comp. *Qing shi bie cai* 清詩別裁. Shanghai: Shangwu yinshuguan, 1958.

Sima Guang 司馬光. *Zhi jia* 治家. Vol. 40 of *Zhonghua sijia cangshu* 中華私家藏書, edited by Xu Han 徐寒. Beijing: Zhongguo gongren chubanshe, 2001.

Sima Qian 司馬遷. *Shi ji* 史記. Beijing: Zhongguo wenshi chubanshe, 2002.

Song Ruozhao 宋若昭. *Nü Lunyu* 女論語. In *Shuo fu* 說郛. Compiled by Tao Zongyi 陶宗儀. Shanghai: Shanghai guji chubanshe, 1988.

Tang Guizhang 唐珪章, comp. *Quan Song ci* 全宋詞. Hong Kong: Zhonghua shuju, 1977.

Tao Qian 陶潛. *Tao Yuanming ji* 陶淵明集. Edited by Lu Qinli 逯欽立. Beijing: Zhonghua shuju, 1979.

Wang Caiping 王采蘋. *Duxuanlou shigao* 讀選樓詩稿. 1894. Copy in Shanghai Library.

Wang Duanshu 王端淑, comp. *Mingyuan shiwei* 名媛詩緯. 1667. Copy in the Harvard Yen-ching Library.

Wang Yanhong 王彥泓. *Wang Cihui shiji* 王次回詩集. Taibei: Lianjing chuban shiye gongsi, 1984.

Wang Qishu 汪啟淑, comp. *Xiefang ji* 擷芳集. 1773. Copy in the Harvard Yen-ching Library.

Wang Shilu 王士祿. *Ranzhi ji li* 然脂集例. Vol. 420 of *Siku quanshu cunmu congshu, Jibu* 四庫全書存目叢書, 集部. Jinan: Qilu shushe chubanshe, 1997.

Wang Yanhong 王彥泓. *Wang Cihui shi ji* 王次回詩集. Annotated by Zheng Qingmao 鄭清茂. Taibei: Lianjing, 1984.

Wang Yi 王逸, annot. *Chu ci* 楚辭. Vol. 217 of *Guoxue jiben congshu sibai zhong* 國學基本叢書四百種. Taibei: Taiwan Shangwu yinshuguan, 1968.

Wei Shou 魏收, comp. *Wei shu* 魏書. Taibei: Dingwen shuju, 1990.

Wei Zheng 魏徵, comp. *Sui shu* 隋書. Beijing: Zhonghua shuju, 1977.

Wu Chai 吳茝. *Peiqiuge yigao* 佩秋閣遺稿. 1888. In Ming-Qing Women's Writings Database, edited by Grace S. Fong. http://digital.library.mcgill.ca/mingqing/.

Xu Can 徐燦. *Zhuozhengyuan shi yu* 拙政園詩余. In Xu Naichang, *Xiaotanluanshi huike guixiu ci*.

Xu Huiqi 徐輝琪 et al., eds. *Zhongguo funü yundong lishi ziliao* (1840–1918) 中國婦女運動歷史資料 (1840–1918). Beijing: Zhongguo funü chubanshe, 1991.

Xu Kuichen 許夔臣, comp. *Xiangke ji* 香咳集. 1804. Copy in the Shanghai Library.

Xu Ling 徐陵, comp. *Yutai xinyong [qian zhu]* 玉臺新詠 [箋注]. Annotated by Wu Zhaoyi 吳兆宜. Edited by Cheng Yan 程琰. Collated by Mu Kehong 穆克宏. Beijing: Zhonghua shuju, 1985.

Xu Naichang 徐乃昌, comp. *Xiaotanluanshi huike guixiu ci* 小檀欒室彙刻閨秀詞. 1896.

Xu Shen 許慎. *Shuowen jiezi* 說文解字. In *Sibu congkan chubian suoben* 四部叢刊初編縮本, vol. 5. Taibei: Taiwan shangwu yinshuguan, 1967.

Yang Shulan 楊書蘭. *Hongquyinguan shichao* 紅蕖吟館詩鈔. 1878. In Ming-Qing Women's Writings Database, edited by Grace S. Fong. http://digital.library.mcgill.ca/mingqing/.

Yuan Hongdao 袁宏道. *Yuan Zhonglang quan ji* 袁中郎全集. Taipei: Shijie shuju, 1962.

Yun Zhu 惲珠, comp. *Guochao guixiu zhengshi ji* 國朝閨秀正始集. Hongxiangguan, 1831.

———, comp. *Guochao guixiu zhengshi xuji* 國朝閨秀正始續集. Edited by Miaolianbao 妙蓮保. Hongxiangguan, 1836.

———, comp. *Langui baolu* 蘭閨寶錄. Longwenzhai, 1831.

Zhao Chongzuo 趙承祚, comp. *Huajian ji [jiao]* 花間集 [校]. Edited by Li Yimang 李一氓. Hong Kong: Shangwu yinshuguan, 1960.

Zhu Zhongmei 朱中楣. *Jingge xin sheng* 鏡閣新聲. In Xu Naichang, *Xiaotanluanshi huike guixiu ci*.

———. *Suicao* 隨草. In Li Yuanding and Zhu Zhongmei, *Shiyuan quan ji*, 80–102.

———. *Suicao xubian* 隨草續編. In Li Yuanding and Zhu Zhongmei, *Shiyuan quan ji*, 103–12.

Zuo Qiuming 左丘明. *Chunqiu zuozhuan [zhu]* 春秋左傳注. Annotated by Yang Bojun 楊伯峻. Beijing: Zhonghua shuju, 1981.

WORKS CITED

Althusser, Louis. *Lenin and Philosophy and Other Essays*. Translated by Ben Brewster. London: New Left Books, 1971.

Allen, Joseph. "From Saint to Singing Girl: The Rewriting of the Lo-Fu Narrative in Chinese Literati Poetry." *Harvard Journal of Asiatic Studies* 48.2 (1988): 321–61.

Belsey, Catherine. "Constructing the Subject: Deconstructing the Text." In *Feminist Criticism and Social Change: Sex, Class, and Race in Literature and Culture*, edited by Judith Newton and Deborah Rosenfelt, 45–64. New York: Methuen, 1985.

Berkowitz, Alan. *Patterns of Disengagement: The Practice and Portrayal of Reclusion in Early Medieval China*. Stanford, Calif.: Stanford University Press, 2000.

Birrell, Anne, trans. *Games Poets Play: Readings in Medieval Chinese Poetry*. Cambridge: McGuinness China Monographs, 2004.

———. *New Songs from a Jade Terrace: An Anthology of Early Chinese Love Poetry*. Middlesex, England: Penguin, 1986.

Bray, Francesca. *Technology and Gender: Fabrics of Power in Late Imperial China*. Berkeley: University of California Press, 1997.

Cai Zongqi. *The Matrix of Lyric Transformation: Poetic Mode and Self-Preservation in Early Chinese Pentasyllabic Poetry*. Ann Arbor: University of Michigan Press, 1996.

Chang, Kang-i Sun. *The Evolution of Chinese Tz'u Poetry from Late T'ang to Northern Sung*. Princeton, N.J.: Princeton University Press, 1980.

———. "Gender and Canonicity: Ming-Qing Women Poets in the Eyes of the Male Literati." In *Hsiang Lectures on Chinese Poetry*, vol. 1, edited by Grace S. Fong, 1–18. Centre for East Asian Research, McGill University, 2001.

———. *The Late-Ming Poet Ch'en Tzu-lung: Crises of Love and Loyalism*. New Haven: Yale University Press, 1991.

———. "Liu Shih and Hsü Ts'an: Feminine or Feminist?" In Yu, *Voices of the Song Lyric*, 69–87.

———. "Ming and Qing Anthologies of Women's Poetry and Their Selection Strategies." In Ellen Widmer and Kang-i Sun Chang, eds., 147–170.

———. "Ming-Qing Women Poets and Cultural Androgyny." *Tamkang Review* 30.2 (1999): 11–25.

———. "Ming-Qing Women Poets and the Notions of Talent and Morality."

In *Culture and State in Chinese History: Convention, Accommodations, and Critiques*, edited by Theodore R. Huters, R. Bin Wong, and Pauline Yu, 236–58. Stanford, Calif.: Stanford University Press, 1997.

———. *Six Dynasties Poetry*. Princeton: Princeton University Press, 1986.

———. "Women's Poetic Witnessing," In *Dynastic Decline and Cultural Innovation: From the Late Ming to the Late Qing*, edited by David Wang and Wei Shang, 504–22. Cambridge: Harvard University Asia Center, 2005.

Chang, Kang-i Sun, and Stephen Owen, eds. *The Cambridge History of Chinese Literature*. Cambridge: Cambridge University Press, 2010.

Chang, Kang-i Sun and Haun Saussy, eds. *Women Writers of Traditional China*. Stanford: Stanford University Press, 1999.

Chen Bangyan 陳邦炎. "Ping jie nü ci ren Xu Can ji qi Zhuozhengyuan ci" 評介女詞人徐燦及其拙政園詞. In Cheng Yuzhui, *Xu Can ci xinshi jiping*, 1–25. Beijing: Zhuoguo shudian, 2003.

Chen Dongyuan 陳東原. "Zhongguo de nüzi jiaoyu" 中國的女子教育. In Pao Chia-lin, *Zhongguo funü shi lunji xuji*, 241–57.

Chen Yu-shih. "The Historical Template of Pan Chao's *Nü Chieh*." *T'oungpao* 82 (1996): 230–57.

Cheng Yuzhui 程郁綴, ed. *Xu Can ci xinshi jiping* 徐燦詞新釋集評. Beijing: Zhongguo shudian, 2003.

Chou, Chih-p'ing. *Yüan Hung-tao and the Kung-an School*. Cambridge, Mass.: Cambridge University Press, 1988.

Chu, Madeline. "Interplay between Tradition and Innovation: The Seventeenth-Century Tz'u Revival." *Chinese Literature: Essays, Articles, Reviews* 9 (1987): 71–88.

Chung Huiling 鐘慧玲. *Qingdai nü shiren yanjiu* 清代女詩人研究. Taibei: Liren, 2000.

Cong Xiaoping. "From 'Cainü' to 'Nü jiaoxi': Female Normal Schools and the Transformation of Women's Education in the Late Qing Period, 1895–1911." In *Different Worlds of Discourse: Transformations of Gender and Genre in Late Qing and Early Republican China*, edited by Naxiu Qian et al., 115–46. Leiden: Brill, 2008.

Deng Hongmei 鄧紅梅. *Nüxing ci shi* 女性詞史. Jinan: Shandong jiaoyu chubanshe, 2000.

Doleželová-Velingerová, Milena, and Oldřich Král, eds. *The Appropriation of Cultural Capital: China's May Fourth Project*. Cambridge, Mass.: Harvard University Asia Center, 2001.

Ebrey, Patricia. *The Inner Quarters: Marriage and the Lives of Chinese Women in the Sung Period*. Berkeley: University of California Press, 1993.

Egan, Ronald. *The Literary Works of Ou-yang Hsiu (1007–72)*. Cambridge: Cambridge University Press, 1984.

———. *Word, Image, and Deed in the Life of Su Shi*. Cambridge, Mass.: Council on East Asian Studies, Harvard University, and the Harvard-Yenching Institute, 1994.

Fan Wei 范褘. "Lun Zhongguo bodai funü zhi zhidu" 論中國薄待婦女之制度. *Zhongguo funü yundong lishi ziliao (1840–1918)*. In Xu Huiqi et al., *Zhongguo funü yundong lishi ziliao*, 198–204.

Felski, Rita. *Beyond Feminist Aesthetics: Feminist Literature and Social Change*. Cambridge, Mass.: Harvard University Press, 1989.

Fong, Grace S. "Alternative Modernities, or a Classical Woman of Modern China: The Challenging Trajectory of Lü Bicheng's Life and Song Lyrics." *Nan Nü: Men, Women, and Gender in China* 6.1 (2004): 12–59.

———. "Engendering the Lyric: Her Image and Voice in Song." In Yu, *Voices of the Song Lyric*, 138–43.

———. "Female Hands: Embroidery as a Knowledge Field in Women's Everyday Life in Late Imperial and Early Republican China." *Late Imperial China* 25.1 (2004): 1–58.

———. "Gender and the Failure of Canonization: Anthologizing Women's Poetry in the Late Ming." *Chinese Literature: Essays, Articles and Reviews* 26 (2004): 129–49.

———. "Persona and Mask in the Song Lyric." *Harvard Journal of Asiatic Studies* 50 (1990): 459–84.

———. *Herself an Author: Gender, Agency, and Writing in Late Imperial China*. Honolulu: University of Hawai'i Press, 2008.

———. "Inscribing Desire: Zhu Yizun's Love Lyrics in *Jingzhiju qinqu*." *Harvard Journal of Asiatic Studies* 54.2 (1994): 437–60.

———. "Signifying Bodies: The Cultural Significance of Suicide Writings by Women in Ming-Qing China." *Nan Nü: Men, Women, and Gender in Early and Imperial China* 3.1 (2001): 105–42.

———. "Writing and Illness: A Feminine Condition in Women's Poetry of the Ming and Qing." In Fong and Widmer, *The Inner Quarters and Beyond*, 19–48.

———. "Writing from Experience: Personal Records of War and Disorder in Jiangnan during the Ming-Qing Transition." In *Military Culture in Imperial China*, edited by Nicola Di Cosmo, 257–77. Cambridge, Mass., and London: Harvard University Press, 2009.

———. *Wu Wenying and the Art of Southern Song Ci Poetry*. Princeton, N.J.: Princeton University Press, 1987.

Fong, Grace S., and Ellen Widmer, eds. *The Inner Quarters and Beyond: Women Writers from Ming through Qing*. Leiden and Boston: Brill, 2010.

Francis, Mark E. "Canon Formation in Traditional Chinese Poetry: Chinese Canons, Sacred and Profane." In *China in a Polycentric World: Essays in Chinese Comparative Literature*, edited by Zhang Yinjing, 50–70. Stanford, Calif.: Stanford University Press, 1998.

Frankel, Hans H. "Cai Yan and the Poems Attributed to Her." *Chinese Literature: Essays, Articles, Reviews* 5.1–2 (1983): 133–56.

Furth, Charlotte. "The Patriarch's Legacy: Household Instructions and the Transmission of Orthodox Values." In *Orthodoxy in Late Imperial China*, edited by Liu Kuang-Ching, 187–221. Berkeley: University of California Press, 1990.

———. "Poetry and Women's Culture in Late Imperial China: Editor's Introduction." *Late Imperial China* 13.1 (1992): 1–8.

Fusek, Lois, trans. *Among the Flowers: The Hua-chien chi*. New York: Columbia University Press, 1982.

Gao Feng 高峰. *Huajian ci yanjiu* 花間詞研究. Nanjing: Jiangsu guji chubanshe, 2001.

Gong Xianzong 龔顯宗. *Nüxing wenxue bai jia zhuan* 女性文學百家傳. Tainan: Zhenping qiye, 2001.

Grant, Beata. *Daughters of Emptiness: Poems of Buddhist Nuns*. Somerville, Mass.: Wisdom Publications, 2003.

———. "Little Vimalakirti: Buddhism and Poetry in the Writings of Chiang Chu (1764–1804)." In *Chinese Women in the Imperial Past: New Perspectives*, edited by Harriet Zurndorfer, 286–307. Leiden: Brill, 1999.

Handlin, Joanna. "Lü K'un's New Audience: The Influence of Women's Literacy on Seventeenth Century Thought." In *Women in Chinese Society*, edited by Margery Wolf and Roxane Witke, 13–38. Stanford, Calif.: Stanford University Press, 1975.

Harris, Windell. "Canonicity." *PMLA* 106.1 (1991): 110–21.

Hay, John, ed. *Boundaries in China*. London: Reaktion Books, 1994.

Hightower, James R. "The Songwriter Liu Yong." In Hightower and Yeh, *Studies in Chinese Poetry*, 168–268.

Hightower, James R., and Chia-Ying Yeh, eds. *Studies in Chinese Poetry*. Cambridge, Mass.: Harvard University Asia Center, 1998.

Ho, Clara Wing-chung. "The Cultivation of Female Talent: Views on Women's Education in China during the Early and High Qing Periods." *Journal of the Economic and Social History of the Orient* 38.2 (1995): 191–223.

Hong Huasui 洪華穗. "Huajian ci de yixiang biaoxian ji qi ganjue" 花間詞的意象表現及其感覺. In Li Gong and Gui Qun, *Huajian ci*, 223–75.

Hsiung, Ann-Marie. "The Image of Women in Early Chinese Poetry: The Book of Songs, Han Ballads and Palace Style Verse of the Liang Dynasty." *Chinese Culture* 35.4 (1994): 81–90.

Hu Shi 胡適. "Sanbai nian zhong nü zuojia" 三百年中女作家. In *Hu Shi wenji* 胡適文集, vol. 4: 585-91. Beijing: Beijing daxue chubanshe, 1998.

Hu Ying. "Re-Configuring Nei/Wai: Writing the Woman Traveler in the Late Qing." *Late Imperial China* 18.1 (1997): 72-99.

———. *Translation of Tales: Composing the New Woman in China, 1899-1918*. Stanford, Calif.: Stanford University Press, 2000.

Hu Wenkai 胡文楷. *Lidai funü zhuzuo kao* 歷代婦女著作考. Shanghai: Shanghai guji chubanshe, 1985.

———. *Lidai funü zhuzuo kao zengdingban* 歷代婦女著作考增訂版, with supplements. Edited by Zhang Hongsheng 張宏生 et al. Shanghai: Shanghai guji chubanshe, 2008.

Huang Liling 黃麗玲. "Nü si shu yanjiu"《女四書》研究. M.A. thesis. Jiayi, Taiwan: Nanhua daxue, 2003.

Huang, Martin. "Sentiments of Desire: Thoughts on the Cult of Qing in Ming-Qing Literature." *Chinese Literature: Essays, Articles, Reviews* 20 (1998): 153-84.

Huang Yanli 黃嫣梨. "Zhongguo funü jiaoyu zhi jinxi" 中國婦女教育之今昔. In Pao Chia-lin, *Zhongguo funü shi lunji xuji*, 259-85.

Hummel, Arthur, ed. *Eminent Chinese of the Ch'ing Period*. New York: Paragon, 1943.

Idema, Wilt L., trans. *Heroines of Jiangyong: Chinese Narrative Ballads in Women's Script*. Seattle: University of Washington Press, 2009.

Idema, Wilt L., and Beata Grant. *The Red Brush: Writing Women of Imperial China*. Cambridge, Mass.: Harvard University Press, 2004.

Israel, Larry. "The Prince and the Sage: Concerning Wang Yangming's 'Effortless' Suppression of the Ning Princely Establishment Rebellion [Wang Yangming (1472-1529)]." *Late Imperial China* 29.2 (2008): 68-128.

———. "To Accommodate or Subjugate: Wang Yangming's Settlement of Conflict in Guangxi in Light of Ming Political and Strategic Culture [1527]." *Ming Studies* 60 (2009): 4-44.

Judge, Joan. *Precious Raft of History: The Past, the West, and the Woman Question in China*. Stanford, Calif.: Stanford University Press, 2008.

———. "Talent, Virtue, and the Nation: Chinese Nationalisms and Female Subjectivities in the Early Twentieth Century." *The American Historical Review* 3 (2001): 765-803.

Kang Zhengguo 康正果. *Fengsao yu yanqing* 風騷與艷情. Shanghai: Shanghai wenyi chubanshe, 2001.

Ko, Dorothy. *Every Step a Lotus: Shoes for Bound Feet*. Berkeley: University of California Press, 2001.

———. "Lady-Scholars at the Door: The Practice of Gender Relations in

Eighteenth-Century Suzhou." In *Boundaries in China*, edited by John Hay, 198–216. London: Reaktion Books, 1994.

———. "Pursuing Talent and Virtue: Education and Women's Culture in Seventeenth- and Eighteenth-Century China." *Late Imperial China* 13.1 (1992): 9–39.

———. *Teachers of the Inner Chambers: Women and Culture in Seventeenth-Century China*. Stanford, Calif.: Stanford University Press, 1995.

Kong Yingda 孔穎達, ed. *Maoshi zhengyi* 毛詩正義. In *Shi san jing zhu shu* 十三經注疏. Beijing: Zhonghua shuju, 1980.

Kwong, Charles. *Tao Qian and the Chinese Poetic Tradition: The Quest for Cultural Identity*. Ann Arbor: University of Michigan Press, 1994.

Legge, James. *The Book of Poetry: Text and English Translation*. New York: Paragon Book, 1967.

———, trans. *The Four Books: Confucian Analects, The Great Learning, The Doctrine of the Mean, and The Works of Mencius*. New York: Paragon Book Reprint Corp., 1966.

Li Chi. "The Changing Concept of the Recluse in Chinese Literature." *Harvard Journal of Asiatic Studies* 24 (1962–63): 234–47.

Li Fang 李昉 et al., eds. *Taiping guang ji* 太平廣記. Beijing: Zhonghua shuju, 1961.

Li Gong 里功 and Gui Qun 貴群, eds. *Huajian ci* 花間詞. Beijing: Yanshan chubanshe, 2001.

Li Xiaorong. "Engendering Heroism: Ming-Qing Women's Song Lyrics to the Tune *Man jiang hong*." *Nan Nü: Men, Women, and Gender in Early and Imperial China* 7.1 (2005): 1–39.

———. "Gender and Textual Politics during the Qing Dynasty: The Case of the *Zhengshi ji*." *Harvard Journal of Asiatic Studies* 69.1 (2009): 75–102.

Li, Wai-yee. "Early Qing to 1723." In *The Cambridge History of Chinese Literature*, edited by Kang-i Sun Chang and Stephen Owen, vol. 2: 152–244. Cambridge: Cambridge University Press, 2010.

———. "History and Memory in Wu Weiye's poetry." In *Trauma and Transcendence in Early Qing Literature,* edited by Wilt L Idema, Wai-yee Li, and Ellen Widmer, 99–148. Cambridge, Mass., and London: Harvard University Asia Center, 2006.

———. "Women Writers and Gender Boundaries during the Ming-Qing Transition." In Fong and Widmer, *Inner Quarters and Beyond*, 179–214.

Lian, Xinda. *The Wild and Arrogant: Expressions of Self in Xin Qiji's Song Lyrics*. New York: P. Lang, 1999.

Liao Xiuzhen 廖秀真. "Qing mo nüxue zai xuezhi shang de yanjin ji nüzi xiaoxue jiaoyu de fazhan" 清末女學在學制上的演進及女子小學教育的發展. In *Zhongguo funü shi luwen ji* 中國婦女史論文集, edited by Li Youning 李又寧 and Zhang Yufa 張玉法, vol. 2: 203–55. Taibei: Taiwan shangwu yinshuguan, 1988.

Lin, Shuen-fu, and Stephen Owen, eds. *The Vitality of the Lyric Voice: "Shih" Poetry from the Late Han to the T'ang.* Princeton, N.J.: Princeton University Press, 1986.

Liu, James J. Y. *Major Lyricists in the Northern Sung A.D. 960–1126.* Princeton, N.J.: Princeton University Press, 1974.

Liu, Kuang-Ching, ed. *Orthodoxy in Late Imperial China.* Berkeley: University of California Press, 1990.

Liu Na 劉納. *Shanbian: Xinhai geming shiqi zhi wusi shiqi de zhongguo wenxue* 嬗变: 辛亥革命时期至五四时期的中國文學. Beijing: Zhongguo shehui kexue chubanshe, 1998.

Liu Ning 劉寧. *Tang Song zhi ji shige yanbian yanjiu: Yi Yuan Bai zhi Yuanhe ti de chuangzuo yingxiang wei zhongxin* 唐宋之際詩歌演變研究: 以元白之元和體的創作影響為中心. Beijing: Beijing shifan daxue chubanshe, 2002.

Liu Ningyuan 劉寧元, ed. *Zhongguo nüxing shi leibian* 中國女性史類編. Beijing: Beijing shifan daxue, 1999.

Mair, Victor H., ed. *The Shorter Columbia Anthology of Traditional Chinese Literature.* New York: Columbia University Press, 2000.

Mann, Susan. "Classical Revival and Gender Question: China's First Querelle des Femmes." *Jinshi jiazu yu zhengzhi bijiao lishi lunwen ji*, part 1, 377–411. Taipei: Institute of Modern History, Academia Sinica, 1992.

———. "'Fuxue' (Women's Learning) by Zhang Xuecheng (1738–1801): China's First History of Women's Culture." *Late Imperial China* (1992) 13.1: 40–56.

———. "The Lady and the State: Women's Writings in Times of Trouble during the Nineteenth Century." In Fong and Widmer, *Inner Quarters and Beyond*, 283–314.

———. *Precious Records: Women in China's Long Eighteenth Century.* Stanford, Calif.: Stanford University Press, 1997.

———. *The Talented Women of the Zhang Family.* Berkeley: University of California Press, 2007.

Marney, John. *Liang Chien-wen Ti.* Boston: Twayne Publishers, 1976.

Mather, Richard B, trans. *A New Account of Tales of the World.* Minneapolis: University of Minnesota Press, 1976.

Meng zi zhu shu 孟子注疏. Edited by Zhao Qi 趙歧 and Sun Shi 孫奭. Shanghai: Zhonghua, 1934.

Meyer-Fong, Tobie. "Packaging the Men of Our Times: Literary Anthologies, Friendship Networks, and Political Accommodation in the Early Qing," *Harvard Journal of Asiatic Studies* 64.1 (2004): 5–56.

Miao, Ronald. "Palace-Style Poetry: The Courtly Treatment of Glamour and Love." In *Studies in Chinese Poetics*. San Francisco: Chinese Materials Center, 1978.

———, ed. *Studies in Chinese Poetics*. San Francisco: Chinese Materials Center, 1978.

Minford, John, and Joseph S.M. Lau, eds. *An Anthology of Translations: Classical Chinese Literature*. Vol. 1, *From Antiquity to the Tang Dynasty*. New York: Columbia Press; Hong Kong: The Chinese University Press, 2000.

Moi, Toril. *Sexual/Textual Politics: Feminist Literary Theory*. London and New York: Methuen, 1985.

Mote, Frederick. *Imperial China: 900–1800*. Cambridge, Mass.: Harvard University Press, 1999.

Owen, Stephen. *The Late Tang: Chinese Poetry of the Mid-ninth Century (827–860)*. Cambridge, Mass., and London: Harvard University Press, 2006.

———. *Readings in Chinese Literary Thoughts*. Cambridge, Mass.: Harvard University Press, 1992.

———. "The Self's Perfect Mirror: Poetry as Autobiography." In Lin and Owen, *The Vitality of the Lyric Voice*, 71–102.

———. *Traditional Chinese Poetry and Poetics: Omen of the World*. Madison: University of Wisconsin Press, 1985.

Palumbo-Liu, David. *The Poetics of Appropriation: The Literary Theory and Practice of Huang Tingjian*. Stanford, Calif.: Stanford University Press, 1993.

Pao Chia-lin 鮑家麟. "Minchu de funü sixiang (1911–1923)" 民初的婦女思想 (1911–1923). In *Zhongguo funü shi lunji xuji*, edited by Pao Chia-lin, 305–36.

———, ed. *Zhongguo funü shi lunji xuji* 中國婦女史論集續集. Taibei: Daoxiang chubanshe, 1991.

Qian, Nanxiu. *Spirit and Self in Medieval China: The Shih-shuo hsin-yü and Its Legacy*. Honolulu: University of Hawai'i Press, 2001.

———. "Xue Shaohui and Her Poetic Chronicle of Late Qing Reforms." In Fong and Widmer, *Inner Quarters and Beyond*, 339–74.

Rankin, Mary Backus. "The Emergence of Women in China at the End of Ch'ing: The Case of Ch'iu Chin." In Wolf and Witke, *Women in Chinese Society*, 39–66.

Reilly, Thomas H. *The Taiping Heavenly Kingdom: Rebellion and the Blasphemy of Empire*. Seattle and London: University of Washington Press, 2004.

Robertson, Maureen. "Changing the Subject: Gender and Self-inscription in

Authors' Prefaces and Shi Poetry." In Widmer and Chang, *Writing Women in Late Imperial China*, 171–217.

———. "Voicing the Feminine: Constructions of the Gendered Subject in Lyric Poetry by Women of Medieval and Late Imperial China." *Late Imperial China* 13.1 (1992): 63–110.

Ropp, Paul S. "Ambiguous Images of Courtesan Culture in Late Imperial China." In Widmer and Chang, *Writing Women in Late Imperial China*, 17–45.

———. *Banished Immortal: Searching for Shuangqing, China's Peasant Woman Poet*. Ann Arbor: University of Michigan Press, 2001.

———. "'Now Cease Painting Eyebrows, Don a Scholar's Cap and Pin': The Frustrated Ambition of Wang Yun, Gentry Woman Poet and Dramatist." *Ming Studies* 40 (1998): 86–110.

———. "The Seeds of Change: Reflections on the Condition of Women in Early and Mid Ch'ing." *Signs* 2 (1976): 5–23.

———. "Women in Late Imperial China: A Review of Recent English-Language Scholarship." *Women's History Review* 3.3 (1994): 347–83.

Rouzer, Paul F. *Articulated Ladies: Gender and the Male Community in Early Chinese Texts*. Cambridge, Mass.: Harvard University Press, 2001.

———. "Watching the Voyeurs: Palace Poetry and the *Yuefu* of Wen Tingyun." *Chinese Literature: Essays, Articles, Reviews* 11 (1989): 13–34.

———. *Writing Another's Dream: The Poetry of Wen Tingyun*. Stanford, Calif.: Stanford University Press, 1993.

Rowe, William T. *Saving the World: Chen Hongmou and Elite Consciousness in Eighteenth-Century China*. Stanford, Calif.: Stanford University Press, 2001.

———. "Women and the Family in Mid-Ch'ing Social Thought: The Case of Ch'en Hung-mou." In *Family Progress and Political Progress in Modern Chinese History*, part 1. Taipei: Institute of Modern History, 1992.

Ruan Yuan 阮元, ed. *Shisanjing zhushu: Fu Jiaokan ji* 十三經注疏: 附校勘記. Beijing: Zhonghua shuju, 1980.

Scott, Joan W. "Gender: A Useful Category of Historical Analysis." *American Historical Review* 91.5 (1986): 1053–75.

Samei, Maija Bell. *Gendered Persona and Poetic Voice: The Abandoned Woman in Early Chinese Song Lyrics*. Lanham, Md.: Lexington Books, 2004.

Scheck, Helene. *Reform and Resistance: Formation of Female Subjectivity in Early Medieval Ecclesiastical Culture*. Albany: State University of New York Press, 2008.

Schmidt, J. D. *Within the Human Realm: The Poetry of Huang Zunxian, 1848–1905*. Cambridge: Cambridge University Press, 1994.

"Shanghai xinshe nüxuetang zhangcheng" 上海新設女學堂章程. In Xu Huiqi et al., *Zhongguo funü yundong lishi ziliao*, 102–6.

Showalter, Elaine. "Feminist Criticism in the Wildness." In *The New Feminist Criticism: Essays on Women, Literature and Theory*. London: Virago, 1986.

———. *A Literature of Their Own: British Women Novelists from Brontë to Lessing*. Princeton, N.J.: Princeton University Press, [1977] 1999.

Sielke, Sabine. *Fashioning the Female Subject: The Intertextual Networking of Dickinson, Moore, and Rich*. Ann Arbor: The University of Michigan Press, 1997.

Sommer, Matthew H. *Sex, Law, and Society in Late Imperial China*. Stanford, Calif.: Stanford University Press, 2000.

Struve, Lynn. *The Southern Ming 1644–1662*. New Haven, Conn.: Yale University Press, 1984.

———. *Voices from the Ming-Qing Cataclysm*. New Haven, Conn.: Yale University Press, 1993.

Swann, Nancy Lee. *Pan Chao: Foremost Woman Scholar of China*. New York: Century, 1932.

Swartz, Wendy. "Rewriting a Recluse: The Early Biographers' Construction of Tao Yuanming." *Chinese Literature: Essays, Articles, and Reviews* 26 (2004): 77–98.

Tian, Xiaofei. *Beacon Fire and Shooting Star: The Literary Culture of the Liang (502–557)*. Cambridge, Mass.: Harvard University Press, 2007.

———. *Tao Yuanming and Manuscript Culture: The Record of a Dusty Table*. Seattle: University of Washington Press, 2005.

Tu, Kuo-ch'ing. *Li Ho* (Li He). Boston: Twayne Publishers, 1979.

Twitchett, Denis, and John K. Fairbank, eds. *The Cambridge History of China*. Vol. 10. Cambridge and New York: Cambridge University Press, 1978.

Wakeman, Frederic E. *The Great Enterprise: The Manchu Reconstruction of Imperial Order in Seventeenth-Century China*. Berkeley: University of California Press, 1985.

Waley, Arthur, trans. *Book of Songs*. New York: Grove Press, 1960.

Wang, David Der-wei. "Chinese Literature from 1841 to 1937." In Chang and Owen, *The Cambridge History of Chinese Literature*, 413–564.

Wang Yunxi 王運熙 and Gu Yisheng 顧易生. *Zhongguo wenxue piping shi* 中國文學批評史. Taibei: Wunan tushu chuban gongsi, 1991.

Wang Zheng 王政, Gao Yanyi 高彥頤, and Liu He 劉禾. "Cong Nüjie zhong dao 'nanjie zhong': Nanxing zhuti, guzu zhuyi yu xiandai xing" 從《女界鍾》到"男界鍾": 男性主體, 國族主義與現代性. In *Bainian zhongguo nüquan sichao yanjiu* 百年中國女權思潮研究, edited by Wang Zheng 王政 and Chen Yan 陳雁, 1–29. Shanghai: Fudan daxue chubanshe, 2004.

Watson, Burton. *Chinese Lyricism: Shih Poetry from the Second to the Twelfth Century, with Translations*. New York: Columbia University Press, 1971.

Wei Xiumei 魏秀梅. *Qingdai zhi huibi zhidu* 清代之迴避制度. Taibei: Taipei: Institute of Modern History, Academia Sinica, 1992.

Widmer, Ellen. *The Beauty and the Book: Women and Fiction in Nineteenth-Century China*. Cambridge, Mass.: Harvard University Press, 2006.

———. "Considering a Coincidence: The 'Female Reading Public' circa 1828." In Zeitlin, Liu, and Widmer, *Writing and Materiality in China*, 273–314.

———. "The Epistolary World of Female Talent in Seventeenth-Century China." *Late Imperial China* 10.2 (1989): 1–43.

———. "Ming Loyalism and the Woman's Voice in Fiction after *Hong lou meng*." In Widmer and Chang, *Writing Women in Late Imperial China*, 366–396.

———. "The Rhetoric of Retrospection: May Fourth Literary History and the Ming-Qing Woman Writer." In Milena Doleželová-Velingerová and Oldřich Král, *Appropriation of Cultural Capital*, 193–225.

———. "Xiaoqing's Literary Legacy and the Place of the Women Writer in Late Imperial China." *Late Imperial China* 13.1 (1992): 111–156.

Widmer, Ellen, and Kang-i Sun Chang, eds. *Writing Women in Late Imperial China*. Stanford, Calif.: Stanford University Press, 1997.

Wolf, Margery, and Roxane Witke, eds. *Women in Chinese Society*. Stanford, Calif.: Stanford University Press, 1975.

Workman, Michael E. "The Bedchamber Topos in the Tz'u Songs of Three Medieval Chinese Poets: Wen T'ing-yün, Wei Chuang, and Li Yü." In *Critical Essays on Chinese Literature*, edited by William H. Nienhauser. Hong Kong: Chinese University of Hong Kong; Honolulu: University of Hawai'i Press, 1976.

Wu, Fusheng. *The Poetics of Decadence: Chinese Poetry of the Southern Dynasties and Late Tang Periods*. Albany: State University of New York Press, 1998.

Wu, Shengqing. "'Old Learning' and the Refeminization of Modern Space in the Lyric Poetry of Lü Bicheng." *Modern Chinese Literature and Culture* 16.2 (2004): 1–75.

Xie Zhengguang 謝正光 and She Rufeng 佘如豐, comps. *Qingchu ren xuan qingchu shi huikao* 清初人選清初詩彙考. Nanjing: Nanjing daxue chubanshe, 1998.

Yang, Binbin. "Women and the Aesthetics of Illness: Poetry on Illness by

Qing-Dynasty Women Poets." Ph.D. dissertation, Washington University in St. Louis, 2007.

Yeh, Chia-ying. "Ambiguity and the Female Voice in Hua-chien Songs." In Hightower and Yeh, *Studies in Chinese Poetry*, 115–49.

———. "The Ch'ang-chou School of Tz'u Criticism." In Hightower and Yeh, *Studies in Chinese Poetry*, 439–61.

———. "Ch'en Tzu-lung and the Renascence of the Song Lyric." In Hightower and Yeh, *Studies in Chinese Poetry*, 412–38.

———. "Li-Shang-yin's 'Four Yen-T'ai Poems'." In Hightower and Yeh, *Studies in Chinese Poetry*, 56–111.

You Zhenzhong 尤振中 and You Yiding 尤以丁, eds. *Qingci jishi huiping* 清詞紀事會評. Hefei: Huangshan shushe, 1995.

Yu, Pauline. "Allegory, Allegoresis, and the Classic of Poetry." *Harvard Journal of Asiatic Studies* 43.2 (1983): 377–412.

———. "Song Lyrics and the Canon: A Look of Anthology of *Tz'u*." In *Voices of the Song Lyric*, 70–103.

———, ed. *Voices of the Song Lyric in China*. Berkeley: University of California Press, 1994.

Zeitlin, Judith. "Disappearing Verses: Writing on Walls and Anxieties of Loss." In Zeitlin, Liu, and Widmer, *Writing and Materiality in China*, 73–132.

Zeitlin, Judith, Lydia H. Liu, and Ellen Widmer, eds. *Writing and Materiality in China: Essays in Honor of Patrick Hanan*. Cambridge, Mass., and London: Harvard University Asia Center, 2003.

Zhang Hongsheng 張宏生. "Jingdian queli yu chuangzuo jiangou: Mingqing nü ciren yu Li Qingzhao" 經典確立與創作建構: 明清女詞人與李清照与李清照. *Zhonghua wenshi luncong* 中華文史論叢 4 (2007): 279–313.

———. *Qingdai cixue de jiangou* 清代詞學的建構. Nanjing: Jiangsu guji chubanshe, 1999.

Zhang Huijian 張慧劍. *Qingdai Jiangsu wenren huodong nianbiao* 清代江蘇文人活動年表. Shanghai: Shanghai guji chubanshe, 1986.

Zhang Jian 張健. *Qingdai shixue yanjiu* 清代詩學研究. Beijing: Beijing daxue chubanshe, 1999.

Zhou Zuoyan. *Androgyny in Late Ming and Early Qing Literature*. Honolulu: University of Hawaii Press, 2003.

Zurndorfer, Harriet T., ed. *Chinese Women in the Imperial Past: New Perspectives*. Leiden: Brill, 1999.

INDEX

Italic page numbers refer to figures.

Analects for Women (Nü lunyu), 6, 7
androgyny, cultural, 74, 84
anthologies, 32–38, 48, 53–54, 55. See also *New Songs from a Jade Terrace*
The Anthology of Correct Beginnings by Inner-Chamber Talents of the Present Dynasty (Guochao guixiu zhengshi ji): agenda, 54, 55–58, 59, 73; boudoir plaints, 67–73; boudoir topos, 52, 84, 143, 176; compilation, 53–54, 56–57, 115; contents, 17–18, 19, 54, 59, 86; editor, 53, 54, 55–58, 59, 85, 86; normative purpose, 53, 85, 184; poems, 59–73, 74–78, 82–83
The Anthology of Poems Written among the Flowers (Huajian ji), 32–38
autonomy, 13–14, 189n41

Ban Chao, 139, 141
Ban Zhao: allusions to, 124; *Precepts for Women* (Nü jie), 6, 7
Bao Linghui, 22
beauty, 30, 53, 65, 66
bedchamber (*fang, guifang*), poems set in, 24–26
Bing Yue, 79–81, 97–98
"The Biography of Li Mi," 107
Book of Rites (Li ji), 6, 9, 55, 149
Book of Songs (Shijing), 21, 23, 48, 55, 57, 73, 85, 123, 128, 144
boudoir plaints (*guiyuan*): conventions, 12, 49–50; by men, 49–50; political aspects, 48, 130; reforms, 153–55; in Tang period, 69, 89, 93, 130; use of term, 26; written to absent husbands, 67–73, 90–92, 94–95, 136–37

boudoir poetry: articulation modes, 14–15; of courtesans, 18–19; erotic, 59; feminine and masculine styles, 62, 63, 93, 102–3, 113; of Gu Zhenli, 88–93; political dimension, 48–49, 50; purposes, 48; sensuous world, 37–38, 59; transformation, 184; of women, 52–54, 58, 59, 61–65, 74–78, 79–81
boudoir topos: in *ci* lyrics, 32–38; complexity, 180–81; conventions, 10–11, 12, 14, 47–48, 49–50, 51, 176–77; establishment, 21–32, 53; Gu Zhenli's use, 88, 112–13; image coding, 63–66, 67–73, 181–82; in late Qing and early Republican periods, 145–46, 170–72; literary reforms and, 153–55; Lü Bicheng's use of, 145–46, 166, 167–68, 170–72, 173–77; male writers and, 10–11, 12, 53, 180, 181; in Palace-Style poetry, 21–23, 26–30; Qiu Jin's use of, 145–46, 157–58, 163–64, 168, 171, 178; reconstruction, 14–15, 52; self-identity, 171–72, 174; in Song *ci*, 38–47; transformation of, 164, 167–68, 169; in wartime, 116–21, 122–26, 129–30, 143–44; in women's poetry, 3, 4, 12, 179–83. See also *gui*
Buddhism, 81, 92–93, 98, 175, 177

Cai Runshi, 120–21
Cao Rui, 76
catkins (*xu*), 64, 90, 141–42, 152
"celebrating objects" (*yongwu*) mode, 26, 36
Chang, Kang-i Sun, 74, 75, 78
Changzhou school, 48
Chao Qianzhi, 33

Chen Hengzhe, 170
Chen Hongmou, *Inherited Guide for My Daughters* (Jiaonü yigui), 7, 147
Chen Shulan, 70–71
Chen Weisong, 50, 87, 102
Chen Yingning, 171
Chen Yunlian, 133–36, 183
Chen Zilong, 50–51, 130, 194n97
ci lyrics: allegorical readings, 48–49; anthologies, 32–38, 48; borrowing of well-known lines, 39, 42; boudoir topos, 32–47; Changzhou school, 48; development of, 12, 32; feminine style, 102–3, 127, 172; gender indeterminacy, 47; "gentle and restrained" (*wanyue*) aesthetics, 38; of Gu Zhenli, 86–111, 130–32; imagery, 34–37, 40; of Lü Bicheng, 165–66, 170, 174; masculine (*haofang*) lyrics, 41, 127, 131; in Ming-Qing period, 50; political expressions, 131; self-expression in, 50; of Song period, 38–47; of women writers, 41–46
Cixi, Empress Dowager, 146, 150
clothing: male, 162; men's, 160; women's, 66, 95–96, 103–4
concubines, 97, 196n44
Confucianism: classics, 6, 9, 21, 129; morality, 54–55; poetics, 58, 85; social and gender norms, 4, 6–7, 57, 67, 150
courtesans, 18–19, 55, 56, 152
cultural androgyny, 74, 84

Daoism, 83, 171
Deng Hanyi, 183
Dickinson, Emily, 11, 112, 113
Ding Chuwo, 168
domestic sphere, 6, 71, 106–7, 142. *See also* gender boundaries; *gui*; women's roles
Dong Baohong, 117–20
Dong Yining, 49–50
drinking motifs, 45, 98–99, 112

education, of women, 146–48, 149–50, 151, 162, 172, 206n7
emotions, 69–70, 96, 112
emptiness, 24–25, 27–30, 38, 76, 79–80, 97–98, 100–101, 137
erotic poetry, 49, 59, 194n87

femininity, 12, 52, 53, 58, 74, 111, 113. *See also* women
feminism, 151, 161, 163, 165, 166–68, 169, 175. *See also* women's roles
feminist scholarship, 16
Four Books for Women (Nü sishu), 7
frontier poetry, 164

Gao Jingfang, 59–62
Gao Susu, 150
gender: Confucian norms, 4, 6–7, 57, 67, 150; cultural androgyny, 74, 84; essentialist view, 173; language and, 180; patriarchy, 12. *See also* men; women
gender boundaries: challenges, 11, 121–22, 130–34, 137–39, 161–62; male views, 8, 9, 144; physical separation, 6–8, 149; restrictions on women's political activity, 132–34, 135–36, 138, 155, 163; transcending, 73–74, 83–84, 182–83. *See also* women's roles
Gilbert, Sandra M., 11–12
Gong'an school, 79, 109
"green window" image, 34–35, 125
Gu Zhenli: boudoir topos, 88–93, 112–13; *ci* lyrics, 86–111, 130–32; emotions expressed, 96, 112; heterodoxy, 130–31; life of, 99, 101–2, 107–8, 109–10; marriage, 94–97, 101, 106–7; nonconformity and eccentricity, 86–87, 100–101, 103–7, 108, 109–11, 112–14, 183; published works, 87; self-critique of writing, 102–3; self-representation, 86–87, 88, 90–92, 93–101, 108, 109–11, 131–32, 183; *shi* poems, 86, 87; sickness, 104, 106; on women's roles, 130–32
Gubar, Susan, 11–12
gui (boudoir or inner chambers): activities, 58, 61–62, 64–65, 74–75, 78, 84, 121, 125, 176–77; association with new citizen, 167–68; association with women, 5–6; coldness, 28–29; confinement in, 4, 94, 97, 99, 130, 137–38, 163; descriptions of space, 27, 28, 34, 81, 84, 176; as discursive space, 4–5, 9, 10, 178, 180; emptiness, 24–25, 38, 76, 79–80, 97–98, 100–101, 137; guests, 64–65, 158; ideological-didactic construction of, 7–10; meanings, 5–6, 27; moods associated with, 45; outward gaze, 182; physical separation, 7–8, 10; as refuge, 83; resentment of, 15, 18; as sanctum, 80, 177; symbolism, 11. *See also* boudoir topos
guiren (person dwelling within inner quarters), 10, 160, 173, 181

Index

guixiu (talented of the inner chambers): activities, 125, 176; cultural androgyny, 74, 84; culture, 52, 57, 182; education, 148, 155; identity, 58; in late Qing and early Republican periods, 149; meanings, 13, 56–57; modern criticism of, 151–53; poets, 14, 74–75, 78, 155–58; social status, 56–57, 58; in wartime, 117–26. *See also* women writers; *The Anthology of Correct Beginnings*
guiyuan. *See* boudoir plaints
Guo Jie, 63–64

Hai Rui, 10
hairpin (*chai*), 39, 59–60, 62–63, 196n31
Han Wo, 49, 65
Handlin, Joanna F., 8, 10
He Guochen, 142–43, 181
He Huisheng: commentaries on, 152; marriage, 136, 139–40, 142; poems, 136–37, 138–40, 163; *The Poetic Drafts from the Plum-Blossom Immortal's Studio* (Meishenyinguan shicao), 140–43; poetic transformation, 142–43; suicide, 140
hermits, 82–83, 110–11, 177
houses, inner quarters, 5, 7, 10
Hu Shi, 3–4, 12, 185
Hu Wenkai, 18
Hu Yinglin, 21–22
Huang Daozhou, 121
Huang Youqin, 74
Huang Yuanjie, 121–22
Huang Zunxian, 168–69
husbands. *See* marriages

L'Impartial (Dagong bao), 165, 166, 175

Jiang Da, 141
Jiang Shumin, 162
Jiang Yan, 131
Jianwen, Emperor. *See* Xiao Gang
Jin Changxu, 89
Jin Tianhe, *Women's Bell* (Nüjie zhong), 150, 151, 153, 159, 160, 161, 167, 173

Kang Guangren, 146
Kang Tongbi, 175–76
Korean women writers, 57
Kristeva, Julia, 113

Li Bai, 98–99, 199n31

Li He, 32, 39, 200n37
Li Qingzhao, 41–46, 89, 203n49
Li Shangyin, 32, 39, 49, 62, 172
Li Yingzhou, 71–72
Li Yu, 13, 46, 130
Li Yuanding, 128, 129
Li Zhi, 109
Li Zhiling, 87
Liang Qichao, 146, 149–50, 151–52, 168–69, 173, 185
Lin Bu, 110–11
Literary Association (Wenxue Yanjiu Hui), 170
literary reforms, 153–55
literati: boudoir imagery, 10–11, 12, 49–50, 53, 180, 181; cult of *qing*, 70; cultural androgyny, 74; culture and lifestyle, 107, 108–9; poetry, 21–23, 33, 103; self-cultivation, 74, 78, 79, 82; withdrawal from public life, 78–79, 82
Liu Na, 169
Liu Renlan, 152–53
Liu Rushi (Liu Shi), 19, 50, 51, 56–57, 130, 194n97
Liu Shu, 132
Liu Yong, 42, 172
Liu Yuxi, 81, 128
Long Jidong, 140–41
Long Qirui, 136, 140, 142
Lü Bicheng: boudoir topos used by, 145–46, 166, 167–68, 170–72, 173–77; Buddhism, 175; *ci* lyrics, 165–66, 167–68, 170, 174, 175; essays, 172–74; essentialist view of gender, 173; later poetry, 169–72, 175–77; life of, 165, 175–76, 177–78; poetic transformation of *gui*, 164, 167–68, 169, 170, 177–78; *shi* poetry, 164–65, 166–68, 170, 174
Lu Cui, 150
Lü Kun: *Records on Practical Government* (Shizheng lu), 10; *Regulations for the Inner Chambers* (Gui fan), 8–10, 9, 147
Lu You, 108–9, 197n77
lyrics. *See ci* lyrics

Mao Huifang, 82, 83
Mao Shuzhen, 71
marriages: dowries, 95–96; "longing wife" (*sifu*), 67–68; poetic exchanges, 94, 140; wives' poems to absent husbands, 67–73, 90–92, 94–95, 136–37; women's education and, 147
masculine (*haofang*) lyrics, 41, 127, 131

May Fourth Movement, 3, 147, 148–49, 151, 170, 173, 185
men: critics of women's poetry, 3–4, 11, 144, 183; female voice used in poems, 153–55; teachers of women writers, 8. *See also* gender; literati; marriages; officials
Meng Guang, 66, 72, 196n40
Ming period: gender role shifts, 8; individuality, 109; literati, 78–79; officials, 67, 196n43; women writers, 18, 65
Ming-Qing transition: life during, 15, 97, 115, 117; Ming loyalists, 50–51, 54, 121, 127–30, 132; women writers' responses, 116, 120–21, 127–30, 131–32
minority literature, 184
Moore, Marianne, 112, 113
morality: female beauty and, 65; in poetry, 54–55, 57
Mulan, 133–34

nationalists, 150, 161, 165, 167
New Culturalists. *See* May Fourth Movement
New Songs from a Jade Terrace (Yutai xinyong; Xu Ling), 21–32; audience, 22, 190n12; boudoir topos, 22, 26–32, 76; depiction of women, 68; female authors, 22; imagery, 50; poems, 24–26, 27–29, 67, 76, 159; preface, 22, 124; reprinted editions, 49
newspapers, 148, 165
"new woman" (*xin nüxing*), 151, 159–60, 164, 168, 173, 177–78
"Nineteen Old Poems" (Gushi shijiu shou), 24–26, 27
Northern Song, masculine (*haofang*) lyrics, 41
nostalgia, 34, 44, 94, 97, 102, 120, 121–22, 126, 130, 140
nuns, 18, 19, 56

officials, 67, 69, 72–73, 129–30, 134, 136, 140, 196nn43–44
Opium War, 115, 134–35
orchids, 70, 158
Ouyang Jiong, 33
Ouyang Xiu, 39, 40–41, 62

"palace lyrics" (*gongci*), 124
Palace-Style poetry (*Gongti shi*): boudoir topos, 21–23, 26–30; criticism of, 32, 33, 66; influence on women poets, 59–62; influences on, 23–26; legacy, 32, 33
Pan Suxin, 72
Pan Xuan, 148
Pan Yue, 25–26
peach blossoms, 63–64
Peach Blossom Spring, 121, 126, 202n31
periodicals, 148, 163, 167
plum blossoms and trees, 82, 110–11
Poetic Revolution (Shijie Geming), 168–69
poetics: Confucian, 58, 85; ideals, 54–55; of women's poetry, 57–58
poetry: allegorical readings, 48–49, 50, 194n87; correctness, 54–55; erotic, 49, 59, 194n87; female laments, 23–25, 27, 30; frontier, 164; of Han period, 23–25; intent expressed in, 13; modernization, 169; morality in, 54–55, 57; regulated verse, 160; sentimental, 173; of Wei period, 23, 25; *yuefu*, 23, 76, 118, 133, 137. *See also* anthologies; boudoir poetry; *ci* lyrics; *shi* poetry
politics: concerns of women writers, 127–30, 159–61, 164, 165, 170, 178; engagement with, 127–30; periodicals, 148, 163, 167; poetic references, 48–49, 50, 130, 131; propaganda, 163; restrictions on women's involvement, 132–34, 135–36, 138, 155, 163; women's roles, 132, 138–39, 150, 182. *See also* May Fourth Movement
Precious Records from the Orchid Boudoir (Langui baolu), 61
propaganda, 163

Qin E, 99
Qin Guan, 89–90
Qin Liangyu, 132, 207n54
Qin Puzhen, 69–70
qing (feelings and emotions), 69–70. *See also* emotions
Qing period: anthologies, 54; late, 145–47, 149–50, 151, 155, 159–60; officials, 67, 129–30, 134, 136, 140, 196n43; Opium War, 115, 134–35; Poetic Revolution, 168–69; reforms, 146–47, 148–49, 170, 182, 185; women writers, 18. *See also* Ming-Qing transition; Taiping Rebellion
Qiu Jin: boudoir topos used by, 145–46, 157–58, 163–64, 168, 171, 178; execution, 160, 163, 164; life of, 155, 158–61, 165, 177–78;

Index

marriage, 158–59; poetry, 155–58, 159, 160, 161–63; political activities, 159–61, 164, 165, 170, 178; textual revolution, 160–64, 168, 169, 178
Qu Yuan, 70, 136, 144

reclusion, 83, 110–11, 177
regulated verse (*lüshi*), 73
Regulations for the Inner Chambers (Gui fan), 8–10, 9, 147
Republican period, 145–49, 170. See also May Fourth Movement

"scented dress-case style" (*xianglian ti*), 49
Shan Shili, 3
She Yongning, 8–9
Shen Cai, 200n45
Shen Deqian, 49–50, 55, 56
Shen Huiyu, 106
Shen Yifu, 39
Sheng shi, 72–73
shi poetry: conventions, 12; domestic subjects, 193n84; erotic, 49; of Lü Bicheng, 164–65, 166–68, 170, 174; of Qiu Jin, 161–62. See also Palace-Style poetry; *The Anthology of Correct Beginnings*
Sielke, Sabine, 112, 113, 184
Sima Guang, 6
Sima Xiangru, 96
"small window" image, 15, 125, 127, 130, 182
social change, 15, 18, 145, 163, 182, 185. See also war and chaos; women's roles
Song Ruozhao, *Analects for Women* (Nü lunyu), 6, 7
song lyrics. See *ci* lyrics
Song period: *ci* lyrics, 38–47; gender segregation, 6
Songs of the South (Chuci), 21, 48, 129
suicide, 135–36, 140
Sun Shou, 106

Taiping Rebellion: social disruption, 115, 117, 125; women writers' responses, 15, 116, 117–20, 122–26, 135–36, 138–39, 144, 205n104
Tang Jingxian, 59
Tang Qingyun, 74–75, 78
Tang poetry: boudoir plaints, 69, 89, 93, 130; *ci* lyrics, 41; frontier poetry, 164; "palace lyrics" (*gongci*), 124; Palace-Style poetry and, 32

Tao Qian, 66, 82–83, 108, 198n85, 202n30
teachers, 8, 147, 149. See also education
Tong Feng, 64–65
travel, 175–76

vernacular movement, 169, 170
virtue, female, 18, 57, 65, 70, 73, 81, 82–83, 106

Wang Caipin, 144, 205n104
Wang Changling, 69
Wang Jiefu, *Record of Female Exemplars* (Nüfan jielu), 7
Wang Nairong, 57
Wang Wei, 83
Wang Yanhong, 49
Wang Yaofang, 75
war and chaos: boudoir topos and, 116–21, 122–26, 129–30, 143–44; displacement, 15, 117–18, 122, 125, 126; engagement with wider world, 126–30; gender-marked accounts, 117; Opium War, 115, 134–35; refuge from, 122–23, 124, 125, 126; suicide as response, 136; women writers' responses, 115–26, 127–37, 138–40, 141–42, 143–44. See also Ming-Qing transition; Taiping Rebellion
Wei Chengban, 37–38
Wei Yingwu, 66
Wei Zheng, 21
Wen Tingyun, 32, 34–36, 39, 48
Weng Guangzhu, 65–66
West: Opium War, 115, 134–35; travel to, 175–76; women writers, 11–12, 16, 112, 113
wives. See marriages
"woman of new China," 149, 151, 160, 161
"woman of talent" (*cainü*), 151–52
women: abandoned, 23–24, 27–30, 46, 53, 99, 159, 181; artistic activities, 74–75, 78; beauty, 30, 53, 65, 66; bound feet, 103–4, 200n45; Chinese words used for, 13, 151; clothing, 66, 103–4; didactic texts for, 7, 8–10, 147; education, 146–48, 149–50, 151, 162, 172, 206n7; illnesses, 106, 110; literary images, 12; "new woman" (*xin nüxing*), 151, 159–60, 164, 168, 173, 177–78; palace ladies, 22; readers, 22, 75, 190n12; social status, 10, 66, 184. See also feminism; gender; marriages

women's roles: changes, 7–8, 150, 161–62, 182; citizenship, 146, 149, 150; criticism of, 105–6, 111; employment, 122, 147–48; motherhood, 68, 72–73, 146–47, 149–50; political, 132, 138–39, 150; reforms, 145, 146–48, 149, 150–51, 153, 183; socialization, 104–5. *See also* domestic sphere; gender boundaries

Women's World, 163, 167

women writers: agency, 13–14, 183–84; anthologies, 53–54, 55; the anxiety of authorship, 11; catalogs, 3, 18; of *ci*, 41–46; courtesans, 18–19, 55, 56, 152; creativity, 13–14; criticism of, 3–4, 11, 185; families, 4, 18; image coding changed by, 62, 63–66, 67–73, 181–82, 196n33; influences on, 51; Korean, 57; literary culture, 12, 14, 18, 52, 107, 170–71, 177, 181, 182; male teachers, 8; minority status, 184; modern, 170; nuns, 18, 19, 56; of Palace-Style poetry, 22; poetic exchanges with husbands, 94, 140; political concerns, 127–30; revisionists, 183; scholarship on, 3, 5; self-images, 14, 53–54, 58, 66, 70–72, 74, 84–85; social status, 18, 55, 56–57, 67, 81–82, 189n51; subjective experiences, 14, 15, 16, 179–80; subjectivity, 13, 16–17, 113, 174; themes, 3, 4; tradition and, 172–74, 179, 183–84; Western, 11–12, 16, 112, 113. *See also guixiu*

writers. *See* literati; women writers

Wu Chai, *Posthumous Manuscripts from the Pavilion of Autumn Sash*, 122–26

Wu Weiye, 122

Wu Zhaoyi, 23, 49

Xian, Mme., 138
Xiao Gang, 21, 22–23, 26, 27–28, 32, 59–60, 61–62, 64
Xie Daoyun, 106, 140, 141–42, 152, 156
Xie Yi, 42
Xin Qiji, 135, 200n56
Xu Can, 127–28, 130
Xu, Empress, *Instructions for the Inner Quarters* (neixun), 7
Xu Ling, 21, 22, 23, 66, 124, 196n42
Xu Xiaoshu, 161–62
Xu Zaipu, 83
Xu Zhenyi, 144
Xu Zihua, 161–62, 163–64

Yan Shu, 45, 46–47
Yang Sushu, 70
Ying Lianzhi, 165, 166
Yu Menghua, 125–26
Yu Xin, 66, 196n42
Yuan Hanhuang, 81–82, 83
Yuan Hongdao, 78–79
Yuan Mei, 11
yuefu (Music Bureau songs), 23, 76, 118, 133, 137
Yun Zhu, 53, 54, 55–58, 59, 61, 67, 81, 85, 86. *See also The Anthology of Correct Beginnings*

Zhang Huiyan, *Anthology of Ci* (Ci xuan), 48
Zhang Jinyong, 141–42
Zhang Lingyi, 76–78
Zhang Xuecheng, 11
Zhou Qiong, 109, 183
Zhou Shi, 154–55, 169, 181
Zhou Yao, 68
Zhou Zuoren, 169
Zhu Yizun, 50, 51
Zhu Zhongmei, 62–63, 127–30

www.ingramcontent.com/pod-product-compliance
Lightning Source LLC
Chambersburg PA
CBHW030619230426
43661CB00053B/2065